WOMEN, FILM, AND LAW

LAW AND SOCIETY

Law and Society Series

W. Wesley Pue, Founding Editor

We pay tribute to the late Wes Pue, under whose broad vision, extraordinary leadership, and unwavering commitment to socio-legal studies our Law and Society Series was established and rose to prominence.

The Law and Society Series explores law as a socially embedded phenomenon. It is premised on the understanding that the conventional division of law from society creates false dichotomies in thinking, scholarship, educational practice, and social life. Books in the series treat law and society as mutually constitutive and seek to bridge scholarship emerging from interdisciplinary engagement of law with disciplines such as politics, social theory, history, political economy, and gender studies.

Recent books in the series:

Amanda Nelund, *A Better Justice? Community Programs for Criminalized Women* (2020)

Trevor C.W. Farrow and Lesley A. Jacobs, eds., *The Justice Crisis: The Cost and Value of Accessing Law* (2020)

Jamie Baxter, *Inalienable Properties: The Political Economy of Indigenous Land Reform* (2020)

Jeremy Patrick, *Faith or Fraud: Fortune-Telling, Spirituality, and the Law* (2020)

Obiora Chinedu Okafor, *Refugee Law after 9/11: Sanctuary and Security in Canada and the United States* (2020)

Anna Jane Samis Lund, *Trustees at Work: Financial Pressures, Emotional Labour, and Canadian Bankruptcy Law* (2019)

Shauna Labman, *Crossing Law's Border: Canada's Refugee Resettlement Program* (2019)

Peter McCormick and Marc D. Zanoni, *By the Court: Anonymous Judgments at the Supreme Court of Canada* (2019)

For a complete list of the titles in the series, see the UBC Press website, www.ubcpress.ca.

WOMEN, FILM, AND LAW
Cinematic Representations of Female Incarceration

Suzanne Bouclin

UBCPress · Vancouver · Toronto

30 29 28 27 26 25 24 23 22 21   5 4 3 2 1

Printed in Canada on FSC-certified ancient-forest-free paper (100% post-consumer recycled) that is processed chlorine- and acid-free.

Library and Archives Canada Cataloguing in Publication

Title: Women, film, and law : cinematic representations of female incarceration / Suzanne Bouclin.
Names: Bouclin, Suzanne, 1975– author.
Series: Law and society series (Vancouver, B.C.)
Description: Series statement: Law and society series | Includes bibliographical references and index.
Identifiers: Canadiana (print) 20200380710 | Canadiana (ebook) 20200380907 | ISBN 9780774865869 (hardcover) | ISBN 9780774865883 (PDF) | ISBN 9780774865890 (EPUB)
Subjects: LCSH: Women prisoners in motion pictures. | LCSH: Prisoners in popular culture. | LCSH: Women in motion pictures. | LCSH: Women on television.
Classification: LCC PN1995.9.W66 B68 2021 | DDC 791.43/6526927—dc23

Canadä

UBC Press gratefully acknowledges the financial support for our publishing program of the Government of Canada (through the Canada Book Fund), the Canada Council for the Arts, and the British Columbia Arts Council.

This book has been published with the help of a grant from the Canadian Federation for the Humanities and Social Sciences, through the Awards to Scholarly Publications Program, using funds provided by the Social Sciences and Humanities Research Council of Canada.

Printed and bound in Canada by Friesens
Set in Warnock Pro and Futura by Apex CoVantage, LLC
Copy editor: Stacy Belden
Proofreader: Judith Earnshaw
Cover designer: David Drummond

UBC Press
The University of British Columbia
2029 West Mall
Vancouver, BC V6T 1Z2
www.ubcpress.ca

Contents

Illustrations

Acknowledgments

This book would not be possible without Anne McGillivray, who suggested I look into "those old movies about girls in prison" as a possible LLM thesis topic. Thank you sincerely, Anne, for scrupulously reading drafts, improving my research, buying monthly lunches, and shepherding me through graduate school. A warm thank you to George Toles and Brenda Austin-Smith from the University of Manitoba's Faculty of English, Theatre, Film, and Media for welcoming me into their mind-expanding film classes, recommending readings, and providing thorough feedback on my work.

I also owe a debt of gratitude to Debra Parkes, who provided invaluable mentorship and comments at earlier stages of this research and who has always supported my work, as well as to Rebecca Johnson, a model of academic rigour and generosity who also happened to introduce me to the field of law and film.

A special thanks to Bruce Ryder for sharing his archival research on the Motion Picture Production Code, which greatly enriched my chapter on *Ann Vickers*. Thanks to friends and colleagues whose research has profoundly deepened my thinking about film, legal pluralism, and feminism: Marie-Claire Belleau, Ruth Buchanan, Kim Brooks, Gillian Calder, Sheryl Hamilton, Ummni Khan, Jennifer Koshan, Sonia Lawrence, Rod Macdonald, Jessica Silbey, Will Straw, and Alanna Thain.

Hearty thanks to my wonderful friends and colleagues who have – over the span of fifteen years – indulged my obsession with prison movies and provided support, reading suggestions, and constructive feedback and, especially, for remaining enthusiastic about this project when my resolve was waning: Tamar Ditzian, Kristin Bright, Colleen Harrington, Annie Rochette, Yves LeBouthillier, Doris Buss, Constance Backhouse, Peter Oliver, Emmanuelle Bernheim, Daniel Rosenblatt, Patrick Gauthier, Shoshana Magnet, Florian Grandena, and Joe Roach. Thank you to Teresa Scassa for providing me with the precise information at the precise moment, to Ellen Zweibel for okaying the book's readability, and to Penelope Simons and the University of Ottawa's Faculty of Law Research Office staff for the support.

I am grateful to the Social Sciences and Humanities Research Council for the generous financial assistance.

I so appreciate Rick Harkin, librarian at the University of Ottawa, for his exceptional skills in finding esoteric sources, and Genevieve Maxwell, reference librarian at the Academy of Motion Picture Arts and Sciences, for sharing materials.

I had two brilliant research assistants who dove into this project with me: the indefatigable Lindsay McLellan and the unrelentingly enthusiastic Bo Kruk. I have also received great insights from other law students – too many to name – whose comments in my film seminars constantly blow my mind. A number of these also provided research support: Cara Bally, Samantha Clarke, Stéphanie Desjardins, Alana Guy, Catherine Nadeau Mijal, Jessica Narda Saris, and Dahlia Hudson Shuhaibar.

I have immense gratitude for the external reviewers, who provided careful and rigorous comments. Thank you to Randy Schmidt, senior editor, to Michelle van der Merwe, production editor, and to the rest of the team at UBC Press for their commitment to bringing this work to publication and their enthusiasm for this project.

I have also had the great fortune of working with Colette Stoeber, an outstanding editor.

And, of course, my deep love and thanks to my family for every kind of support imaginable and to Morag the Dog, my faithful writing companion, who came into my life the year I began to put these ideas onto paper.

WOMEN, FILM, AND LAW

Introduction

Female incarceration in the United States is expanding at an alarming rate. With a staggering 700 percent increase between 1980 and 2014, women are the fastest-growing demographic of the American carceral population.[1] These numbers do not reflect a growth in crime but, rather, increased reliance on correctional control to address deeply entrenched social problems and inequities. Women who are confined in correctional facilities are among the most marginalized members of society. While they come into contact with the criminal law for a range of reasons, the vast majority of incarcerated women have committed minor offences.[2] There are other shared commonalities among this diverse population. Women who are confined in correctional facilities tend to come from neighbourhoods or countries[3] that are entrenched in poverty and that have faced systematic dismantling of social services, such as decreased school funding. These women are, more likely than not, members of a racial/cultural/ethnic minority that is over-policed and aggressively prosecuted.[4]

Incarcerated women have pre-existing histories of trauma, systemic racism, child sexual abuse and other forms of sexual, economic, and physical violence as well as experiences with foster care and having their own children removed by the state. Almost one-third of women in prison have been treated for psychiatric issues before incarceration, over one-third have attempted suicide and one-half suffer from serious mental illness or depression, and approximately 10 percent live with schizophrenia or other psychoses.[5] Once serving their sentence, women may further experience physical, sexual, psychological, and economic violence in the form of intimidation, harassment, and sexual coercion by guards and other correctional employees; have their basic privacy interests denied; live in dire conditions characterized by overcrowding, cutbacks to educational programs, and inadequate health services; and be grossly underpaid for high-profit-generating labour.

These various experiences are often punctuated by prescription medication use, illicit drug use, and/or alcohol dependence as coping or survival mechanisms. Consequently, women are most likely to be in jail or prison for drug-related or minor offences in which they engaged out of necessity, desperation, or pragmatism. Most women in jail and prison are mothers of children under the age of eighteen and are often the head of single-parent homes.[6] Finally, as US Supreme Court Justice William J. Brennan noted decades ago, "prisoners are persons whom most of us would rather not think about. Banished from everyday sight, they exist in a shadow world that only dimly enters our awareness."[7] Similarly, Angela Y. Davis has written that "the realities of imprisonment are hidden from almost all who have not had the misfortune of doing time."[8] Other feminist criminologists have confirmed how such invisibility is more acute with incarcerated women.[9]

At first blush, films and television series about women housed in correctional facilities, with their divided commitments to entertainment and the generation of profits, may seem to contribute little to a meaningful engagement with such appalling facts. However, I believe that popular representations that tell stories about women's imprisonment may play a role in shedding light on the multiple forms of marginalization, social exclusion, and oppressions experienced by criminalized women. Assuming, as I do, that film is a creative force that generates legal meaning,[10] the artefacts – a mix of television series and films – that I refer to in shorthand as "women-in-prison" (WIP) movies do have the potential to leave viewers feeling unsettled about the existence of prisons, empathetic towards the women who are warehoused in them, and troubled about the crimes of which such women have been accused. This body of representations comes in various visual modalities – from theatre screenings to on-demand content – and takes multiple forms – including film, television series, and music videos.

I maintain that, as a whole, these cultural texts bring into view the legal, economic, and political structures that target already marginalized women and criminalize these women differently than men. To ground this assertion, I identify a genealogy of the WIP genre and propose a corresponding grammar of WIP movies.[11]

In her excellent study of representation and crime, Nicole Rafter asserts that "until recently, if one wanted to see a film about women in prison, there were only two choices: *I Want to Live!* and soft pornography." While she rightly acknowledges that there are multiple iterations of the WIP film, Rafter establishes the boundary of the existing oeuvre to "babe-behind-bars" movies, furthering the view that the WIP genre neither "develop[s] [n]or sustain[s] a women's point of view on incarceration." Instead, WIP films merely "substitute women for men" to appeal to a broader audience.[12] Rafter's perspective on the WIP genre, however, is somewhat narrow. The artefacts that I define as WIP films are significantly more diverse than Rafter suggests. In fact, I trace the WIP genre back to one particular film: Carl-Theodor Dreyer's distinct vision of Joan of Arc in *La Passion de Jeanne d'Arc/The Passion of Joan of Arc* (*The Passion*) (1928).[13] As portrayed by Dreyer's film, Joan was a devout seventeen-year-old white peasant who believed she was under the counsel of saints when she led the French to victory against the Anglo-Burgundian armies during the Hundred Years' War. In 1429, the Bishop of Beauvais launched an inquisition into possible heretical claims on Joan's part. While the condemnation depositions reveal the state of grace and exaltation in which Joan found herself both in combat and during her trial, they also reveal that, while in custody at Rouen, she was held in chains and iron fetters, suffered humiliating taunts and trauma, and was sexually and physically assaulted. On May 30, 1431, after three months of gruelling interrogations and appalling prison conditions, Joan was finally executed by being burned at the stake. Not only have her honour and innocence since been restored, but she has also become a feminist icon and a Catholic saint.[14] Through the iconic film representation of her remarkable life, the WIP genre was born.

Joan of Arc's life has been chronicled in manifold iterations, including several films: *Jeanne d'Arc* (1900), *Joan of Arc* (1948), *Saint Joan* (1957), *Procès de Jeanne d'Arc/The Trial of Joan of Arc* (1962), and *Jeanne d'Arc/The Messenger: The Story of Joan of Arc* (1999). These representations interest me because each expression of the mythical and/or real Joan of

Arc speaks to various modes of policing and imprisoning women in sexist societies, such as confinement to the private sphere, economic infantilization, and emotional, sexual, and physical violence. These films also illustrate the punishment meted out to women who transgress norms of femininity. Yet Dreyer's distinct vision of Joan of Arc in *The Passion* remains one of the most powerful and sympathetic exploration of how women exercise agency within conditions of formal and structural inequality. Joan's resilience and unwavering faith are depicted in an allegory of female resistance, transcendence, and vindication. She stands in for all women who are confined, showcasing the subversive and disruptive strategies imprisoned women deploy in the face of such constraints. Thus, Dreyer's film is not only a strong story that reveals the consequences of women's persecution, incarceration, and resistance, but it is also the cinematic precedent for the subject of this book: the WIP genre.[15]

The Passion is the prototype that established some familiar WIP codes and conventions through Dreyer's striking construction of the Joan of Arc myth as one of innocence destroyed. One prominent convention of the WIP genre, exemplified in *The Passion*, is that a wrongfully convicted woman whose head is shaved as a form of public humiliation will subsequently be freed from normative femininity and will experience a deeper inner transformation. The ritualistic head shaving has become a staple of the genre and has appeared, for example, in *Caged!* as well as in *Orange Is the New Black* (*OITNB*) (2013–19).[16] Dreyer uses cinema's language to elicit empathy for his protagonist: close-ups of Joan's (Renée Maria Falconetti's) luminous face are juxtaposed in stark contrast to that of her tormentor, Cauchon (Eugène Silvain), whose repulsiveness is heightened through canted angles. In addition, *The Passion* remains an iconic depiction of women's literal and metaphoric imprisonment. One instance of its lasting influence can be seen in Jean-Luc Godard's *Vivre sa vie/My Life to Live* (1962), in which Nana, a struggling actor, single mother, and occasional sex worker, is brought to tears as she watches Dreyer's film. Nana's internal monologue ("I think we are always responsible for our actions. We're free") is suggestive of what I view as one of the WIP genre's guiding principles: even in the most repressive conditions, there are always possibilities for resistance and redemption. Despite the prevalence of this theme of personal emancipation, WIP films are not simply stories about individual transgressions; these films may also provoke viewers to question systemic injustices and consider whether prisons for women should exist at all.

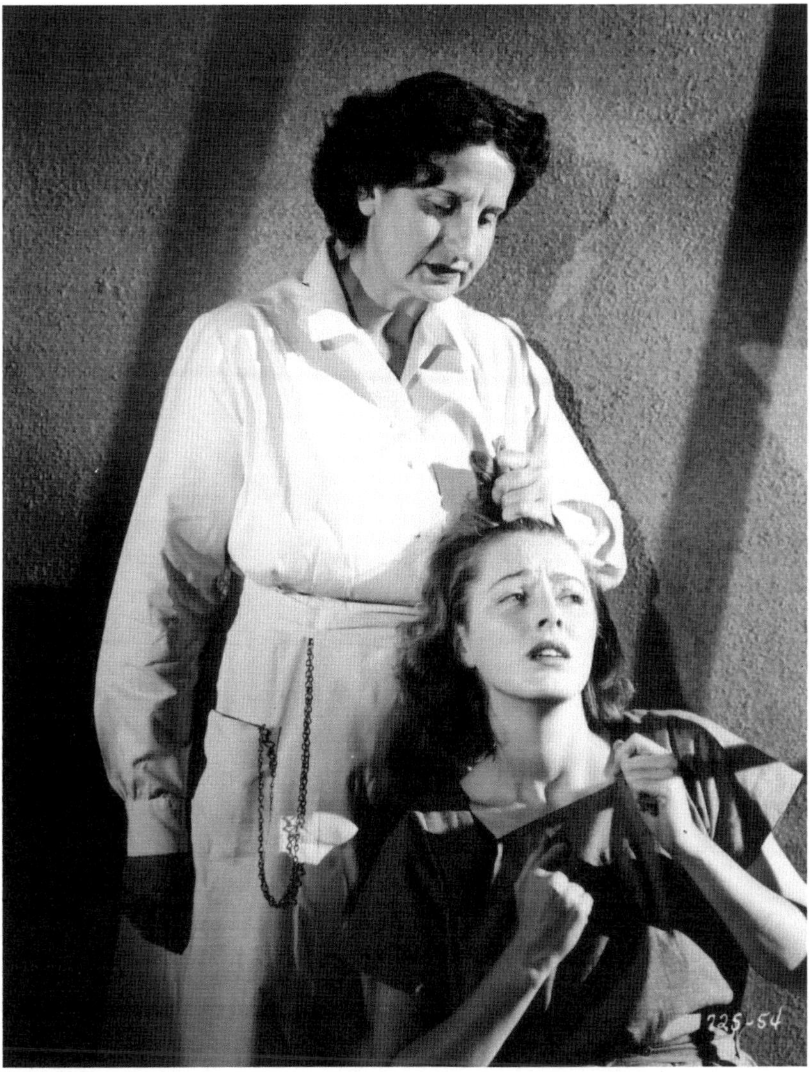

Figure 1 Evelyn Harper (Hope Emerson) shaving Marie Allen's (Eleanor Parker) head in *Caged!* (1950). Licensed by Warner Brothers Entertainment (all rights reserved).

Why Care about Women in Prison Movies?

Law and visual culture are both integral aspects of the contemporary human experience. Law is an artefact born of human creativity and constituted through interactions. It is one mode of establishing and organizing knowledge about human relationships and, thus, one symbolic expression of how to make sense of the world in which we live. Like any other sociocultural artefact, law confronts, competes with, and is inextricably intertwined with countless other ways of organizing such knowledge. Audio-visual representations – film and television mainly – have their own vocabulary and representational norms, tell stories about law, and reflect and shape its institutions. They are one of law's most visible and accessible expressions.

Audio-visual representations symbolize how we govern and how we are governed. They may circulate and reinforce deep-seated assumptions; they may also destabilize and confront ideology. They may invite visceral responses to human suffering; they may also help to justify indifference or inaction in the face of such suffering. By extension, WIP films may symbolize how women are policed and criminalized; they may also explore how women themselves constitute norms and rules for interaction with the prison space. They may be cautionary tales to women who misbehave or infringe traditional gender expectations, or they may be allegories of female liberation. They may be read as tacit approval of oppressive institutions, or they may be read as a direct indictment of such repression. They may also produce all of these effects at the same time. The WIP genre thus shapes and reflects women's actual and metaphoric imprisonment in contemporary society and is an important site of the cultural and legal construction of criminalized women. Yet this body of representations remains unmined for what it reveals about these themes. While scholars have historically taken considerable interest in the male prison genre, they have often overlooked women's prison films.[17]

My purpose is not to assess whether WIP films reveal anything about the actual conditions of incarcerated women. In fact, as Mariana Valverde might argue, to ask whether the portrayal of women's prisons is true to life is to assume that people consume popular culture to obtain accurate information about crime and justice, which is contrary to most available evidence.[18] Yet a common feminist critique of the WIP genre remains that these films distort the actual experiences of real women serving sentences specifically because they feature normatively attractive, white, heterosexual, middle-class protagonists who are, for all intents and purposes, wrongfully convicted. Consequently, WIP films can abstract the reality that Indigenous women, racialized women, lesbian, gay, bisexual, transgender, queer, and two-spirited people, women with learning disabilities, and women navigating mental health challenges are more likely to be living in poverty, more often subjected to high fines for minor offences, more often disproportionately impacted by police interventions, and, thus, more likely to be incarcerated.[19] Therefore, the argument goes, WIP films circulate dangerous stereotypes about criminalized women. As feminist media, film, and cultural theorists have noted, the problem with this kind of argument is not the critique of the stereotypes but, rather, the solution offered for such problematic representations: the production of more "realistic" images of women in prison. As Christine Gledhill has explained, the focus on real women begs the question: which women, what reality, and according to whom?[20]

Even though WIP movies are not direct reflections of the social world, imaginary prisons are an expressive, metaphorical, and symbolic mode of representation that have a constitutive role in shaping our understandings of "prison" as a cultural signifier. This signifier should not be confused with real-life prison, but it can nonetheless suggest new understandings about hegemonic structures, such as the criminal justice system, that govern women's actual lives. While WIP films grapple with women's liberation and subjugation, sexuality and sexual identities, forbidden desires, and physical and emotional imprisonment through the prison signifier, WIP films are also full of potential critical legal readings around the construction of the "female criminal" and the crimes with which stock characters are charged. These crimes range from morality offences, such as accessing illegal abortions and engaging in prostitution, to violent crimes, such as killing a rapist. Doubtless, some WIP movies reproduce the gendered operations and assumptions of the criminal law. However, many, and even most, WIP films simultaneously expose the prison as an institutionalized apparatus of power, presenting women who refuse to accept the law that is externally imposed upon them or denying the legitimacy of the legal actors who enforce that law – whether these are wardens, child and welfare service workers, or medical practitioners.

In this book, however, I focus on six exemplary fictionalized and mediated versions of prison that, on at least some level, challenge the criminal justice apparatus and the criminalization of particular women. These six "WIP movies" (five films and one television series) challenge inhumane and violent state or legal practices and suggest the existence of broader gender, race, and class injustices that make certain women more vulnerable to criminalization and incarceration. These six texts also circulate discursive formations that reproduce and reflect damaging stories about criminalized women, stories that are themselves constructed and circulated through formal legal doctrine addressing issues such as reproductive rights (*Ann Vickers* [1933]), transactional sex (*Caged!* [1950]), mental illness (*Caged Heat* [1974]), motherhood (*Stranger Inside* [2001]), institutionalized racism (*Civil

Brand [2002]), and drug use (*OITNB* [2013–19]). Each film provides a psychic and artistic space to explore, shape, and refine beliefs about women who are in fact criminalized because they exercised the choice to abort a foetus or engaged in prostitution as a mode of survival, women who navigate mental health challenges as a result of being criminalized, women who are labelled "bad mothers" as a result of their interactions with the law, and women whose criminalization is a result of systemic racism and its manifestation through the war on drugs.

My discussion of these six texts is located within a general ethos of critical legal pluralism. My methodology is situated at the nexus of law and cinema and begins from the assumption that film is law. My method of inquiry and analysis is to examine how particular films, as part of a genre of their own, exist in transtextual relationships.

Interpretive Frameworks

Legal pluralism refers to a broad set of assumptions and research practices organized around the reality that there are multiple legal orders within the same socio-spatial arena. In Sally Engle Merry's words, legal pluralism is "a situation in which two or more legal systems coexist in the same social field." Accordingly, legal systems are meant to include state institutions and actors, such as courts and judges, as well as "nonlegal forms of normative ordering," such as family, etiquette norms, and religious beliefs.[21] Critical legal pluralism builds on this insight by exploring normative sites, modes, and instruments that are sometimes overlooked within a more classical pluralist view of law. To critical legal pluralists, law is polycentric, in that various normative forms overlap in the same normative universe, but it is also dynamic, meaning that law is rule-governed behaviour that shifts with individuals' beliefs, commitments to rules, and interpretations and applications of the law. This dynamism is crucial: whereas much law and society scholarship has focused on how individuals are marginalized by, or subjected to, law, critical legal pluralists reframe law's subjects as its agents – as law generating, and constituting laws through interactions with others.

A further insight from legal pluralism is that we define acceptable behaviour and interact in ways that capture our fluid, competing, and multiple notions of self. Our sense of self shifts and varies through our interactions – our morphing locations along axes of race, class, gender, age, ethnicity, sexuality, culture, and nationality – and materializes in "myriad nooks and crannies of everyday life."[22] We are socio-spatial, self-monitoring, self-reflexive creatures, always in formation, always in the process of becoming. As such, our normative commitments vary depending on our various configurations of self, which in turn are shaped and informed by our personal motivations, bonds to others, institutional affiliations, and identity markers. Each of these aspects of our selves – the plurality of identities by which we live – is variably self-ascribed and prescribed by others. Of course, stories, including those circulated in cinema and through law, shape and impact how we self-ascribe and prescribe identities onto others.

Similarly, work at the nexus of law and film is generally concerned with the doctrinal, pedagogical, and jurisprudential relevance of film to law. Some law and film methodologies assume and reinforce the positivist view that film provides an external perspective on law and legal processes. There is, nonetheless, a more complex understanding among most scholars working in the field that neither social phenomena nor the disciplines that study them are self-governing or self-sustaining. I will briefly discuss the former positivist view; however, I will emphasize the latter perspective, building upon it to show that film is law. Within the broader ethos of legal pluralism, I suggest four ways we can and do think through the relationships between law and film, using the following terms to describe them: (1) film's law; (2) law in film; (3) law and film; and (4) cinematic law.

It is commonly assumed that most people develop at least some of their understandings and expectations about law through popular media, including television and cinema.[23] Law and film scholars tend to share, on the one hand, an idealized view of movies as a means of generating empathy and as part of a broader pedagogy in legal ethics and, paradoxically, on the other hand, a more cynical view of cinema as a medium that distorts reality or misleads audiences/students into holding law to unreasonable standards. As a result, law and film studies have emerged as a diverse field generally concerned with the doctrinal, pedagogical, and jurisprudential relevance of film to law and, occasionally, of law to film. Rosemary Coombe has cautioned that "law and" explorations "will not be fruitful" unless they can transcend, transform, and disrupt categories like "law" or "culture."[24] Nevertheless, there are a number of ways to meaningfully talk about the points of contact between these two disciplines and sociocultural processes.

First, what I call "film's law" refers to the control of film production and cinematic practices through a complex matrix of formal, explicit, informal, or implicit modes of governance. For instance, film's law can include how film production and cinematic practices are governed through legislation or judicial decisions that balance the claims of competing groups in a copyright claim. However, film's law can also refer to formal economic and cultural regulations that have shaped the film industry, such as the moral regulation of the Motion Picture Production Code ("Production Code") or the legislated racial segregation and discrimination of the Jim Crow laws in the United States.[25] Film's law can further be understood as the implicit norms that govern film production, such as the moral codes of each person involved in the production or the informal norms developed through filmmakers' collective practices, which develop over time.

Second, "law in film" is the most common subject of film discussion by legal scholars. Despite the promise of pluralistic analyses of law and film, the overwhelming majority of legal scholarship on film situates itself within the study of law in film. Broadly speaking, law in film concerns itself with films "about" law. In the legal academy, students are often asked to turn their minds to the truthfulness of the law as represented in the diegesis; law is usually limited to formal, state-sanctioned written rules and legal practices. This focus is unsurprising given that fact determination remains a fundamental strategy of legal method. The assertion that film is a legal text – even if it is limited to a single text with fixed content to be discovered or described – is in itself provocative insofar as it destabilizes what counts as legal authority, legal sources, and the skills and attributes necessary for good lawyering. Nonetheless, normative judgments about a film's legal veracity or relevance still inevitably occur in areas such as the use of appropriate precedents ("factual accounts"), the accuracy of legal details (doctrine or legal concepts), and the believability of the protagonist (as a "real" lawyer). Such a narrow range of interpretive lenses is limiting. As historian Robert Rosenstone explains, "our notions [of cinema] come directly out of our training and practice as academics. Our first reaction is to think a film is really a book somehow transferred to the screen, and that it should do what we expect a book to do: get things right."[26] Nevertheless, as Ruth Buchanan and Rebecca Johnson argue, looking at law in films can be a means of confronting the jurisprudential belief that formal legal processes can actually divine truths about law.[27]

Third, "law and film" scholarship highlights the mutually constitutive and intertextual relationship between two sociocultural artefacts and fields of inquiry: law and film.[28] Less concerned with questions of methodological unity or factual depictions, law and film scholars call attention to how these two sociocultural formations, discursive practices, and modes of representation can share a number of features, including narrative strategies; a desire for truths, whether factual, analogous, or metaphorical; interpretive techniques; and world-building functions. Law and film can also retain their own communicative modes, technologies, apparatuses, and unique sensory, spatial, and temporal means of persuasion.[29] In highlighting such continuities and disjunctions, scholars wrestle with the intertextual dialogue between law and film that permits each narrative regime to shed light on how the other functions.[30]

Fourth, as I argue, films capture our legal imagination and become a fundamental aspect of our legal lives as "cinematic law." Contrary to more orthodox law and film approaches, considering what is legal about film and what is cinematic about law turns our attention to the aesthetic and affective dimensions of both law and film. While content analysis and close reading still hold currency in both film and legal studies, moving beyond the text nudges us to think about how films work on us and how they may produce, as Johnson and Buchanan explain, "structures of feeling that help to cohere [or destabilize] contemporary legal and political institutions."[31] Cinematic law refers to the plurality of normative commitments and expectations that each individual viewer navigates and is best examined in terms of the production of norms through the interpretation, evaluation, and reconfiguration of generic conventions.

Each mode of engaging law and film points to some of the competing normative orders that characterize any film. These orders include the regulatory frameworks in which the film is produced, the norms of the constructed world described and lived in the film's diegesis, the film's fixed order of sounds and images, the ideologies and normative commitments that inform directorial discretion, and the rules of genre that constitute a normative site. The six visual representations that I explore in this book present their own hypothesis about women's criminalization; each is also an invitation to sense and feel law cinematically, anchoring legal theories, which have historically elided or misrepresented women's experiences, in women's emotional lives.

I use a transtextual analysis to highlight how these films explore the dynamic and shifting relationship between law and film. Film analysis that attends exclusively to either its veracity or its textual qualities is insufficient for my purposes. Nevertheless, I borrow from poetics to develop an interpretive method for my inquiry. In the following chapters, I explore the transtextual relations (a term coined by French literary theorist Gérard Genette) between, and among, films. Working in reference to Mikhail Bakhtin and Julia Kristeva, Genette defines transtextuality as "all that sets the text in a relationship, whether obvious or concealed, with other texts."[32] Bakhtin developed the notion of dialogism to convey the idea that textual meanings are not merely located within authorial intent but are also constituted through the relation of utterances (any complex of signs, such as a spoken sentence or a poem) to other utterances.[33] Dialogism has since been translated and revised by Julia Kristeva as "intertextuality" or the "mosaic of quotations" found in any text.[34] A film is not simply the fruit of an individual filmmaker auteur, and a screenplay is not simply the sum of its sources. A film, like any other text and like the law, "cannot exist as a hermetic or self-sufficient whole, and so does not function as a closed system"; instead, it engages in the "absorption and transformation" of other surrounding texts, elaborating new meanings, giving those texts "new way[s] of being," and constituting "its own signification."[35]

Genette expanded and codified Kristeva's intertextuality into transtextuality and developed a theory of its multiple modes and sites, of which there are at least four: paratextuality, metatextuality, hypertextuality, and architextuality.[36] Paratextuality is the relation between a text and that which surrounds the body of the text. Paratextuality is the surrounding framework, or the "ether," of a text, including its promotional material, its score, the credit sequence, and the subtitles used for various audiences. It includes the peritext ("around text" or the physical appearance of the printed work) and the epitext ("above text" or the writings that provide context to a text).[37] Christine Gledhill provides concrete examples of paratexts, including "journalist features, 'letters to the editor', classroom lectures, critical responses, changes in distribution or publication policy, [and] more critical activity."[38] Metatextuality is the explicit and direct commentary of one text on another text. Metatextuality may also be done implicitly, "without summoning," naming, or citing the original or other text. Hypertextuality is the relationship between a particular text (hypertext) and the broader genre from which it emanates (hypotext). Hypertextuality is a process through which the hypertext parodies, imitates, and satirizes the hypotext, thereby elaborating, extending, and ultimately transforming it. Finally, architextuality is an umbrella that covers a text, whether a type of discourse or, for our purposes, its generic framing.[39]

The first chapter, "A Genre of One's Own," is devoted to the WIP genre's architextuality – that is, its generic conventions. I introduce the logic of WIP movies, which are transgeneric: comprising multiple genres and transcending them at once. WIP movies draw on conventions and codes from melodramas, film noir, Blaxsploitation, the rape-revenge film, documentary cinema, comedy, the western, and, of course, the prison movie. WIP movies also constitute their own rules and invite normative assessments from their unique viewing communities. Consequently, I define and historically situate the formal WIP norms and four overlapping cycles of the WIP genre: melodramas/social problem films, exploitation flicks, realist dramas, and dramedies.[40] Based upon the logic of the genre that develops when taking a distant view of these four moments, the remaining chapters in this book do not provide a general review of the treatment of women's prisons in film. Instead, I deploy the modes and sites of transtextuality to provide a close and contextualized reading of five films and one television series: *Ann Vickers, Caged!, Caged Heat, Stranger Inside, Civil Brand,* and *OITNB*.

In *Ann Vickers,* the titular character is a feminist prison reformer, standing in for white middle-class women who were inspired by the revolutionary fervour at the turn of the twentieth century and who mobilized to attain suffrage, paid employment, and some reproductive freedoms. The movie features long sequences within various women's correctional facilities, but the focus of my discussion is on how the film maps WIP's generic law onto the canonical (written) law. I concentrate on multiple modes and sites of law, especially the regulation of film content under the Production Code, the formal prohibition of abortion, and the societal norms that privilege monogamy.

Caged!, the second melodrama/social problem film that I discuss, is one of the most highly regarded movies about prisons. It is a transitional film that reproduces earlier social problem WIP conventions while fundamentally altering and ultimately defining the most recognizable tropes of WIP films: an unimpeachable protagonist who is transformed by her time in prison and a sadistic authority figure (whether a matron or a guard) with Sapphic inclinations. *Caged!* also features many of the genre's key signifiers, including the shower scene, the prison mascot, and the riot. Unlike most earlier films, *Caged!* contains no easy resolution, and its protagonist is not redeemed through the love of a good man; in fact, she resigns herself to working as a prostitute. As a result, it offers a painful, complex, and nuanced illustration of an intersectional understanding of human agency, in which women's life choices are contextual, relational, and dependent on multiple power dynamics that exist in any given moment or situation.

I turn to the exploitation flick *Caged Heat* in order to examine how fan communities generate meanings about WIP films by reflecting and informing film aficionados' expectations of the genre. The exploitation cycle of WIP films has been dismissed by some feminists as explicitly misogynistic or, at the very least, as crass artefacts that circulate stereotypical views of femininity and sexuality. On the one hand, *Caged Heat* seems to confirm the idea that WIP movies are merely using the prison as a pretext to shackle women and exploit nudity. On the other, it may be a self-reflexive parody of the WIP genre that irritates its intended fan base and appeals to unintended audiences – specifically, queer women. I explore how these critical elements are reproduced and expanded in more explicitly feminist satires such as Lady Gaga and Beyoncé's video for the song *Telephone* (2009).

Unlike the other cinematic representations I consider in this book, the fourth and fifth films, *Stranger Inside* and *Civil Brand* were written and directed by Black American women. Cheryl Dunye's *Stranger Inside* explores incarceration from a Black lesbian standpoint. I explore one of the film's more overt political messages: in prison, there are new configurations of "motherhood" and of "family." I compare the stories it tells about mothering – specifically, the stories of queer Black mothers – to those presented in *OITNB* and other representations that feature "mother-child prison programs." Neema Barnette's *Civil Brand* depicts the prison as being integral to America's systems of social and racial inequality or, as Michelle Alexander puts it, "The New Jim Crow."[41] Barnette's film may be a corrective in a mainstream popular culture that has often underplayed, or even ignored, how Black women are more likely to be arrested when using self-defence against abusive intimate partners and have become the largest population currently under control of the correctional system, and, during their tenure behind bars, are more likely to be denied basic rights and freedoms than their white counterparts.[42] I locate both films within an industry and a genre that has pushed race to the margins (especially in the melodrama cycle) while simultaneously remaining obsessed with Black women's bodies (especially in the exploitation cycle).

Finally, the last chapter is devoted to the television series *OITNB,* Jenji Kohan's adaptation of Piper Kerman's memoir that was commissioned by Netflix and produced by Lionsgate. I include this series, while not a WIP film proper, in the genre because it brings together, builds on, and reconfigures many of the WIP genre's themes, codes, and conventions. *OITNB* features a flawed warden who is driven by a desire to reform, but unlike similarly minded characters such as Ann Vickers, Mary Ellis from *Convicted Woman* (1940), or Ruth Benton in *Caged!,* Joe Caputo is a man. He is profoundly dysfunctional, often power hungry, and sometimes weak-willed. He is also profoundly well meaning, often compassionate, and sometimes kind. Like *Caged!* and *Stranger Inside,* the show uses the loss of a child as a driving motivator for key characters. However, from the first moment of Episode 1 – a shower scene – it displays allegiances to the exploitation aesthetics over those of the melodrama. Nevertheless, unlike *Caged Heat,* it broadens the ambit of desirous bodies, explores gender fluidity, and casts an objectifying gaze onto the male characters. Like *Civil Brand, OITNB* features implicit and explicit commentary on how particular bodies in the globalized capitalist and neocolonial world are marked by criminality. Indeed, the incursion of the prison industrial complex in the lives of racialized, poor, and otherwise marginal women is at the core of much of *OITNB.* The show's subsequent seasons shift its attention away from the young, white, middle-class protagonist to tell stories from the standpoint of racialized women, ethnic minority women, older women, women navigating disabilities, and poor women. I explore the implications of this shift for the myths we construct about the women warehoused in prison and argue that the show advances the feminist prison abolitionist conversation that guides the object of inquiry of this book – namely, should women's prisons exist at all?

In each chapter, I discuss the films that have become precedents of the WIP genre and show how each is embedded in a broader WIP aesthetic as well as its own socio-historical moment. The social problem films, which include *Ann Vickers* and *Caged!,* span the 1920s to the 1950s and portray the "new woman" navigating feminist concerns such as employment equity and reproductive rights. *Caged Heat* and the exploitation flicks of the new Hollywood era reflect and respond to the concerns of radical feminism – gender equality and the abolishment of patriarchy – and also reflect and respond to the backlash against it. *Stranger Inside* is the only WIP film told from the standpoint of queer Black women. In contrast, *Civil Brand,* while also emanating from the experience of incarcerated Black women, is the first WIP film to call out the prison industrial complex. Finally, *OITNB* connects the promise of a modified social problem aesthetic with the campiness of the exploitation cycle and, thereby, explores new modes of gender inequalities. Each of these iterations of the WIP film is dynamic insofar as it generates new codes and conventions while remaining squarely fixed within the broader structure and ethos of the genre.

While it is true that I hold these visual representations up because of their implicit and explicit interactions and their novel contributions to the WIP genre, I have ultimately selected films and a show with which I have fallen in love, each for different reasons. Despite the prevalence of scepticism within much of the feminist scholarship that tackles WIP movies, each of the representations I have selected is not only worthy of scholarly consideration but also of attention to what Susan Sontag calls an "erotics of art" or "the pure, untranslatable, sensuous immediacy of some of its images."[43]

My aesthetic preference is for well-written work that tells a compelling story, which is occasionally, though not necessarily, inspired or grounded in fact; that has visual appeal and is narrativized beautifully and symbolically through light, colour, sound, and shape; that navigates dramatic structure and psychic tension; and that features compelling female characters, all of whom are, as film scholar George Toles writes, "concerned with the artful lifting of life's burdens."[44]

These six cinematic texts have had prominent and constitutive effects on the WIP genre and invite feminist engagement with the physical and metaphorical space of the women's prison. In the WIP movies I discuss, women are simultaneously vulnerable and powerful; their vulnerability is not reified as victimhood, nor, importantly, is their power unadulterated emancipation. Consequently, I have chosen these representations because they speak to my aesthetic preferences and normative commitments: they are impressive, bold, and sometimes ironic portrayals of strong and beautiful, flawed and complex women who engage in disruptive strategies and assert selfhood and agency as they navigate conditions of constraint and inequality.

1 A Genre of One's Own

A genre is a system of inclusion and exclusion that organizes the conventions – settings, iconography, and stock characters – of a fictional world. In film theory, genre refers to codes that group representations with similar storylines, settings, themes, approaches, and emotional affects and, correspondingly, viewer expectations. These expectations arise from our familiarity with conventions – with a body of signifiers and signs. The combinations of, and relations between, these signs and signifiers, as Christine Gledhill has explained, generate a "process of constantly shifting combinations and differentiation," which in turn constitute and reconstitute the genre's membership.[1] In legal theory, when a limit is established, as Jacques Derrida reminds us, "norms and interdictions are not far behind"; accordingly, genre translates into dos and don'ts and is always contiguous with rules and laws.[2] If generic conventions are laws like any other, they are subject to appeals, debates, and new iterations. To speak of generic transgressions or contestations necessarily implies a genre's ongoing pertinence and revitalization. Film theorists have pointed out that the rigid narrative taxonomies of traditional genre analysis may overlook the importance of cinematic codes related to montage, editing, light, and sound. When engaged in a more cinematic register, however, genre theory can invite a re-examination of what may at first seem like a static and immutable body of rules.

The exploration of women-in-prison (WIP) movies in this book adds a fresh sense of inquiry into the process of genre making. I argue that these representations, rather than a distaff version of the prison genre, actually constitute a genre of their own. Turning to genre has enabled me to foreground salient commonalities of style, formula, composition, and form in this body of films. To establish the WIP genre's themes, codes, and conventions, I draw boundaries and exclude certain films, at times for heuristic purposes. I also constitute an imagined viewing community whose familiarity with, and expectations of, the genre develop by virtue of generic traditions that repeat or vary over time. In the following discussion, I trace the generic development, and shifting logic, of the WIP genre. Film theorists point to some of the challenges of generic analysis. To Andrew Tudor, for example, inquiry into genre is "the end point of the critical process," and slotting together movies with superficial similarities offers little insight into how a film works.[3] Why then insist – as I do throughout this book – that WIP movies compose not only a genre of their own but also one that merits scholarly attention?

Focusing in particular on *A Room of One's Own,* in which Virginia Woolf insists on the urgency of providing women with the intellectual and financial resources to articulate their worldviews, I argue, on one level, that WIP movies can constitute such a unique cultural and psychic space because they can, at times, examine gendered criminalization through a feminist lens.[4] In comparison to the prison film, which focuses on men's experience of punishment, the WIP movie has received less theoretical or critical attention and, in this way, reflects the general dearth of scholarly and media attention to "women and punishment." As Pat Carlen explains, "the coupling of 'women' and 'punishment' occurs only infrequently in penological literature ... [B]y and large, even in the literature that has focused on the deliberate imposition of pains or deprivations in return for wrongdoing, there seems to have been a reluctance to conceive of punishments as being gender-specific."[5] This lack of critical exploration is noteworthy from a feminist film studies' perspective, in light of the number and variation of WIP films featuring almost exclusively (and often diverse) female casts and deploying different generic conventions and styles to explore women's metaphoric imprisonment. It is also noteworthy from a law and society perspective, which aims to link popular culture to broader issues of social stratification and social conflict, especially as women are the fastest-growing segment of the prison population globally.[6] On another level, and as I elaborate in each of the following chapters, WIP movies are a unique aesthetic space articulating legal meanings about how and why women experience criminalization.

Delineating the Women in Prison Genre

Without claiming that the WIP genre is a discrete or closed system, I have developed a grammar of WIP movies by establishing the semantics of the genre (its key components and signifiers) while also attending to its syntactic features, which help to provide an "overall meaning" to the genre (the structure within which these components and signifiers are arranged).[7] This development was done in two steps. First, I engaged in what Franco Moretti has called a "distant reading" of over three hundred films and other cinematic representations, such as television programs and music videos that feature women in prison or prison-like institutions. Moretti refers to distant reading as the intentional abstraction of details to suggest something about regulatory patterns and networks of governance. In his view, distance is not an obstacle to knowledge about phenomena but, rather, a unique mode of generating meaning. A distant reading of many films can, unlike a "close reading" of a particular artefact, provide a sense of the connections between people, things, and other elements of life and, by extension, of the relationships between texts.[8] Working within a narrative framework, I drew out patterns, networks, flows, and relationships that give a sense of the overall interconnection throughout the WIP genre, and these fruits of my distant reading are outlined, demonstrating a number of the features that constitute the WIP genre and elaborating how these have developed or shifted over time.

The prison genre, which features men in prison, is certainly one of the most accessible modes through which we imagine, understand, and construct myths about the nature of punishment in contemporary society.[9] WIP movies have often been subsumed under the more widely recognized prison genre. However, my distant reading of a large body of cinematic representations has revealed that, far from being a subgenre, the WIP genre has its own rules, features, and knowledge-producing discourses: WIP films consist of almost entirely female characters, many of whom implicitly and, sometimes explicitly, violate hetero-normative structures and almost all of whom engage in crimes against entrenched notions of femininity. Consequently, WIP movies challenge the gendered nature of the traditional prison film and bring into view legal, social, economic, and political structures that criminalize women differently than men.

The Prison Genre: Themes, Codes, and Conventions

The quintessential male prison movie is an action/drama film that takes its central motifs from classical or contemporary mythology: the journalist or undercover cop bent on exposing corruption or saving an innocent is a modern-day Orpheus; the physical or metaphoric walls that divide lovers or families recall Ovid's *Metamorphoses* and Shakespeare's *Romeo and Juliet*; and the prisoner who experiences a profound transformation, akin to Pygmalion, during incarceration. As Brian Jarvis argues, the prison film is "a stage for the negative oedipal complex, driven by hostility toward the mother and desire for the father."[10] While there were earlier iterations of the prison film, its recurring themes, as well as its technical, narrative, and symbolic elements and rules, are usually traced to the 1930s. Films such as *The Big House* (1930), *Numbered Men* (1930), *Criminal Code* (1931), and *I Am a Fugitive on a Chain Gang* (1932) established what are now the genre's most recognizable codes and conventions. Produced at a time when Americans were feeling the full effects of the Great Depression, and just before the Motion Picture Producers and Distributers of America began regulating content in earnest, films of the prison genre conjure the political consciousness of the "social purpose" film and the overarching ethos of reform.

The genre's core themes include punishment/social control and redemption/resistance, with sub-themes such as upholding the rule of law, the relationship between identity and agency, gender non-conforming sexualities, race and class relations, and the fluidity of belonging. Key narrative elements are organized around the maintenance – or contraventions – of the most immediate and direct form of prison law: the "Convict Code." That is, there are implicit norms generated by prisoners and maintained through their interactions among themselves and with guards. Such rules include displays of loyalty among prisoners (don't snitch; don't be too close to the guards), prohibitions such as "no rubbernecking" (don't concern yourself with things beyond your jurisdiction), and guidelines for survival (do your own time). Within the first few scenes of any prison film, the "new fish" (prison slang for a rookie or first offender) will be initiated into the Convict Code, whether by a guard or a more seasoned prisoner.[11]

The protagonist was historically, and often still is, a white man, who is usually middle class – perhaps a stockbroker, a lawyer, an accountant, or an engineer.[12] Frequently, he has been framed for robbery, counterfeiting, embezzlement, or murder.[13] He may also be ambiguously innocent, such as in *20,000 Years in Sing Sing* (1932), in which a hardened criminal takes a murder rap to protect his girlfriend. Sometimes he has committed a minor, but excusable, crime, like in *Brute Force* (1947), where the lead steals to support his physically disabled wife. The roles are typically situated in good/bad binaries, whether these be the innocent or excusable protagonist/sadistic warden, the solid con/hardened con, or the virtuous warden/pit-bull guard. As protagonists tend to fall on the good side of this dyad, prison films usually elicit empathy for those detained.[14] In the WIP genre, similar binaries emerge in unique gendered configurations.

Breaking Away from the Father: A Grammar of American Women in Prison Films

While film theorists have historically talked about the prison genre as though it is composed only of films about men, several early prison films are actually about women. These films feature complex protagonists navigating sexist social structures, and their themes – namely, women enacting justice and the importance of female solidarity – re-emerge in later cycles of the genre. In the 1923 film *Within the Law* and in its 1939 remake, the protagonist is wrongfully convicted. She metes out her own vision of justice once she gets out of prison. Unlike the heroines of the 1970s female-centred rape revenge movies that *Within the Law* prefigures, Mary vows to get even legally.[15] In *The Lullaby* (1924), Felipa, played by Jane Novak, takes the rap for her boyfriend, who has killed a rival in a jealous rage. She is handed a twenty-year sentence. Unlike the romantic melodramas that it precedes, which end in the reconstitution of a heterosexual union, the story in *The Lullaby* keys in on the reuniting of Felipa and her daughter. Moreover, given

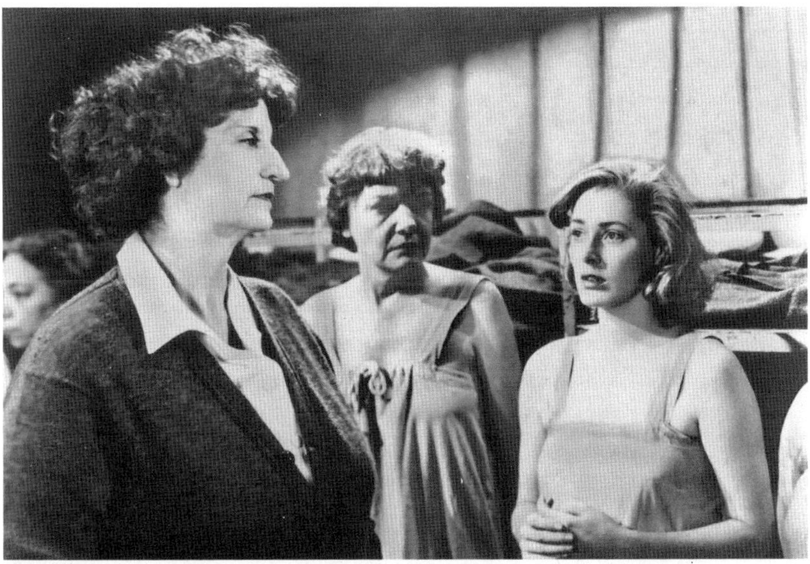

Figure 2 *Caged!* (1950). Licensed by Warner Brothers Entertainment (all rights reserved).

that *La Passion de Jeanne d'Arc/The Passion of Joan of Arc* (*The Passion*) (1928) spotlights Jeanne's physical and sexual abuse by guards and the corruption of those who judge the trustworthiness of her claims, I argue that it actually establishes many of the generic rules followed in later iterations of the WIP movie – from John Cromwell's social problem oeuvre, *Ann Vickers* (1933), to Netflix's immensely popular dramedy, *Orange Is the New Black* (*OITNB*) (2013–19).

Yet any genre, semiologists explain, draws on several others, whether by inversion or displacement, or it may overlap and mix with another genre. The films that make up the WIP genre surely borrow from the prison genre. As audience expectations have shifted over time in response to the recurring discursive properties of WIP films, the genre has become more closely aligned with romantic melodramas and social problem films in their earlier incarnations, with teenage exploitation, with rape-revenge movies, with the action movies from the 1960s to the late 1980s, and with an admixture of all of these genres in current movies and television series. In particular, unlike prison films that feature men, the WIP genre has consistently circulated multiple and conflicting proto-feminist or feminist discourses. To this effect, the WIP genre's different styles and structures do not offer a consistent or coherent vision of women's criminalization or of women's agency despite such criminalization. This textual diversity renders WIP films a unique arena for the exploration of a range of empowering and disempowering images of women and the intersecting and shifting hegemonic structures that operate to criminalize women's survival tactics. I divide the genre into four cycles, each displaying codes and conventions that can be grouped according to a loose general time frame: melodramas/social problem films (1930s–1950s); the exploitation tradition (1970s–early 1980s); realist dramas (1990s–2000s); and dramedies (mid-2000s–today).

Like any classification, arranging films into cycles may be considered linear and essentialist. Rather than claiming to provide a clear historical trajectory of the genre, I am "proposing its logic," to borrow from Stanley Cavell, by pointing to shifts in audience expectations, formal composition, and narrative over time.[16] I am not suggesting that each cycle is discrete and insular. On the contrary, the romantic melodramas and the realist dramas contain exploitative elements; the exploitation films have romantic subplots; the dramedies often include satire while remaining heavily influenced by the realist aesthetics or use parody to pay homage to exploitation films; and all of the cycles still operate, with varying degrees, within a melodramatic mode. Moreover, every WIP cinematic representation summons up other genres, whether it is gangster, western, action, documentary, film noir, or comedy. Consider *Caged!* (1950), which is often referred to as the prototypical "social purpose" WIP film, drawing on film noir (not simply a type of film but also a worldview and approach that transcends genre) while also setting the conventions for the exploitation films produced two decades later.[17] Similarly, Neema Barnette's realist drama *Civil Brand* (2002) relies heavily on the tropes of exploitation to convey its critique of the prison industrial complex.

Finally, each cycle includes parodic repetitions of the genre's conventions. Sapphic "girls in reformatories" films emerged during the melodrama cycle and again as made-for-television movies but more often than not, they were self-reflexive spoofs of the exploitation movies in the 1980s, and cheeky responses to the serious aspirations of the reality-based dramas.[18] *Reform School Girls* (1986) marketed itself as a parody of the genre ("the loveliest girls in the history of socially conscious cinema"). Fox Television's short-lived satirical comedy *Women in Prison* (1987–88) has episode names like "Vicky Does Prison" and "Goldfingers." Its protagonist Vicky Springer (Julia Campbell), who is framed by her lawyer/husband because it was cheaper than getting a divorce, lists "most likely to be pictured running naked in slow motion on a beach" on her resume and laments that her looks must be fading because no guard will sexually harass her.[19] In *Slammer Girls* (1987), Matron Crabapples (Veronica Hart) says to the innocent protagonist: "Put that back in an old Susan Hayward movie," referring to the Academy award-winning critique of capital punishment, *I Want to Live!* (1958). Finally, Lady Gaga/Beyoncé's video for *Telephone* (2009) and *OITNB* are both firmly within the WIP genre and function as meta-critiques of the genre itself. In *Telephone,* Lady Gaga is sent to the "Prison for Bitches" where she makes out with her norm-defying girlfriend, played by performance artist/body builder Heather Cassils, only to be busted out by her partner, Beyoncé, who drives the "Pussy Wagon" from *Kill Bill: Volume 1* (2003). *OITNB* shamelessly reproduced some of the exploitation tropes through the character of George "Pornstache" Mendez (Pablo Schreiber) who, during intake, regularly utters phrases such as: "When they first come through, we should check their assholes" (pausing for effect) "thoroughly."[20] Finally, the short film *Condemned* (2010) features a night guard (Ashlie Atkinson, who could be a doppleganger of Hope Emerson) who embodies the sexually ambiguous and terrifying matron in *Caged!*

All to say, I avoid a strict taxonomic approach by measuring the general drift of WIP films released over decades and by providing a punctuated overview of some of the continuities and discontinuities that appear in four different, but overlapping, cycles of the genre.

Melodrama Cycle (1930s–50s)

The first cycle of WIP films were often melodramas with a social purpose ("social purpose films"), in which protagonists confront institutional injustices. The melodrama was the mainstay of film production in the early silent era (1915–29) and reproduced theatrical conventions including the domestic sphere, familial tensions, the hero/villain dyad, a suffering female protagonist, and the struggle of good against evil. The melodrama genre underwent a redefinition in the 1940s when it became primarily a vehicle for stories told from a female point of view, which were renamed "weepies" or "women's pictures."[21] Social purpose films may also be considered a genre in which protagonists navigate injustice; their focus and form shifted from morality tales in the early 1900s, to depression-era class struggles in the 1930s, peaking in the late 1940s when filmmakers grappled with the aftermath of the Second World War.[22]

WIP melodrama and social purpose films released before the 1950s grapple with the emergence of the "new woman" or, in later iterations, film noir that reappraised changing gender roles. Some of these films were distributed during the laxer regulatory era prior to the release of the Production Code, which ended around 1934. Other WIP films emerged when the Production Code was in full effect. While the explicit lesson of some of these later films is that prison can restore a "fallen woman," many feature scenes directly violating the Production Code's prohibition of sexually suggestive content and invite audiences to side with lawbreakers.

Exploitation Cycle (1970s–early 1980s)

Social consciousness/melodrama WIP movies, such as *Caged!,* claimed through advertising to depict "the story of a women's prison today."[23] In contrast, *Caged Heat* (1974), the exploitative reboot produced twenty-five years later, promised in its trailer to expose "caged passions igniting in carnal confinement and exploding into violence."[24] The second cycle of WIP films (the "exploitation" cycle) is generally composed of B features intended for the drive-in theatre or the grindhouse theatre, produced during the New Hollywood era of the 1970s and targeting young heterosexual male audiences. Responding to a decrease in cinema's popularity, filmmakers and production companies shifted towards narratives of sexual exploitation and revenge. They also modified their distribution methods, especially towards television and direct to video, in order to attract and sustain a new audience base.

Exploitation WIP films of the 1970s reflect an overarching anxiety due to the disruptive social and political consequences of a number of social movements (such as second-wave feminism, the new left, civil rights, and gay and lesbian rights); the rise of postmodern and post-structural theories in the academy, which challenged entrenched understandings of authority and truth; the Vietnam War; the Watergate scandal; and a debilitating economic recession. They may also be considered part of a counter-narrative against a slate of "new women" films, such as *Alice Doesn't Live Here Anymore* (1975) and *An Unmarried Woman* (1977), about female protagonists with difficult or limited life choices. The exploitation WIP films opted instead for a formula: women enduring victimization, having their consciousness awoken, and then enacting revenge on their oppressors, usually while topless.[25]

Realist Drama Cycle (1990s–early 2000s)

The melodrama/social consciousness films tend to wane after the 1950s, but they re-emerge in the late 1970s with the release of a variety of television series, beginning with Australia's *Prisoner* (1979–86) and its reboot as *Wentworth* (2013–present), which follows many conventions of the soap opera.[26] Similarly, in the British dramatic television series *Bad Girls* (1999–2006), written and directed by Maureen Chadwick and Ann McManus, two "do-or-die, go-to-the-wall, in-your-face feminists" explicitly use television to educate the public on women's imprisonment.[27]

Compare this purpose to the exploitation films of the 1970s, many of which were aimed at male audiences and directed by men, who were not exactly compelled to educate the masses on the cruel reality of women's incarceration. Nevertheless, since the release of *Bad Girls,* there have been a few WIP films that reproduce the conventions of the social purpose film while still catering to a more censured version of the voyeuristic demands of the exploitation cycle. *Stranger Inside* (2001) and *Civil Brand* are directed by Black women and told from the standpoint of criminalized Black women. The scripts were workshopped with women who were or had been incarcerated and the story was shot, at least in part, in actual women's prisons. According to Cheryl Dunye, her film reproduces the exploitation cycle's elements in order to "reach an audience beyond the converted-supporters." Dunye explains that "she did a lot of soul-searching and digesting of the history of [women's] prison movies ... [and] knew that all sorts of people [were] going to be watching the film." Consequently, "along with the sadistic guard there are one or two fight scenes."[28]

The realist dramas are films that respond to changing expectations and preferences of audiences, who want representations of prison to "feel" real and be socially aware while still displaying a range of female bodies and telling dramatic stories. For instance, unlike earlier iterations of the genre that follow an "innocent" white protagonist, Treasure (Yolonda Ross), the lead character in *Stranger Inside,* is a young, Black, lesbian gang member who navigates what Black feminist scholar and activist Beth E. Richie calls "the cumulative negative impact of stigmatized racial, class, sexual, and gendered identities."[29] In several of the films from this cycle, the criminalization of the characters, similar to Treasure, is embedded within a larger trajectory of intergenerational incarceration, unsupportive social services, rejection from community, and marginalization from peers. The realist dramas also introduce a new character to the WIP roster: the psychopathic female offender, who is an exception to the usual depiction that women who are incarcerated for murder have killed abusive men. Troublingly, these characters, such as Suzy Kurosawa (Susie Elene) in *Cage without a Key* (1975) and Brownie (Davenia McFadden) in *Stranger Inside* are racialized and seem to derive pleasure from the senseless murders they commit.[30]

Dramedies (Mid-2000s–Today)

The dramedy is an evolving hybrid genre that melds comedic conventions and characteristics (for example, gags, props, repartee, exaggerated situations) and dramatic conventions and characteristics (for example, serious storylines, realistic settings, and complex characters). Rather than simply including "some cross-genre features," as Leah Ekdom Vande Berg explains, there is a self-reflexive and "sustained fusion" of the elements of each genre in dramedies.[31] In some ways, the dramedy cycle has crossed over with the satire. The satirical, feminist show *Women in Prison,* for instance, used the tropes of the social purpose film with narrative elements of the exploitation cycle to critique the under- and stereotypical representation of women in the television and film industry more broadly. However, unlike the dramedies that would follow it in the 2000s, the show had no aspirations of revealing actual injustices faced by incarcerated women.

Dramedies are a cycle that began before the advent of *OITNB*. However, the series has become not only the quintessential WIP dramedy, it may well be the most recognizable and widespread cinematic representation of women in prison ever made. Consider the first season of *OITNB* by the on-demand streaming platform Netflix. Like some of the newer iterations of the melodrama, especially *Bad Girls, OITNB* has feminist pretensions and, as some media scholars point out, "[has] contribute[d] to consciousness raising about the conditions in women's prisons, the inequities of the U.S. justice system, and the situation of female subjects as protagonists in control (or not) of their own life stories."[32] At the same time, Netflix marketed the show as a comedy and even won the Emmy in 2014 for "Outstanding Casting for a Comedy Series." Despite the creator of the show's desire to draw the audience's attention to the lived realities of criminalized women through humour, Season 1 left me sceptical about *OITNB*'s critical potential. The show, in large part as a response to audience expectations, has since represented the prison space as a complex spatio-temporal matrix of race, sexuality, and femininity and as a site of feminist solidarity across difference, largely through complex, hitherto non-existent, leading characters, such as Sophia Burset (Laverne Cox), a Black transgender woman played by a Black transgender woman and a vocal advocate for gender self-determination.

Narrowing the Field: Conventions of the WIP Genre

With these four cycles of WIP cinematic representations in mind, I now articulate the genre's conventions and explain, at least in part, how a body of films can convey multiple, sometimes conflicting, sometimes subversive, meanings about women's criminalization and how these meanings shift over time. To do so, I have narrowed the scope of my inquiry and will explain what actually constitutes a WIP movie. Richard Altman argues that the first step in discussing a genre is to establish as widely as possible a "preliminary corpus" of films to be analyzed and filtered.[33] For my purposes, the preliminary WIP corpus includes any film in which women find themselves in a jail or prison. To further distil the genre, I narrow down the kinds of narrative forms, themes, settings, plots, and stock characters. These are the conventions that define the WIP genre, that shape and inform shared audience expectations, and that, to some degree, have been followed, referred to, or twisted by the makers of other cinematic representations.

Narrative Form: Fiction Films and Television

Women have historically been, and continue to be, subjected to multiple forms of informal regulation, such as social norms around sexuality, cultural conditioning about femininity, and paternalist assumptions around employment equity and reproductive freedoms. However, compared to men, only a relatively small number of women will directly encounter explicit formal regulation in the form of the criminal justice system. Following upon both of these points, the question of whether films about women's prisons are realistic is less interesting than the question of whether – and, if so, how – WIP films invite viewers to question the function of women's prisons within hegemonic structures based on gender, race, class, and other forms of domination that metaphorically and concretely circumscribe women's choices.

Consequently, the WIP genre, as I define it, does not include documentaries about women in prison. Concern for authenticity and realism looms large in the documentary genre and tradition. Yet documentary filmmakers do blur the boundaries between fiction and fact through editing, the use of music, and voice-overs. There is a tension between the ideal – that documentaries capture an unmediated reality – and the practical fact that the act of filmmaking may incite change in the subject's behaviour and in the outcome of events. A number of documentary films about prison exist, and many of these have been used as vehicles to alter public perception about incarceration. These documentaries can be thought-provoking accounts of women's criminalization and can contribute, or already have contributed, to political mobilization to abolish prisons. There are excellent documentaries produced in the United States that grapple with the subject of women in prison, several of which feature women discussing difficult themes, such as racism and the dehumanization that results from the prison experience.[34] However, as documentary filmmaker Alexandra Juhasz points out, others may re-victimize incarcerated women and feed a voyeuristic desire in mainstream audiences.[35]

Other law and film scholars have discussed the blurring between fictional and non-fictional narratives in film and the vexing question of what documentary film's relationship to law and regulatory practices is or ought to be.[36] However, the representations that interest me are not, nor do they claim to be, documentaries, even though some of the films I discuss are inspired by factual events. *Caged!* is partly based on the life of Dr. Miriam Waters, a feminist warden from Massachusetts; *Stranger Inside*'s screenplay is grounded in conversations and workshops with residents and staff in a state prison; and, of course, *OITNB* was inspired by the memoir of the same name, which details Piper Kerman's thirteen months in a women's prison.[37] Regardless of whether they are grounded in factual events, I am less concerned with the extent to which these WIP films are accurate depictions of female criminalization and incarceration than I am with what we can draw from the intertextual relationships between these different representations as well as with the dialogical relationship between criminal law, the criminalization of particular groups of women, and fictional stories about women's incarceration.

Lastly, film and television have historically existed within very different and often competitive regulatory contexts; have had their own production, distribution, and exhibition modalities; have generated different relationships to audiences; and have favoured particular acting styles. For example, film was traditionally intended as a shared viewing experience in a theatre, whereas television was a private, intimate experience within the home. The advent of videocassette recorders and DVDs, so-called "prestige" television with more sophisticated content, fluidity in stardom from television to film and vice versa, and on-demand streaming have blurred the clear distinction between these two media forms. Nonetheless, whereas films generally take place within a fixed time frame (usually ninety minutes) and rely on generic conventions of familiarity to cut out large segments of time or character development, television generally requires "that the ending of one episode is the beginning of the next, so that the meaning of events is never easily pinned down."[38]

Since television series can run for several years, this medium permits more complex narrative arcs and more dramatic shifts in character motivations. What I have found is that television is the newest form of WIP film and could possibly even compose its own cycle. And, indeed, most series are realist dramas. However, rather than carving one media off from the other, I have included the fiction television series as part of, and constitutive of, the WIP genre. In particular, I discuss *OITNB* according to various seasons, which vary in their allegiances to different WIP cycles. For instance, Season 1, particularly episodes 1–4, reflects an exploitation aesthetic, whereas Season 5 seems to be a satire of that cycle and is much more explicitly focused on circulating messages of social change (like the social purpose films) and exploring the experiences of characters who could be actual incarcerated women (like the realist dramas).

Themes: Spatialized Material and Symbolic Imprisonment

Film and law are two ways of symbolizing anxieties and expectations about how the prison space is, or should be, experienced. A film organizes the prison space within its diegesis (meaning the story within the film, including shots, narrative sequences, and geographic relationships between various settings). Law confronts and articulates prison space through the attribution of the legal label ("prisoner") and the associated restrictions on mobility. In tracing the contours of the WIP genre, I sought out films that deploy prison space metaphorically in ways that resist dominant legal constructions of femininity as passive, domestic, and heterosexual or dominant legal subjectivities such as victim (in the sense of someone who has directly or indirectly suffered harm as a result of a crime) or criminal (in the sense of someone who has directly or indirectly inflicted harm as a result of a crime).

Consequently, I limit my inquiry into the WIP genre according to some spatial characteristics. For instance, I do not discuss the miniseries *Bangkok Hilton* (1989) or the film *Brokedown Palace* (1999), which concern white, middle-class women from the global North charged with drug offences held in brutal "foreign" prisons. These stories often implicitly or explicitly invite comparisons between the archaic other(ed) jurisdiction and the inevitably more just and procedural Western common law system. Given that the American style of retributive penology is leading the global trend in the explosion of women's prison populations,[39] it is more useful to examine the filmic representation of American-style penology in action to help untangle questions around women's criminalization generally. To this effect, I engage in a close reading of two WIP films – *Ann Vickers* and *Caged!* – that centre on the efforts of American prison reformers at the beginning of the twentieth century and that expose the brutality of women's prisons and question their utility altogether. I distinguish these WIP films from others that simply deploy the prison as a narrative device through which to develop a romantic relationship between the protagonist and a male love object.

Other themes that emerge when we approach the prison space as a metaphor are the nature of motherhood and domesticity; feminist responses to the sexual assault and sexual domination of girls and women; heterosexual male anxieties about women's emancipation; resistance in the face of injustice; allegorical condemnation of conservative norms that restrict women's mobility; hierarchies among women along axes of privilege and disadvantage; vengeance; and the revolutionary potential of women's solidarity across symbolic boundaries of race/ethnicity/culture, class, sexual identity, and gender expression.

Setting: Women's Incarceration in the United States

The WIP genre's conventions are defined and enabled by spatial metaphors for time and temporal metaphors for space – being inside, doing time, being behind the wall, and so on. I limit my field of inquiry to fictional narratives whose majority running time and diegetic space remain "within" women's prisons located in the United States. To this end, I exclude from the WIP genre films that bear similar markers of incarceration – the basement, the psychiatric ward, the Magdalene laundries – but are not "prisons" in the sense of formally recognized, government-regulated punitive spaces.[40] These films may well grapple with notions of psychological and physical imprisonment in complex ways, but they do not further the study of how the cinematically rendered space of a "women's prison" and the legal institution of a "women's prison" that exists beyond the film world are mutually constitutive. I also do not include films about residential and boarding institutions that have been used as instruments for the cultural assimilation of Indigenous peoples, though they have certainly been compared to prisons.[41]

The films I have selected for in-depth discussion are based in American prisons. I do occasionally extend my inquiry beyond the American context in this book. Most notably, I claim that the WIP genre originated with Dreyer's *The Passion,* which takes place in medieval France. I may also refer to texts from other jurisdictions insofar as they provide compelling complementary stories or poignant counter-narratives.[42] However, my focus is American-centric because the United States still has one of the highest incarceration rates in the world. The Bureau of Justice Statistics found that, in 2015, almost seven million Americans (715 per 100,000 people) were under supervision, whether in jail, in prison, on probation, or on parole. And women are currently the fastest-growing segment of that American carceral population. Therefore, in this book, I talk about the WIP genre as films taking place in the Western world, and I focus on those films depicting life in American prisons.

The series of WIP films produced by New World Pictures under Roger Corman and a number of reboots by other production companies are, accordingly, excluded from my discussion. These films were shot in, and set in, the Philippines or other developing countries because of their lower production costs, including low-paid, non-unionized labour. While the B films about women "in bondage" on "exotic islands" probably began in Europe with Jesús Franco's *99 Women* (1969), New World soon dominated the market with the release of its WIP catalogue beginning with *The Big Doll House* (1971), followed by *Women in Cages* (1971) and *Big Bird Cage* (1972).[43] These films portray American women in prison, of which at least one protagonist is Black and often played by Pam Grier, who is a fan favourite. The stories unfold as follows: unjustly imprisoned in an unnamed Southeast Asian dictatorship or an otherwise colonial and imperial regime, women attempt to escape and are eventually captured or killed in a shoot-out. The women, cast as freedom fighters and revolutionaries, are usually resisting male-dominated power structures, though occasionally, as in the case of

Women in Cages, in which Pam Grier plays a sadistic warden, they may also be resisting other women who are complicit in their oppression. The jungle WIP movies are interesting because of these themes and are relevant insofar as they helped to establish the codes around marginalized sexual orientation and normalized female nudity found in the dramedies that followed a few decades later. However, the jungle prison variation of the exploitation WIP cycle is less significant to this book, which is interested in shifts in women's prison reform in the global North and the United States, in particular.

Temporal restrictions exclude prison "exiting" films, such as *Girls on Probation* (1938), *The Company She Keeps* (1956), and the Canadian independent film *Délivrez-moi* (2006). In the latter film, Annie (Céline Bonnier) is released from jail and tries to rebuild a relationship with her daughter. While the actual prison is only shown twice in the film (once as it currently exists and once in a flashback shower scene), the metaphor of prison permeates the movie and chronicles much about who occupies the space known as prison in reality: working-class women, survivors of violence, and women with little-to-no post-secondary education. These films poignantly foreground and confront the difficulties of reintegration into society after incarceration. Similarly excluded are "prison break" films such as *Black Mama White Mama* (1973), transport movies such as *Five Bold Women* (1960) in which a marshal must ensure the safe transfer of five violent women, or furlough movies like *Prison Girls* (1973), which also feature characters who violate orthodox gender norms, but all of these genres tend to be more closely aligned with road movies – and the existential questions of freedom and movement that they explore – than with the warehousing and immobility of prison films. Finally, for a film to fall within my definition of a WIP film, a significant amount of the film's narrative must occur in prison. For instance, films that merely feature a protagonist who lands herself in jail for a brief time are excluded.[44]

Plot Structure

According to law professor David Black, films that depict people "rotting away in prison, deprived of their narrative agency" are rarely interesting unless something else happens.[45] In early WIP films – popular melodramas or "women's films" with a backlight of social protest about the conditions of women's prisons – that "something else" is what feminist film theorists call "recuperation" plots that historically contained the threat posed by unattached women. To a large extent, but with some important exceptions that I explore later, the melodramas of the 1930s to the mid-1950s reproduce many of the characteristics of a classical Hollywood narrative.[46] There are often cause-and-effect connections – namely, the "good" girl will be proven innocent or the "bad" girl will be saved, after atonement, from her profligate lifestyle.[47] In either iteration, the protagonist shifts from being a criminal subject to being a love object, and there is usually a tidy resolution in the form of a romantic heterosexual union.[48] Despite variations in the cinematic vocabulary, for much of the genre's existence, the (otherwise "respectable" and invariably white) protagonist is either innocent (wrongfully convicted);[49] in an unhealthy relationship with, and taking the rap for, a boyfriend;[50] or is found guilty of being an accessory to a crime committed (usually by a man to whom she is romantically attached).[51] The first season of *OITNB* introduces the prison through the eyes of Piper Kerman, and despite the variance that she has been set up by her girlfriend rather than by a man, she remains the figure of the white woman who feels woefully out of place with the real criminals.

The most recognizable and popular character arc is the following: the film chronicles the depersonalization that each woman must endure once in prison, as she dons a prison uniform, is given her identification number, and told to hand over her personal belongings, especially her wedding ring.[52] As a "new fish," the protagonist is confused and overwhelmed. She discovers that she is "expecting company" or is "in a jam" – that is, pregnant. Unable to find a guardian for her child while she completes her sentence, she is forced to hand her baby over to child and family authorities. This causes her distress and she becomes jaded.[53] In another cycle, she discovers corruption within the institution and is then subjected to cruelty by a matron or another prisoner when she tries to speak up.[54] Usually, she attempts to break out for noble purposes or she is cajoled into an escape plan by more seasoned cons.[55] More often than not, her bitterness subsides through the love or kindness of a good man, whether a chaplain or minister who wants to save her soul, a doctor who teaches her life lessons, a reporter trying to expose corruption and cruelty within the prison, or a lawyer convinced of her factual or moral innocence.[56] In later iterations of the genre, such as in *OITNB*, this story will shift to a well-meaning, but ineffectual, interloper – in this case, a white male reporter:

> Do I lie awake at night fantasizing that I personally take down an institution that is the single greatest stain on the America collective conscience since slavery with the awesome power of my words. Sure. But it's the daytime and I've accepted that that's not going to happen.[57]

A few films tell the story of women who can be considered neither factually nor morally innocent. These may be cautionary tales exposing the dangers of being a "wild child,"[58] but they may also include sympathetic protagonists sent to prison for engaging in criminalized survival acts, such as larceny, forging cheques, or vagrancy.[59] Here, too, the protagonist usually has a life-changing experience in jail and leaves rehabilitated, resolved to be a good person, and, more often than not, a good wife and mother.[60]

While these are redemption scenarios, there are contradictory messages circulating within each of these films.[61] *Ladies They Talk About,* for instance, ends with Nan Taylor, played by the quintessential femme fatale Barbara Stanwyck, accepting an evangelist's marriage proposal. Yet Stanwyck's screen presence – her ability to be vulnerable and impenetrable at once – suggests that her decision may be born in equal measure from genuine affection and pragmatism.[62] In addition to these core conventions, audiences can expect some other formulaic scenes: an introductory speech for the "new fish" about the prison rules, a hunger strike, women working in laundry facilities, the development of close bonds between prisoners, and a conversation in the dorm or basin room that tells audiences what crime each woman has been charged with. While the Production Code prohibited "sex perversion or any inference to it," queer connotations – whether suggested or explicit – have always been a core element of the WIP genre's risqué dialogue. More than any other WIP film of its era, *Caged!* provides the prototype for this, including the mandatory shower scene and a matron of questionable sexual appetites, and plays with heterosexual anxieties around women's changing social status.

With the exploitation cycle of the 1970s and early 1980s, the WIP genre shifts from comprising "women's films" to being composed of "men's films." This cycle promises young, attractive, topless women coming into conflict with sadistic lesbian guards and/or lecherous male wardens, rioting or possibly escaping, and taking several showers along the way. Put differently, in this articulation of the WIP genre, the "something" that keeps audiences engaged is "Rape, Riot and Revenge!"[63] WIP exploitation films unfold in three parts: victimization, radicalization, and violent retribution.[64] Women endure abuse and humiliation in the corrupt justice system that has landed them in prison and then in the institution itself, where they undergo cavity searches, electro-shock therapy and other forms of torture, as well as sexual assaults by male or female guards, the warden, or other prisoners, all while taking many, many showers.[65] Technically, the first shower scene is in *Paid* (1930), in which audiences get a glimpse of women's calves through a panning sequence. That scene is quoted in *Caged!*, which also shows women in their slips waiting in line before the camera pans to their legs/calves in the shower stalls. In the exploitation flick *Women in Chains* (1972), which features nudity throughout, the shower scene is in direct reference to these earlier depictions, and the women are only shown from the legs down. Finally, the satirical film *Prison-A-Go-Go!* (2003) has a clock in the bottom corner of the frame indicating when the next shower will occur.

Like the melodramas, these films may portray a morally or legally innocent character; however, unlike that cycle, in exploitation films she is rarely the main protagonist. The protagonist nonetheless makes some loyal friends[66] and tries (usually unsuccessfully) to keep out of the "queen bee's" (the alpha female) way or to remain quiet after witnessing institutional violence or corruption.[67] She rallies other prisoners to voice their complaints through "legitimate" channels (a sympathetic guard, a firm-but-fair warden, or a kind doctor), but she is unsuccessful.[68] Tensions build, and a riot or escape attempt ensues.[69] With a few exceptions, such as *Caged Heat*, several, if not all, of the main characters die or are recaptured and brought back to complete their prison sentences.[70] These key narrative moments and codes – shower scenes in which guards are confronted with their own desires; bondage/humiliation relationships and their multiple inversions; rape fantasies; "cat fights" that result in romantic liaisons; and the eroticism of solitary confinement – put into sharp relief the exploitation cycle's major themes: the relationship between marginalized (non-normative) sexual identities and punishment and the changing configurations of gender that accompany women's shifting position in society.

I differentiate, somewhat tenuously, between exploitation WIP films that are essentially soft-core pornography, which exploit female nudity and sexuality to sexually arouse viewers for commercial purposes, and those that tend towards more singular expressions of sado-masochistic fantasies and desires and in which the prison setting is incidental to the plot. Given that the initial research for this book began over a decade ago, when movie rental stores still existed, my inclusion criteria for exploitation WIP movies were either those that I could find in the aisle of a video store rather than in the "adult" section and those listed on various fan website pages. One fan similarly explained a distinction between niche exploitation series, such as *Ilsa She-Wolf of the SS* (1975) and the New World Pictures prison camp trilogy, in this way:

> Where is the turn-on in a Nazi slave labor camp? Or a cruel Japanese wartime prison for that matter? In these settings we seem to cross the line from

> the taboo/power narrative into the arena of full-blown degradation. Is there really a large market for that? Maybe it is just me, but I think there is a qualitative difference between standard women-in-prison movies and movies like *Ilsa* [*She-Wolf*] ... Although Puritans of both the left and right might not see the difference, it seems pretty clear to me.[71]

At least one scholar flips this assertion on its head: whereas WIP films exhibit sadistic tendencies in which women are the object of violence, the *Ilsa* series is more accurately masochistic insofar as "the pain is turned against the subject," a presumably male viewer.[72]

Rather than make a clear statement on the phenomenology of WIP films, I have simply excluded from my data set those films that are set in a desolate "jungle prison" (because they do not engage with the prison as an institution) or in a Nazi extermination camp (because fans have determined that they do not fall within the generic criteria).[73] I am not attempting to evaluate whether exploitative cinema plays a role in shaping troubling discourses around violence against women. It is certainly not beyond the realm of possibility that some of them do, and several fans of the genre will admit that therein lies much of its appeal. As a commentator who goes by the name "Borris Lugosi" writes, "if you're a radical feminist you won't get much out of this sleazefest, and even the sensitive side of your old Uncle Boris flinched at a couple of the scenes in this one, but look, brutality to women goes with the territory of this genre." Correspondingly, I leave it to other feminist scholars to explore how the more explicitly fetishistic cinematic constructions may be a source of pleasure and sexual emancipation for a broad array of spectators.[74] While I do read a few films that fall within the exploitation cycle as campy and subversive, and they may playfully raise questions about sexual difference, normative femininity, and gender roles, I leave it to another time to ask in what ways the exploitative cycle of WIP films "works" on its targeted audience: young, heterosexual males.[75] Suffice to say that I am of the view that such fantasy spaces and "alternative societies" are, in and of themselves, a fruitful realm for critical exploration of the relationship between law and cinema[76] and of how women's sexuality and legal subjectivities are constituted through film.

Finally, films explicitly about women's executions might make up a genre of their own.[77] These films tend to cast a critical lens on a particular sentencing practice – state executions – rather than to grapple with the specific issue of women's criminalization. Nonetheless, they do share some of the WIP melodrama's conventions, including the development of a bond between the protagonist and a man who tries to "save" her, whether he be a defence attorney, a psychiatrist, a journalist gathering evidence of wrongful conviction, or a spiritual guide.

Stock Characters

As one of the few film genres that feature almost entirely female casts, WIP movies offer a venue for articulating, interrogating, and re-articulating how women negotiate their identities and legal subjectivities within conditions of relative constraint. Fluid gender identities, sexual orientation, and gender expressions are key elements of the WIP genre. In early WIP films, for example, notions of womanhood mark differences and produce meanings around character types. Usually, a "butch" lesbian whose identity and gender expression reflect dominant understandings of normative masculinity (usually a warden or a matron) is matched with a "femme" whose identity and gender expression reflects the dominant understandings of normative femininity (usually a "new fish").[78] In some of the exploitation WIP films of the 1970s, the more one-dimensional depictions of lesbians shift in ways that offer both familiarity and novelty: the heroine may be gender non-conforming and sexually liberated, whereas the warden/matron may be "femme" and sexually repressed.[79] These new configurations produce more complex meanings about the criminalization of non-normative sexualities. While stock characters in WIP films may reproduce dominant binaries, they also invite audiences, through parody and inversion, to interrogate assumptions about the nature of those binaries.

As a consequence, the main characters in WIP films are sometimes stereotypical forms for expressing gendered expectations or anxieties about women's changing social status. As short forms, they can reproduce the discourse that women in prison are "less dangerous and socially less injurious" than men.[80] The innocuous nature of many of the crimes women commit has become a guiding convention or organizing principle of the WIP genre. Women are charged with morality offences, such as bigamy or prostitution; addiction-related petty offences; or physician-assisted suicide. Other protagonists are political prisoners or labour rights activists. Others still have committed gendered violent crimes, such as infanticide and maternal filicide.[81] These characters question jurisprudential principles involving the nature of culpability and challenge the class and gender biases embedded in the criminal justice system. In *Hold Your Man* (1933), for instance, a socialist in jail for "criminal syndicalism" asks: "What right have they got to put her in here? Or you? Or me? We haven't done anything those society debutants don't do but do you ever hear of a society girl being sent up. No! It's the system!" Other characters, such as those who have killed abusive male partners, trouble the victim/offender dichotomy because their crimes are depicted as reasonable survival mechanisms.[82] These women invite questions about the assumptions that shape individual culpability under the law and disturb the good girl/bad girl dichotomy that continues to govern girls' and women's lives in many ways. Occasionally, the movies contain women who commit seemingly senseless violent acts while still exhibiting gendered norms of femininity and honour: Mary Hilton (Diana Dors) in *Yield to the Night* (1956), for example, murders a woman she believes to be sleeping with her boyfriend; in *OTINB,* Tiffany Doggett (Taryn Manning) kills an abortion provider.

Every WIP film has a queen bee – a woman in a dominant position within the group – and she often presents as butch or as otherwise gender non-conforming.[83] Every WIP film also features at least one character struggling with severe mental health issues and often delusions.[84] Finally, the most recognizable of all of the WIP stock characters of the early films is the sadistic matron who embodies law and lawlessness at once, insofar as she may signify social disorder, sexual deviance, and moral decay. She stands in for the authority of the state and wields that authority in an arbitrary manner. Most often a "mannish" lesbian, she has developed with time into a more androgynous figure and a source of pleasure for viewers and, importantly, for queer viewers.[85] Compare, for instance, the depiction of Evelyn Harper (Hope Emerson) in *Caged!* with that of Amazon (Stacy Cunnigham) in the kitschy/exploitation reboot *Stuck!* (2009).

While the melodramas tend to chronicle the life of one protagonist, the "innocent,"[86] the exploitation films and the realist dramas follow several characters, thereby casting a wider net for audience sympathies for diverse criminalized women. With the exploitation cycle, new characters are also introduced: an anti-authoritarian "soul sista" who plays a pivotal narrative role; a political prisoner; and a woman who has committed crimes against the state and leads the others in an escape.[87] In these films, some characters still find their way to prison for having committed serious crimes against the "patriarchy" (male-dominated legal, political, and social relations and structures), such as killing a rapist, but the majority of women's criminal behaviour is linked to more subtle, implicit, and pervasive forms of victimization, such as feminized poverty.[88] The exploitation WIP films emerged at the same time as Blaxploitation films of the 1970s and share some of their features. Blaxploitation films showcased, and were produced by, African

American talent. They were explicitly intended for young, predominantly male, Black audiences and exploited humour, sexuality, and violence to explore themes of racial oppression. The WIP exploitation cycle also features strong, complex Black characters, often driving the narrative. These female protagonists were in stark contrast to the more traditional roles afforded to women in action movies (often narrow and without much character development) and the caricatured treatment of Black women in cinema more broadly (often personifying racist stereotypes such as the mammy, Aunt Jemima, Jezebel, Sapphire, and, more recently, the welfare mom). Pam Grier, most notably, became not only a feminist icon with her role in Blaxploitation classics *Coffy* (1973) and *Foxy Brown* (1974) but also a mainstay of the WIP exploitation cycle, such as *Big Bird Cage*,[89] in which she played characters who, when faced with a corrupt legal system, will carve their own laws and exact justice.[90]

Having established, through my distant reading of a large body of films, the basic feel of what makes a cinematic or televisual text fall into the WIP genre, I now engage in a close reading of those texts that add complexity and layers to the genre's themes, codes, and conventions. Of these, I have selected four movies and one television series for a more detailed discussion. These closer readings make up the next five chapters.

2 Reforming Prisons, Transforming Women: *Ann Vickers*

Ann Vickers (1933) is the story of an unconventional woman's coming of age at a time of great social upheaval in American society.[1] The film, which is an adaptation of Sinclair Lewis's novel, portrays a complex feminist character whose identity is inextricably linked with the desire for economic independence.[2] As mentioned in Chapter 1, the movies discussed in this book use the prison as a metaphor to explore women's various and often conflicting personal commitments and how these complicate their exercise of autonomy at different social, historical, and economic moments. These are struggles that persist today in new and shifting modalities. In this chapter, I examine how *Ann Vickers,* set against the backdrop of the progressive reform movement, grapples with women's symbolic imprisonment in their struggles for complete emancipation through meaningful work and fulfilling relationships.

Multiple sites and modes of law regulate *Ann Vickers* – namely, the informal, but effective, rules of the melodramatic and women-in-prison (WIP) genres and the resulting expectations of a predominantly female audience. There are also the formal, but often ineffective, rules of the Production Code during a period of lax regulation. The canonical, written criminal law that has historically curtailed women's freedoms also gets mapped onto any cinematic depiction of women's criminalization. Finally, there are the implicit and inferential norms around gender and femininity that governed women at the time of the film's release. I explore these various iterations of normativity in *Ann Vickers* through a focused discussion of the formal and informal prohibition of abortion as well as of the legal and cinematic regulation of non-normative heterosexual unions.

Synopsis of *Ann Vickers*

The film opens in lower New York City on the cusp of the First World War. At a time when opportunities for advancement for women were few, Ann Vickers (Irene Dunne), or Annie to her friends, a handsome and clever twenty-something social worker, is leaving her job as assistant head resident for an advanced better-paid position in Rochester.[3] In the first five minutes of the movie, Ann receives a marriage proposal from a colleague, but tells him work leaves her no time for love; a request to dine from another suitor, Russell Spaulding (Sam Hardy), which she politely declines; and longing glances from one of the residents (a cameo by director John Cromwell), to whom she remains oblivious. Then, just moments after explaining to her friend and confidante Dr. Melvina Wormser (Edna May Oliver) that "grabbing me is the only way I'll be gotten," she is approached by Captain Lafayette "Lafe" Resnick (Bruce Cabot), who is shortly going into combat training. The camera draws us from his boots to his chiselled face and then cuts to Ann, who is in a dazed swoon. Love struck, she puts off taking her "very important job" so they can date. He proposes, promising "not to interfere" with her career. She declines, not wanting him to resent her while he is overseas, and promises instead to marry him when he returns. By the time Ann discovers she is pregnant, Lafe's correspondence has already dwindled. While out for dinner with Melvina, Ann conveys her disillusionment:

> I have discovered you can read into someone else all the things you want them to be. And you can love those things and think that you're loving the person. Blind to the truth that you've never once seen and never heard him. But you can read into boastful whining all the wise gallantry you've always longed for in a man. And into his glittering eyes an authentic passion that was not his at all, but only a projection of your own desire.

Moments later, Ann is confronted with what until then was conjecture: Lafe sitting in the corner with "a dashing young brunette." When hers and Lafe's eyes meet, he reluctantly excuses himself from his date, claiming that he has recognized "an old friend" with whom he must speak. He approaches Ann's table, kisses her hand, and, in a lacklustre tone, says: "Darling. How marvellous. I got into town half an hour ago. Was going to call you up right away." The two are captured in the same frame. He has been made a major and transferred to personnel and may not be going to France for several months after all. Ann confronts him:

> ANN: Are you engaged to her, Lafe?
>
> LAFE: [Chuckles] Engaged? Good heavens no.
>
> ANN: [Flat] Then are you and I to be joyously married?
>
> LAFE: I must say, my good woman that you don't sound as though you were so devilishly keen about it!
>
> ...
>
> [Cut to mid-shot of Ann, eyes lowered, fidgeting with her napkin.]
>
> ANN: It's just that you and I should perhaps be married right away.
>
> [Cut to Lafe, registering annoyance.]
>
> LAFE: What a break.
>
> [Cut to Ann, stripped of any illusions.]
>
> [Cut to Lafe, looking away.]
>
> LAFE: All right we'll get married. I'll marry ya. I'll keep my word.
>
> [Cut to Ann, wounded but in possession of herself.]
>
> ANN: That's all I wanted to know, Lafe. Goodnight.

If the cool correspondence left her unsure about the status of their romance, his brusque and off-hand proposal leaves her with no doubt. She accepts her personal lot but holds a critical attitude towards women's broader position in society:

[Shot in a single take, Melvina and Ann sit in a cab; Ann cups her face in her hands as though to cry but instead begins to laugh.]

> ANN: My dear doctor, you have beside you the perfect specimen of innocent country girl fooled by city slicker who engaged to heiress is reluctant to marry his victim.
>
> MELVINA: So that's the plot. Well why aren't you weeping and distraught my girl?
>
> ANN: I should be. I should get out the family shotgun I suppose and do some New England father with a chin whisker. But as a matter of fact, I don't want to weep.
>
> MELVINA: Well that's something to be thankful for.
>
> ANN: I did until I saw him. It's amazing ... how in just a few words he freed me of him completely.
>
> MELVINA: Yes. Some men have a gift that way.

ANN: I mean he freed me of him mentally, spiritually [pauses], physically. It's as though I never knew him. It's as though I'd never known him.
MELVINA: You didn't quite obviously.
ANN: Nice spot for a rising young social worker. Well it's something to know you've been a damned fool. One thing, Melvina, more than ever I'm determined to go on with my work: careers for women. That's the answer.

There is a dissolve to Melvina's summer home and the intertitle "later." Ann is recovering from having terminated her pregnancy, and while hurt and confused by the failed romance, she explains her decision not to force Lafe's hand into marriage and, instead, to take the position as assistant warden at a prison for women:

> I almost regret not using the regulation women's wiles and luring him into making love to me ... I know, if I want a man, I must lure, flatter, be ecstatically impressed by all he says or does, be coyly aloof, wistful, fluttered by his handclasp, arousing him to the conviction that I'm a swooning mystery which he must understand or die. No. I'm hanged if I will. Copperhead Gap may be terrible but I won't have to use women's wiles on it.

The warden, Dr. Addington Slenk (Murray Kinnell) is, by his own admission, a "gadabout" and engages in some mundane sexual harassment, telling his deputy, Captain Waldo Drindle (Mitchell Lewis), that Ann "is in for the comparatively minor crime of being a sociologist" and, thus, ought not to be given "the dark cells, at least not yet." Waldo actually runs the reformatory and imparts his approach to reforming women: "I'd like to get back some of the good old punishment. If I could brand incorrigibles, slash them ... a little trophy so that it would be a warning to everybody ... Use a real cat-o-nine-tails ... Say, if I could do that I'd sure cure crime in a jiffy."

The prison building is as archaic as Waldo's penology. The women are overworked and malnourished. Victims of wholesale brutality administered by the guards, they revolt unsuccessfully for better prison conditions. Suspecting that Ann may go public with what she has seen, Waldo stages a photo of her in a compromising position. In exchange for her resignation, Ann negotiates the release of the rioters from solitary confinement. She then writes an exposé of prison conditions and a training manual for women offenders that is so well received in social work and penal reform communities that she is awarded an honorary doctorate and named superintendent at a new women's reformatory in Manhattan. At its helm, she treats prisoners humanely and offers addictions treatment and work placements.

Ann's career, while fulfilling, leaves her longing for a family. Nevertheless, she refuses to settle for a mundane marriage with Lindsey Atwell (Conrad Nagel), her long-time suitor, even if it could serve to anoint her sexual past and legitimize her. Instead, she meets a socially progressive judge, Barney Dolphin (Walter Huston), who is "tremendously successful with all the ladies except his wife," at a party. It is love at first sight. He cajoles her and convinces her to leave the party with him: "Let's get a drink. We'll kill a policeman. I'll sentence us both and we can live in that pretty little jail of yours." Ann and Barney's relationship flourishes despite the fact that his wife, who has taken a lover herself, refuses to grant him a divorce. They make efforts to keep their relationship clandestine, passing themselves off as partners in the fight to reform prisons. When Ann becomes unexpectedly pregnant, Barney reassures her that he has "never been so happy" and, had they met earlier, that there would be "six of them" by now. Not long afterward, however, he is found guilty of insider trading and sentenced to eight years of hard labour. When the news of her relationship with Barney erupts, Ann is relieved of her position as superintendent because, in the words of her Board of Directors, "the head of a woman's reformatory should herself be above reproach." Her professional reputation tarnished, Ann lives modestly outside the city and supports herself and her son Matthew as a writer. Meanwhile, she lobbies on Barney's behalf, and he is granted a pardon. Ann and Barney are reunited in the final scene.

The Feminist Genealogy of *Ann Vickers*

Ann Vickers carries and conveys multiple and often conflicting meanings to a range of audiences, with their own diverging expectations, assumptions, and values. According to historian Lawrence Levine, *Ann Vickers* is an "'open text' which mandates the cooperation of the audience by compelling them to make a series of interpretive choices that invest the text with meaning and significance."[4] Multiple influences and features lead me to qualify the film as a feminist text, including the worldviews and commitments of a number of people involved in its production, ranging from the author Sinclair Lewis himself, who was regarded as socially progressive in his treatment of gender, race, and class, to the curatorial decisions made by Jane Murfin in her screen adaptation, to the themes that audiences expected from a John Cromwell film, to Irene Dunne's acting choices in her depiction of a feminist character.

First, Sinclair Lewis's novel *Ann Vickers* has been regarded as feminist in tone and in content. It is the culmination of his trilogy of novels with female protagonists in which he projects a proto-feminist voice, writing "about women as persons with identities of their own, not just as appendages to their husbands or lovers."[5] Inspired by Dorothy Thompson, the foreign affairs journalist and feminist advocate who came to be Lewis's second wife, the controversial, sexy, funny, and timely novel depicts the life of a "great woman." In a letter to Thompson, Lewis writes that Ann embodies the intelligence of Shakespeare's Portia, the conviction of Susan B. Anthony, and the femininity of Sarah Bernhardt.[6] Ann Vickers is a suffragist, a feminist social worker, and a pioneering prison reformer; each of these elements of her personality is portrayed sympathetically and with dimension. Nevertheless, some passages in the novel, particularly when Ann discusses her own relationship with feminism, suggest Lewis's multiple and contradictory views about modern women.[7]

It is relevant then that highly regarded theatre and film pioneer Jane Murfin wrote the screenplay for *Ann Vickers*. At a time when women's pictures were generally directed and produced by men, women authors and screenwriters proved to be invaluable in creating narratives that would attract female audiences.[8] Murfin was divorced and moved to Hollywood in the 1920s to make independent films. By the early 1930s, she had penned a string of scripts for Radio-Keith-Orpheum (RKO) and Metro-Goldwyn-Mayer Studios (MGM). She had already collaborated with John Cromwell – on *Spitfire* (1934), which starred a young Katherine Hepburn. She fought for the creation of well-rounded and realistic roles for female leads, such as Ann Vickers as played by Irene Dunne. In the 1930s, Dunne was an icon of melodrama, taking on roles in films that carried progressive social messages.[9] Her acting was minimalistic, yet she was "equally capable of bringing pathos to situations which would play as bathos for most other performers."[10] Kate Cameron of the *New York Daily News* qualified Dunne's acting as "beautiful" and stated that she made the "positive honesty and the capability of Ann [Vickers] shine through" by inviting audiences "to feel the underlying vigor of the girl."[11] It is no surprise then that John Cromwell cast Dunne as his titular character; he considered her his "special favourite" because of her great, yet underrated, screen presence.[12] Early in his career, Cromwell was recognized for his social problem films, depicting issues that preoccupied progressive Americans at that time: racial tensions, gender inequities,

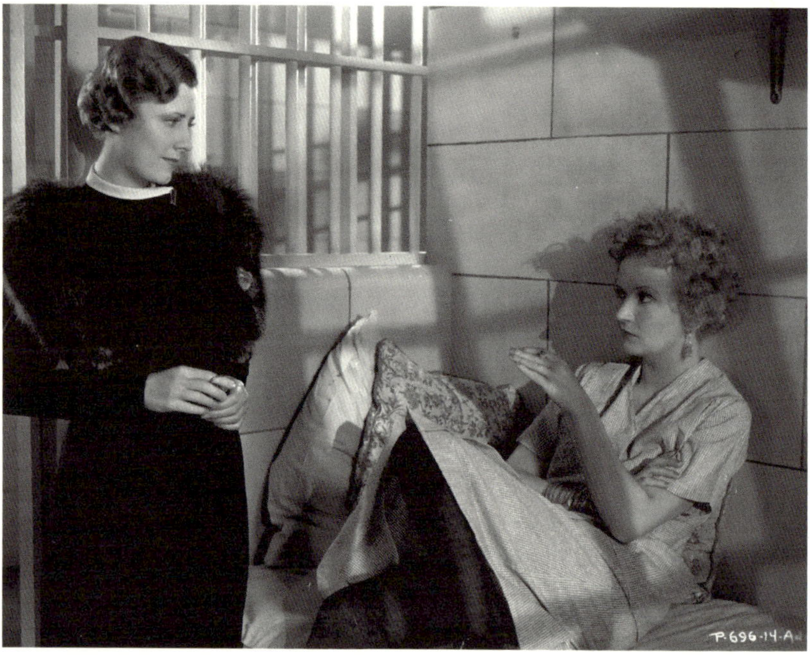

Figure 3 Irene Dunne as Ann Vickers opposite Helen Eby-Rock as Kitty Cognac in *Ann Vickers* (1933). Licensed by Warner Brothers Entertainment (all rights reserved).

industrialization, and extreme poverty.[13] He was also building a reputation for drawing unforgettable performances from his female leads, such as Bette Davis in *Of Human Bondage* (1934) and Eleanor Parker in *Caged!* (1950).

All of these influences help shape *Ann Vickers* as a feminist film about women's literal and figurative incarceration and liberation. The creation of such a filmic universe, driven by a woman who refuses to relinquish her professional identity or her prospects of a loving relationship, was possible in large part because Hollywood was itself in a unique moment in motion picture history, and this moment is often referred to as pre-Code Hollywood.[14]

Censorship and the Motion Picture Production Code: Film's Law

Film production has always been governed through a matrix of formal, explicit, informal, and/or implicit social rules that can be thought of as "film's law." What film's law conjures for most people is legislation (state-based law), such as health and safety standards on sets, or precedent (judge-made law), such as contractual obligations and intellectual property rights. Later in this book, I will discuss how film's law extends beyond legislation or judgments and includes social and cultural regulation of particular groups, such as racialized women, but, at this point, I will focus on another site of film's law: the voluntary industry rating system known as the Motion Picture Production Code or the Hays Code.

The Emergence of the Hays Code

The Hollywood film industry has always been under pressure from religious and political lobby groups who believe that impressionable populations ought to be protected from the harm of being exposed to morally questionable images.[15] By the mid- to early twentieth century, in light of increased state-by-state censorship laws and pressure from lobby groups to consolidate these regulations into one federal legislation, the industry proposed a voluntary code of practice around appropriate content. In 1916, the "Big Five" production and distribution companies – Paramount Pictures, MGM, RKO, Twentieth Century Fox, and Warner Brothers – formed a trade association: the National Association of Motion Pictures Industry. In 1922, this association became the Motion Picture Producers and Distributors of America (MPPDA) and was also commonly known as the Hays Office.

William Hays, a Republican Presbyterian, was elected as its first president, and his mandate was to quell the public's fears around film content while protecting the industry's financial interests. Hays set in motion public relations strategies to legitimize the film industry, which was, in his words, "the epitome of civilization and the quintessence of what we mean by America."[16] He created the Studio Relations Committee/Public Relations Committee (PRC) and tasked it with advising production companies around problematic content. He then put Colonel Jason Joy, known for his diplomacy, at the PRC's helm and held screenings for pressure groups, including the International Federation of Catholic Alumnae, the Young Man Christian Association, and the Central Conference of America Rabbis who would publish favourable reviews or boycott films they "condemned" as offensive.[17]

To encourage consistency in film production and to respond to ongoing concerns from pressure groups, Jason Joy consolidated existing state and regional censorship laws in 1927 into the "Don'ts and Be Carefuls" list, which prohibited the use of "pointed profanity" and "licentious nudity," the inference of sexual perversion or miscegenation, and any reference to "sex hygiene." It also included subjects that should be treated with "good taste," specifically law enforcement. Finally, it discouraged the depiction of "first night scenes," "deliberate seduction of girls," and "surgical operations."

However, the document had no enforcement mechanism and was essentially ignored. Jason Joy resigned and was replaced by James Wingate, a former member of New York State's Department of Education and a school principal, who brought a meticulousness and particular methodology to reviewing scripts in every detail, including going over multiple drafts and scrutinizing the dialogue, the mise en scène, and even the choice of score.

While navigating pressure from censorship lobbyists, the priority of the Hays Office was actually protecting the financial interests of the MPPDA's members in light of the growing formal legal regulation of the industry. Hollywood was in a precarious financial state; as the Great Depression reached its apex and unemployment rates skyrocketed, movie attendance declined dramatically. Yet industry insiders, such as Martin Quigley, editor of the trade journal *Motion Picture Herald,* maintained that the goals of upholding moral standards and turning a profit were not mutually exclusive.[18] Enshrining the values articulated in the Don'ts and Be Carefuls list, he argued, would facilitate the uniform interpretation of motion pictures.[19] The list was ratified as the Motion Picture Production Code in 1930.[20] From that point onward, in theory, no studio could release a feature whose content defied the code's principles.

However, oversight remained lax, and conservative individuals organized to shun morally objectionable movies. A loose affiliation, formalized in 1934 as the Legion of Decency, became "a permanent and disciplined group to keep watch on the talking pictures and to act summarily when breaches of decency occur."[21] Thereafter, the legion would assess films according to their adherence to the Production Code and publish in *Variety* magazine their "white list" – films that were morally acceptable – and "black list" – films they condemned and boycotted for their immoral content. Some sources indicate that box office losses resulted from the boycott, while others indicate that there was no change in ticket sales.[22] Regardless of whether the boycott had a concrete impact, it worked as a symbolic mechanism and was sufficient to elicit a reaction from the industry: the Hays Office created the Production Code Administration (PCA) to enforce the regime. Any film released after July 1, 1934, required a PCA seal of approval, and a penalty of $25,000 would be issued for screening without certification. Joseph Breen, a Christian fundamentalist, staunch anti-Communist, and anti-Semite who was zealous in his pursuit of the suppression of moral indulgences in movies, was appointed the PCA's director.[23] Appeals of his decisions went directly to William Hays.

It is in this context that RKO purchased the screen rights to *Ann Vickers* and submitted a script to the Hays Office for certification.[24]

Ann Vickers and the Hays Office

It should have been no surprise to RKO that their script for *Ann Vickers* would generate controversy. Sinclair Lewis's novel had already been vociferously opposed by the Catholic Church and added to its forbidden reading list. Joseph Breen was convinced that the book was "vile," and during negotiations for certification of the script under the Production Code, he found RKO's proposed screen adaptation "vulgarly offensive," especially in its depiction of extramarital sex.[25] Specifically, the text violated the spirit and the letter of the code, which was intended to protect the "sanctity of marriage and the home" and stipulated that, in the treatment of a "triangle" or "the love of a third party for one already married," movies must not "throw sympathy against the institution of marriage."[26]

After several months of discussions and having made, in its estimation, reasonable changes to adhere to the Production Code, RKO announced in a press release that production of the film would continue.[27] However, while RKO agreed to uphold the principles of the code, the director John Cromwell made use of allusion, juxtaposition, and strategic editing to challenge its moral authority. The opening credits of *Ann Vickers* roll over a bookshelf, upon which the titular novel sits next to other works also labelled obscene by the Legion of Decency, including *Of Human Bondage* by William Somerset Maugham.[28] Further, during Ann and Lafe's amatory interlude, they spend time alone in Lafe's quarters. One night, as she prepares to leave, the couple's embrace is captured by a tight, slow-moving camera, closing in on Lafe's arm around Ann's waist, inching downward as he drops Ann's coat to the floor. In an uninterrupted take, the camera moves to the hotel window where a neon sign outside advertises Cecil B. De Mille's silent film *Joan the Woman* (1916), in which the story of Joan of Arc is retold through the eyes of a First World War solider realizing that his mission may cost him his life. Cromwell then dissolves the scene to draw attention to a shift in time – namely, that Ann has spent a week in her lover's apartment. The marquee title now reads *Shoulder Arms* (1918), Charlie Chaplin's slapstick war film. The juxtaposition of films also suggests that the war hero may be a bit of a clown and that a great woman will be tarnished but will ultimately be redeemed. Finally, while the Production Code issued no clear instructions against the depiction of dishonest legal actors, the film counterposes a corrupt, yet sympathetic, judge – Barney Dolphin, who will ultimately win Ann's heart – with the only "law-and-order" figure in the film – attorney Lindsey Atwell, whose hand Ann will refuse because he is timorous and "without enough red blood in [his] veins to be tempted by anything." In the end, as I elaborate, James Wingate would insist on a few additional "minor trims," but he gave the film a seal of approval in August 1933.[29] *Ann Vickers* opened at New York City's Radio Music Hall in September 1933.

Intertextual Dialogues: Ann Vickers as Criminalized Protagonist

Ann Vickers is situated at the intersection of the WIP melodramatic and social problem cycles. It features a morally innocent, but factually guilty, protagonist within a romantically driven narrative. The film follows a prison reformer who appraises the criminal justice system as an institution that operates in ways that render some women vulnerable to criminalization; the film is consequently an indictment of prisons for women.[30] Unlike the other WIP melodramas explored in this book, however, the protagonist is not a prisoner herself but, rather, a superintendent. In fact, *Ann Vickers* is one of the few WIP films that feature a warden or a superintendent as the main character, but none of the other movies are as effective at casting a critical lens on the prison as a dehumanizing institution. For instance, Yvonne (Edna Best) in *Prison without Bars* (1938) is idealistic, believing that prisons can be made more effective as a tool that "corrects" hardened cons. She becomes a cuckquean,[31] however, when her long-time fiancé tires of her commitment to her job and leaves her for a former prisoner. Otherwise, the warden is ruthless and even psychopathic, as in Ida Lupino's iconic portrayal of Amelia van Zandt in *Women's Prison* (1955),[32] or is condescendingly focused on "salvaging" women "whose natural growth has been marred by bad upbringing [or] bad companions,"[33] as in the matron played by Nora Swinburn in *Good-Time Girl* (1948).

Ann Vickers is also unique in that its titular character, charged with the task of reforming other women, has herself broken the law. Specifically, Ann assaults a police officer during a suffrage rally, she terminates a pregnancy at a time when it is a felony to do so, and she commits adultery. True to Lewis's novel, the film depicts Ann as having committed these acts without experiencing the full regulatory force of the criminal law, due to her social class and standing. While Ann is de facto a criminal, unlike the protagonists in other WIP movies released in the same year – Paramount's *Hold Your Man* (1933) and Warner Brothers's *Ladies They Talk About* (1933) – she is not a fallen woman to be redeemed through incarceration. Ann Vickers will ultimately concede that the prison system is corrupt and ineffectual and that only broader social change – specifically, remunerated work for women – will address the gender inequities underpinning criminalization. *Hold Your Man* and *Ladies They Talk About,* on the other hand, present a more optimistic view of the prison's function in society as a space of personal transformation.[34]

In *Hold Your Man,* Ruby (Jean Harlow) is a working-class woman who gets by with the help of married male benefactors. She falls for Eddie (Clark Gable), a rogue and a con artist, and they get caught up in an accidental homicide. Ruby is sent to a women's reformatory for two years. Inviting audiences to scrutinize and admonish her past behaviour, the film depicts her suffering retribution and then changing while serving time, atoning for her past and finding solace in Christianity and her inner yearning for a family. Eddie too will change his ways to be with Ruby, and the film ends with the couple settling into blissful and quiet domesticity. The prison in *Hold Your Man* is not a space of confinement, dehumanization, and coercion; rather, it is a vehicle for personal growth and a conduit to a heterosexual pairing.

In *Ladies They Talk About,* Nan Taylor (Barbara Stanwyck) is a gun moll arrested for her part in a bank robbery. David Slade (Preston Foster), an evangelist who is convinced of her integrity, lobbies in her favour and convinces the prosecutor to leave her in his custody. When Nan confesses to David, however, he is honour bound and turns her in, effectively, according to the theatrical trailer, changing her "from a lady of leisure to lady number 6142."[35] Nan oscillates between wanting to "go straight" and enacting her revenge on David, but his love and her time in prison save her, and instead of killing him upon release, she accepts his marriage proposal and gives love a chance.

Despite conforming to a more optimistic moral, however, *Hold Your Man* and *Ladies They Talk About* exhibit incongruities and dislocations of the "fallen woman" archetype and, consequently, circulate multiple meanings about feminism and criminal law.[36] Specifically, neither Ruby, who is basically an escort, nor Nan, who is a gun moll, hold much economic capital; they engage in crime out of pragmatism and necessity. Ultimately, however, any critical assessment of women's criminalization in these films – indeed, both depict the prison as a dormitory – is overshadowed by the love stories, and the prison is essentially a narrative vehicle to a happy ending in marital bliss. As discussed earlier, this narrative device became central to a number of WIP films produced after the Production Code took full effect. Like other WIP films, *Ann Vickers* asks jurisprudential questions about the nature of women's culpability when engaging in acts of survival. Unlike the other protagonists in the films explored in this book, Ann's crimes are not related to poverty. Instead, the film evokes her vulnerability to criminalization and regulation through her decision to abort after her liaison with Lafe and her entanglement in an adulterous union.

Suffrage Mobilizing as Civil Disobedience

In the cinematic adaptation, Ann's time as a suffragist is condensed into a comedic interaction between herself and Lafe; she is already firm in her feminist convictions and her passion for social justice when the film begins. However, Lewis's novel spends chapters exploring Ann's formative years; her arrest and the paternalism she experiences as a result will incite in her the desire to reform women's prisons. Ann is found guilty of breaching the peace, using abusive and profane language, causing a crowd to collect, and resisting officers in the discharge of duty. In the cell where she will spend two weeks, Ann does not "feel like a criminal" and "wonder[s] if many prisoners [felt] merely like human beings who had been arrested." This disillusionment is heightened when she discovers that one of her colleagues – a "member of a prominent family and daughter of a bishop" – has her charges dismissed despite her assertions that she was "equally guilty" of a crime. In the county jail, she experiences sexual harassment and describes her cell as "ill lighted, cracked and damp, furnished with a mattress of straw and a rickety chair." She asks herself: "What does the State accomplish by shutting one up here," especially given that the other women are "no more 'criminal'" than she is. Rather, she finds that "poverty, unemployment, early underfeeding ... ha[s] sent them there." Her short stint in jail is sufficient for her to see the futility of incarceration and the myth of rehabilitation: "[W]hat is there about sitting idle for a fortnight among professional prostitutes that is going to make me so gentle, that is going to teach me so much self-restraint, that when I come out the policeman ... will be safe?" As mentioned, the film glosses over her coming of age and the development of her social conscience and her belief that there "are no good prisons." In the cinematic adaptation, unlike the book and unlike other films produced in the same year, it is her defiance *vis-à-vis* gendered social norms – the decision to abort her foetus and, later, her commitment to a non-normative union – that enables transformative moments for Anne.[37]

In other WIP films explored in this book, the narrative revolves around a "good" protagonist who has come to a life of crime because of unfortunate circumstances (poverty or an abusive relationship) and her metamorphosis through encounters with the "other" (whether a well-meaning warden, hardened lifers, or fiendish guards). Ann's transformative encounter, by contrast, is not through an intersubjective dialogue with otherness but, rather, through her own internal struggle as a woman in the early twentieth century who wants great romantic love and a satisfying career. The way she defies, while still conforming to, gender normativity, especially the heterosexual marriage system, sets *Ann Vickers* apart from other WIP movies at the time. The kind of femininity promulgated in the Production Code and the formal legal system in the 1930s was embedded in the belief that women's role was first and foremost to be a mother within the boundaries of a monogamous heterosexual marriage. Yet *Ann Vickers* prompts viewers to identify with an independent woman who directly confronts this version of femininity through her brushes with the law. Ann runs a prison even though she has committed acts characterized at the time as criminal and transgresses primary social norms. As a young woman, she engaged in civil disobedience to obtain suffrage. As an adult, Ann has an unsanctified sexual liaison that results in her opting for an illegal abortion to preserve her dignity and her career. Later, rather than settling for a loveless marriage that would adhere to normative gendered expectations, she will breach adultery laws by choosing an alternative union: monogamous cohabitation with a married man.

The Criminalization of Abortion

When RKO initially asked the Hays Office to certify its script for *Ann Vickers,* Joseph Breen insisted that they remove a number of problematic elements, including any direct reference to Ann terminating her pregnancy. As I elaborate later, RKO's vice-president of production, Merian Cooper, was more pliant in deleting direct reference to abortion than he was regarding the theme of marital infidelity. The final film uses euphemism and metaphor to remain within the dictates of the Production Code while still grappling with Ann's decision to abort. So subtle was Jane Murfin's text and so skilful was John Cromwell's directing that several (male) commentators have incorrectly interpreted the scene as though Ann miscarries rather than terminates her pregnancy.[38]

The scene unfolds as follows. After Ann confides to Melvina that she has been duped by Lafe, she is more than ever determined to carry on advancing career opportunities for all women:

> MELVINA: Now that you belong to yourself once more, what are you going to do about ... [stops herself mid-sentence].
>
> ANN: I don't know. I have to think about what I'm going to do.
>
> MELVINA: I'll tell you. You'll resign your job and take a trip to Havana with me. We leave in about ten days.

Melvina is an obstetrician and equipped to induce the abortion herself. The scene takes place in 1917 as the United States enters the First World War. Taking "a trip to Cuba" refers to the cross-border travel that some "women in trouble" made to access legal abortions.[39] In New York, where Ann and Melvina reside, abortion is widespread,[40] but it remains a felony that carries a sentence of up to four years in a state prison.[41] In fact, at the time the movie was released, every state had statutorily criminalized abortion.[42]

Anti-abortion laws were intended to safeguard the foetus and to promote general deterrence of a "social evil"[43] by "limiting the power of a woman over her own person," punishing any attempt to self-induce a miscarriage, and protecting her "against her own weakness."[44] However, most included a narrow exception where an abortion could be performed to preserve the pregnant woman's life (the "medically necessary" interruption of a pregnancy).[45] New York's law was particularly strict: it did not create such an exception, meaning that abortion was essentially never legally performed, and it extended the crime beyond those who provided the procedure to the women who sought out or self-induced a miscarriage.[46] New York's Penal Code made a "self-induced abortion act" punishable by a prison term of one to four years.[47] There are cases of women being indicted with self-inducing abortions;[48] however, convictions were "virtually unknown."[49] There is little evidence that women were actually being imprisoned for "removing the consequences" of intercourse because the common law regarded them as victims rather than as perpetrators of, or accomplices to, the crime. As explained in *State v Carey* (1904),

> at common law ... it was not an offense in her to so treat her own body, or to assent to such treatment from another; and the aid she might give to the offender, in the physical performance of the operation, did not make her an accomplice in his crime ... It was in truth a crime which, in the nature of things, she could not commit. And so it has been held, under various statutory forms of this offense, that the victim of an attempted abortion could not be an accomplice in a crime which consisted in an operation on her body, with or without her consent, by another person with intent to produce abortion.[50]

Instead, criminal and state regulation focused on abortion providers, whether licensed physicians or midwives or any other person who performed an abortion by means of medicines or the use of instruments.[51] Some legislation allowed for the maximum sentence for manslaughter in the case of the death of the pregnant woman.[52] However, even in states where women might be spared being tried criminally, the consequences of the charges were serious. They would be called out by judges for being "morally at fault"[53] or "an accomplice in the moral sense"[54] and would be left with a public record detailing the private matter of terminating a pregnancy.

Beyond social stigma, a staggering number of women were dying as a result of post-abortion complications.[55] The Children's Bureau of the United States documented maternal deaths in fifteen states between 1927 and 1928, finding that almost one-quarter of them (1,824) "followed some type of abortion."[56] Only a minority of the abortion-related deaths were listed as "legal," while over half were treatable sepsis-related infections, and many were "falsely attributed" to other causes such as pneumonia and heart failure.[57] In her historical exploration of abortion regulation in the United States, Leslie Reagan reveals that women who were hospitalized for life-threatening complications associated with abortion were often harassed and denied treatment until they made "dying declarations." These reports disclosed who performed the abortion, where it occurred, how much it cost, and the name of their sexual partner.[58] However, charges against criminally negligent abortion providers were rare, and convictions were unlikely.[59] In fact, complaints, when entertained, were generally dismissed. On occasion, however, a physician's licence would be suspended.[60]

Consequently, even in the face of public humiliation, stigmatization, and the threat of further regulation, some women or their families attempted to use the civil legal system to obtain redress after a botched abortion.[61] Most jurisdictions would not allow a woman to recover damages against an abortion provider for injuries inflicted when the procedure was not medically necessary to save her life.[62] Wilful participation by a competent complainant in an immoral or illicit activity – here, a "non-therapeutically necessary" abortion – would bar recovery for malpractice or negligence on public policy grounds.[63] Similarly, the person who arranged for the abortion (usually, the male sexual partner) was usually not found liable for injuries sustained by an adult woman who consented to the procedure.[64] In Oklahoma, for instance, a woman was denied damages from her former sexual partner to cover the medical bills she incurred while "she lay for weeks near the point of death" after a botched abortion as well as general damages for "her irreparable injury to her standing in society, to her mental anguish and pain, and humiliation among her friends and acquaintances."[65] Moreover, as a general rule, courts would also deny families of deceased women the right to recover damages from abortion providers to cover funeral expenses[66] or for general pain and suffering.[67] Courts would also bar their access to the deceased's life insurance policies.[68]

Beyond the juridical realm, while the early twentieth century represented a pivotal time for women claiming formal equality, some maternal or conservative-minded feminists supported the strict regulation of women's reproductive capacity. For instance, Lois Weber wrote and directed *Where Are My Children* (1916), a film in which a self-absorbed hedonist terminates a number of pregnancies despite her long-suffering husband's desire to have children; in the end, she is left barren and in a loveless marriage. *Ann Vickers* ends with the protagonist, despite having terminated a pregnancy once in her youth, choosing motherhood when she becomes pregnant from a man she loves. Ann is empowered enough to feel loss. But she is neither ashamed nor full of self-loathing about making a decision that is grounded in a sense of dignity and self-regard – refusing Lafe's tepid offer of marriage simply to avoid embarrassment and, instead, ending their unplanned pregnancy. It is also the only reasonable option available that enables her to escape social stigma, ostracism, and financial ruin. Ann's ambivalence rather than self-reproach in her decision to abort confronts the Production Code's dictates and dominant societal mores, especially Sigmund Freud's popular and influential equation of abortion with a predisposition to hysteria rooted in an "intense load of guilt."[69]

After *Ann Vickers* was released and once the Motion Picture Production Code was in full effect, films that even elliptically broached the subject of abortion would be subject to close scrutiny from Joseph Breen's office. Always implicitly included under "repellent subjects" found in Part XII, abortion was expressly added in a 1956 amendment to the code:

> The subject of abortion shall be discouraged, shall never be more than suggested, and when referred to shall be condemned. It must never be treated lightly or made the subject of comedy. Abortion shall never be shown explicitly or by inference, and a story must not indicate that an abortion has been performed. The word "abortion" shall not be used.[70]

In any event, most filmmakers and producers removed any reference to the practice without protest.[71] When the subject was treated cinematically, pregnant women who had abortions often violently haemorrhaged to death; others would be shamed into carrying the foetus to term.[72] *Ann Vickers* stands out as it is not a cautionary tale of a self-indulgent careerist who will be rebuked; instead, John Cromwell's direction of the story never alienates its protagonist from the audience.

Breaking the Rules of Normative Monogamy

This refusal to alienate audiences from Ann is also true in the depiction of her non-normative pairing with Barney Dolphin. In his correspondence with Merian Cooper, James Wingate pegged away at the story because, in his view, it did not denounce Ann's "loose sex relationships" or her "flaunting of the laws of convention." The titular character should instead, he insisted, serve as a spokesperson "for accepted morality" once realizing the error of her ways. If this role could not fall to Ann, narratively speaking, then a strong subsidiary character should mentor her into leading a life that upholds the values of the Production Code. For Wingate, since no one performed such a function in the film, the "inevitable result" was that the film, in not condemning Ann's behaviour, was "implicitly condoning" or, worse, "advocating" for adultery."[73]

Cooper had always maintained that controversial themes in the film should be treated with complexity and in a way that "did not pander to cheap sex, nor to cheap and vulgar emotions."[74] Wingate, unconvinced, insisted that Ann Vickers condoned adultery "as a justifiable means out of an impasse" – namely, that Ann was in love with, and intended to carry the child fathered by, a man to whom she was not married.[75] The script could be redeemed, however, if Ann was shown to make "an honest statement of remorse for having broken the laws of God" – that is, Ann and Barney should "not be shown to be proud and happy in their adultery."[76] With this response, the president of RKO, Benjamin Kahane, appealed directly to William Hays. He insisted that his studio had met all of Wingate's requirements and that the script adhered to the code's principles.[77] Specifically, in the original adaptation, Ann marries her long-time suitor, Russell Spaulding, at the age of forty and begins her affair with Barney while both of them are still legally married. RKO sanitized this element of the plot by making Ann single when she meets Barney, thereby avoiding "double adultery."[78]

Nevertheless, according to Kahane, Ann is in fact "punished" for choosing a relationship with a married man, insofar as she loses her economic standing and esteemed career when news breaks that the tarnished, still-married judge has fathered her child. RKO put to Hays that the PCA's interpretation of the Production Code was overly narrow and that its aversion to any depiction of adultery, without its "affirmative denouncement," was excessive. Kahane agreed that the subject should not be glorified. However, he maintained that *Ann Vickers* told "a story of human life and frailties," that it approached adultery "in a distinguished and dignified manner," and that it was not a "deliberate resort to salacious material, vulgarity and filth to pander to certain types of patrons."[79] Hays, who unlike Wingate, was himself a film producer, understood the extent of RKO's efforts to take a "thoroughly dangerous story" and make it compliant with the code. Ultimately, though, he agreed with Wingate that RKO's duty to "establish in the minds of the audience that adultery is wrong, unjustified and indefensible" had not been met. Hays urged Kahane to exclude anything from the film that "may fail to fix definitely in the mind of the audience the important social and moral values which, it is always our purpose, to establish and endorse."[80]

As a concession to the censors, *Ann Vickers* does not exactly culminate with Ann and Barney in blissful matrimony. They are reunited after his disgrace, however, and are still in love. Barney's wife, who is equally unhappy in their marriage, finally agrees to a divorce.[81] But whether Ann and Barney's coupling will be a fulfilling one for Ann is left ambiguous. However, two key elements of the film's dénouement resist and complicate the film's apparent adherence to the Production Code and the gendered and legal ideologies that underpin it.

Ann Vickers: Surrender or Defiance?

Throughout the film, Ann Vickers exhibits contradictory views about being a "new woman." She is granted a sexual subjectivity but is allowed to feel conflicted for having aborted her foetus. Instead of locking herself into a mundane marriage – despite the economic security and social legitimacy attached to a union with Russell Spaulding – she guards her freedom. Yet it can be argued that Ann's story ends on a very different note than it began. While she is first portrayed as an ambitious young woman resisting the current of social conventions and sexism, it appears as though Ann ultimately succumbs to the gender and political norms that the contemporaneous society expected. In this reading, while toying with feminist concepts like reproductive rights and economic independence, the film is also wary that such thematic content must adhere to the moral principles governing producers at the time and, in this case, that she be punished for disobeying the gender conformity of her time. As articulated by one reviewer, Ann "stays outside the matrimonial fence but remains a perfect lady."[82] Another reviewer bemoans that "there's no denying that the film's conclusion (in which Ann denounces her ambition and accepts her role as a housewife) can't help but come off as ludicrous and utterly dated."[83]

Indeed, we meet Ann as a socially conscious, former suffragist and a radical thinker who is also fiercely independent of men. By the film's end, she has become domesticated insofar as she is a single mother raising a child on a meagre income. She has also compromised her social position to be with a man of questionable integrity and now inhabits the legal precarity – in terms of property rights and constitutional protections – of a single woman and her illegitimate child in a society that protects monogamy and heterosexual marriage. However, she embraces her new reality, telling Barney that her career was the cage and that she is now free from "the prison of ambition, the prison of desire for praise and success for myself." This shift in perception, however, does not reduce the entire film to what might otherwise be "formulaic pablum," ending with a domesticated female protagonist, but, rather, as Lawrence Levine puts it,

> [*Ann Vickers*'s] formulaic ending, no matter how securely it may have fit in with traditional conceptions of a woman's fundamental place in society, could not in one fell swoop wipe out everything that preceded it concerning Vickers' strength, talent, independence, competence, her important contributions, and the fact that her gender was hardly incidental to all of this but was the basis for much of it.[84]

Ann Vickers was produced at a cultural moment when the cinematic construction of femininity was shifting as filmmakers began to solicit female audiences while also catering to a new fetish: the modern woman. The prison in *Ann Vickers* is a device through which to display and subvert traditional gender arrangements and identities – in this case, access to career opportunities for middle-class white women. Moreover, the film's ending flies in the face of the Production Code's preamble – "law, natural or human, shall not be ridiculed, nor shall sympathy be created for its violation" – and its edict that no "sympathy" shall be "thrown to the side of wrongdoing, evil or sin." Specifically, these characters break adultery laws, choosing to cohabitate and build a family despite Barney's existing marriage. According to New York's Penal Code, the "sexual intercourse of two persons, either of whom is married to a third," including persons "who live or cohabit together" in the state of "fornication,"[85] was a misdemeanour.[86] Historically policed during America's colonial period in order to protect men's property rights in their wives,[87] adultery became a statutory offence punishable by "severe lashing."[88] Gradually, penalties shifted from whipping to fines and imprisonment.[89] Some states, including New York, made the offence a misdemeanour,[90] while others viewed adultery as "a very great crime, once capital ... [and therefore] nearly allied and equal in guilt to felony."[91]

In the end, whereas other WIP films released the same year include redemption stories in which the main characters navigate a repressive and hostile environment to generate the conditions in which they can eventually free themselves of past mistakes, Ann Vickers's choices – to engage in civil disobedience, to terminate a pregnancy, and to embrace an alternative family configuration, all of which happen to be illegal acts – are celebrated rather than punished. As a result, the film highlights the contingency and social construction of what we call "crime" and invites interrogation of how some women who defy norms and break laws are treated differently based on their social and economic location and their moral standing within society.

3 The Unattainability of Reform: *Caged!*

I have suggested that *Ann Vickers* (1933) raises concerns about the criminalization of women by presenting a protagonist who is keenly aware of the full measure of the criminal law while remaining sheltered – by virtue of her social and economic privilege – from much of its force. While *Ann Vickers* follows a feminist prison reformer in her attempts to make women's incarceration more humane, *Caged!* (1950) endeavours to bring the inner world of women's incarceration to light.[1] *Caged!,* like *Ann Vickers,* has a well-meaning superintendent at its moral centre. However, it explores the plight of a young prisoner with limited life opportunities whose options have been further circumvented by the stigma associated with her criminalization. By inviting a variety of interpretive claims around the possibility of prison reform and the impact of the regulation of prostitution, *Caged!* prefigures the feminist intersectional analyses that gained currency in academia decades after the film was released, illuminating how feminist progressive policies and reform movements have historically been most concerned with issues faced by white, middle-class, heterosexual, able-bodied women.[2]

In *Caged!,* director John Cromwell, to whom film theorist André Bazin attributes most of America's most compelling psychological dramas of his time, presents a gritty and unsentimental prison. The film's austerity is in part attributable to Cromwell's ability to bring together the critical impulse of the social problem film and the aesthetic qualities of film noir. He uses diegetic sound (a deafening train whistle, heavy rain, and women whimpering, coughing, and wheezing), claustrophobic camera angles, and high-contrast lighting (close-ups and figures framed with shadows and bars) to introduce and enhance the film's main themes: women's physical and metaphorical imprisonment. However, *Caged!* also offers up an unapologetically queer and campy exploration of the relationships that develop between women living in confined and repressive spaces. The theatrical trailer promised to "reveal the menace of today's prisons" and to "expose" the reality that "each day the criminal courts condemn scores of unfortunate girls to prisons who need reforming more than they do."

Despite the *New York Times*'s dismissal of *Caged!* as a "bleak picture" and "no great shakes" and its modest success at the box office, the film received three Academy Award nominations. It has since been lauded as, and remains, one of the most provocative and intelligent prison films ever made; it has also become the prototype from which later iterations of the women-in-prison (WIP) genre found their conventions and tropes.[3]

Synopsis of *Caged!*

A siren wails as opening credits roll over a van full of women. While the camera lingers on the Women's State Penitentiary, we hear a matron tell the "new fish," including the terrified and disoriented Marie Allen (Eleanor Parker), to "grab [their] last look at freeside." Nineteen-year-old Marie is processed by a disinterested matron, who tells her to "get to the crime." She explains that her husband tried to heist a gas station; she was just meant to be the lookout, but when he was stabbed, she ran to his rescue. For that, she was found guilty of being an accessory to armed robbery, a felony that carries a sentence of one to fifteen years. Marie hands over her wedding ring, is given prison garb, and is told she is now Prisoner 93850. In quarantine, she shares a room with a prisoner dying of tuberculosis who welcomes her to "Lysol Lane." During an invasive physical examination – ("open up. I said wide") – Marie discovers that she is "expecting company" (pregnant). The nurse snickers ("you know who the father is?") and then derides her as a tax on the social system ("another bill for the state"). Shortly thereafter, she is sent to meet Ruth Benton (Agnes Moorehead), a compassionate warden and the moral compass of the film who is trying to effect progressive change to an outmoded and retributive penal system. She takes a keen interest in Marie, whom she believes is "an intelligent girl who knows good from bad" and explains that she should consider her a "friend."

Ruth exhibits a drive to improve conditions for women and their helplessness as she works within and against a corrupt and brutal justice system.

Not the least of her worries is Matron Evelyn Harper (Hope Emerson), who personifies brutality. Evelyn imparts her beliefs about the role of prison:

> This place ought to be run with a piece of rubber hose. Break 'em in two if they talk out of turn. Anyone who doesn't tow the line gets solitary for one month. Bread and water. One funny move from a girl and I'd clip every hair off her head. That's the way it used to be run and that's the way it ought to be run. Just like they're a bunch of animals in a cage.

There is a stench of moral corruption about Evelyn, who is not above extorting and blackmailing her charges. She runs the prison like a private racket, bringing in candy, cigarettes, or anything to quell a "habit that's hard to break." When it becomes clear that Marie has "no dough," Evelyn relentlessly bullies her. While Ruth, considering Marie's delicate state, puts her in the laundry to work as a checker, Evelyn reassigns her to scrubbing floors with lye. Marie eventually "loud talks" (stands up to) Evelyn and catches Kitty Stark's (Betty Garde) eye. Kitty, in for murder, is the hard-bitten, but fair, queen bee who recruits "boosters" for a penny-ante shoplifting syndicate. But while her cellmates have resigned themselves to prison life, Marie is determined to get her life on track, despite Kitty's relentless attempts to win her over ("in this cage, you get tough or you get killed"). She gains respect from her peers as someone who keeps to herself.

However, a series of events leaves Marie disabused about her ability to "go straight." First, she gives birth prematurely and is forced to hand her son over "to the law" (child and welfare services). Her mother, who we only see behind the mesh grid that separates visitors from prisoners, is stuck in a difficult marriage and has no option other than to betray Marie to avoid compromising her "situation" at home:

> Mrs. Allen: I can't leave Gus, there'd be nobody to take care of me until you get out. I'm not getting any younger ...
>
> Marie: [Staring at her mother in disbelief, then fully recognizing the state of affairs] Stop crying! Tom's folks are dead. [Imploring] If you won't take him, they'll put him up for adoption.

Mrs. Allen retreats sheepishly without making eye contact with her daughter. Marie claws at the mesh wire; frantic and crying, she begs her mother not to destroy her family. Shortly thereafter, Marie's one true friend, June (Olive Deering), kills herself after being "flopped back" (refused parole) and goaded about it by Evelyn. Then, her own application for early discharge is denied because the parole board determines she requires additional moral reformation. As one board member tells her, "at your age, with no favourable home conditions and no beneficent influences on the outside, we feel nine months has been too short a time to prepare you for your responsibilities outside." Kitty tells her to get over it because there will be other guys who will "tumble" for her and that she can have another baby as long as she "flops out" (gets parole) as soon as possible; the quickest way to do so, she reminds Marie, is through Kitty's connections to the booster ring. Marie turns Kitty down again, but there is a perceptible shift in Marie's demeanour. Her tone is acerbic and mechanical; she has lost her youthful innocence.

The arrival of Elvira Powell (Lee Patrick), "an institution with a big bankroll," on the cellblock creates palpable tension in the prison. She saunters onto the scene, a shrewd businesswoman doing "a quick stint to take the heat off" and avoid testifying before the grand jury. Elvira is also recruiting for a prostitution ring and immediately tags Marie as a "cute trick." Marie rebuffs her unequivocally: "I'm a big girl and this isn't my first year away from home," but Elvira persists: "You can have real stones anytime if you change your type." Elvira puts Evelyn on her payroll and dethrones Kitty by having her busted for recruiting. After being violently beaten by Evelyn and spending a week in segregation, Kitty comes back to the ward "stir bugs" and half catatonic. Meanwhile, Marie's decline into world-weariness is complete when an uprising breaks out over a stray kitten she has found. Evelyn labels Marie the instigator, beats her, and cuts off her hair down to the scalp. Despite Ruth's ban on the use of segregation, Evelyn will throw Marie in the hole for several days. An angular shot of Marie's pale and sickly face framed in shadows indicates she has lost her grip. When Evelyn returns Marie to her bunk, apathetic but stoic, the other women pound on their footlockers and rattle the prison bars in solidarity. Evelyn's eyes fill with fear.

At the first opportunity, Kitty plunges a fork into Evelyn's neck. Marie snaps. She is captured in a tight close-up, yelling maniacally: "Kill her! Kill her! Kill her! Kill her!" Once her composure is regained, Marie checks Evelyn for a pulse and with bitter satisfaction tells the others to "kindly omit flowers." With ambivalence, Marie will take Elvira's bid; in a scene meant to foretell her life as one of Elvira's girls, she applies thick red lipstick in a heart-shaped mirror. While her cellmates tease her that she is "played the honest John too long anyway," Millie (Gertrude Hoffman) says otherwise:

> I had a first time like you, but I can't remember how long ago. Then a second rap. Then a third. Now I'm a lifer. I'll be seventy-one soon. I've

> been a con for forty years. [Her voice cracks.] Any you know what I think? Nobody got cheated but me. Forty years taken away! So I'm giving it to you straight. Wait a year on dead time. Get a legit job slingin' hash. Then get a good guy. Have a kid. [Mournfully] What I'd give for a sink full of dirty dishes.

Marie is moved by Millie's words, but it is ultimately too late; she will opt for early parole through Elvira's connections. In the final scene, she walks out of the prison gates. Ruth watches her leave through the barred office window and tells her staff to keep Marie's file "active" because "she'll be back." To an extra-diegetic jazz piece, Marie climbs into an expensive car. A man puts his hand on her knee and lights her cigarette.

Capturing Realism

The screenplay for *Caged!* is based on a story that Virginia Kellogg wrote for *Collier's Weekly* magazine. A respected reporter and screenwriter, Kellogg went undercover as Virginia Laurel, who was sentenced to three years for embezzlement; she spent several weeks conducting informal interviews with imprisoned women and observed the prison institution as a whole. Her research revealed that, with the exception of a few honest and incorruptible women, most matrons were "ignorant and sadistic" "broad-beamed Amazonish spinsters" shielded by their political appointment or connections to "men who had influence." She also found neglectful healthcare practitioners, staff under the thumb of organized crime, and women having their hair "clipped to the scalp as a penalty." In her estimation, reformatories were essentially "crime universities for young women," cycling paroled women in and out of the system only to bring them "back to the university for postgraduate work." These insights were directly translated into the final script for *Caged!*[4]

The cinematic text exhibits additional verisimilitude in that one of its main characters, Ruth Benton, stands in for Dr. Miriam Van Waters, who spent a quarter of a century as the superintendent of the Massachusetts State Reformatory for Women, where *Caged!* takes place. The reformatory housed adult women found guilty of misdemeanours carrying a sentence of two years or less, such as being idle and disorderly, public intoxication, and vagrancy, or of a range of "sex" crimes, including giving oneself to "lewdness" (birthing a child out of wedlock), being in a "triangle situation" (adultery), and especially being a "common night walker" (engaging in prostitution).[5] The film quotes actual headlines ("Superintendent under Fire, Demands Public Hearing") from a set of hearings before a special commission of the state's House of Representatives regarding the management of the Massachusetts Correction Institution in Framingham. Under Van Waters's purview, the reformatory had garnered international praise for its radical policies and practices that fostered women's sense of dignity and agency and focused on their emotional, economic, and physical health. These practices included cultural programs, education within and outside the prison, a volunteer treatment program for alcoholics that was open to women within the broader community, active mentorship, and meaningful employment opportunities. Her programs had an especially significant impact on the large number of women charged with misdemeanours who, given their short sentences, would not have received constructive supervision once they exited the reformatory in other jurisdictions.

When Elliott McDowell took over as commissioner of corrections, he was adamant that Van Waters cancel rehabilitative programs and implement unadulterated punitive custody. His directives were, in his and his advisers' view, ignored; as a result, he dismissed Van Waters for misconduct and poor judgment, citing twenty-seven charges, including the misinterpretation of state law around indentured service by enabling prisoners to work outside the reformatory unsupervised and implicitly encouraging recidivism by allowing paroled women to maintain friendships with those still incarcerated. The charge that received the most airtime in the media and during the hearings – and which seemed to most fuel McDowell's animus towards Van Waters – was that she condoned, or at least failed to denounce and punish, salaciousness and sexual perversions (lesbianism) within the institution. Following her dismissal, Van Waters exercised her statutory right to a public hearing before an unpaid commission, which ultimately threw out all charges against her. Regarding same-sex relationships in the reformatory, the commission determined that "while overt acts of homosexuality occurred," she took "prompt and effective steps" to address it. Van Waters was cleared of allegations of encouraging lesbianism within her institution just a few months before *Caged!* was released. However, during the commission's investigations, she walked a tightrope when fielding questions about the regulation of same-sex couples in prison, neither explicitly denouncing nor endorsing them. Her stance on non-normative sexualities in prison was complicated at least in part because she was herself in a long-term committed relationship with Geraldine Thompson.[6]

Queering the WIP Genre

Despite its realist mooring, *Caged!* also provides the prototype for the fantastical exploitation WIP cycle and especially the stock references – both explicit and implicit – to Sapphism. It was produced when the Motion Picture Production Code had banned the representation of "sex perversions" including homosexuality and when the emerging McCarthyism framed same-sex relationships as both the source and outcome of moral depravity and political subversion. Moreover, lesbianism in WIP films reflected criminological scholarship at that time. It was perceived as the manifestation of a gender reversal whereby a "female bully-boy," who adopts mannerisms and attitudes normatively attributed to men, aggressively contaminates heterosexual "innocents" who defy gender norms temporarily in order to survive in a deprived social order.[7] These distorted and reified views about same-sex relationships were those that most often circulated in the cinema of the mid-twentieth century.[8]

Yet even before official production began, *Caged!* could not help but become a queer cinematic text.[9] The role of Marie Allen was intended for Bette Davis, who reportedly refused to play in a "dyke movie," and the character of Ruth Benton was based on a woman who was accused of encouraging "deviant" sexualities and was herself a lesbian. Further, the film includes elements that not only reproduce, but also complicate, the dominant assumptions about non-conforming sexualities and gender identities. Indeed, Vito Russo observed in *The Celluloid Closet* that lesbianism in *Caged!* "appears as a product of an outlaw social structure – it comes with the territory."[10] The film's playful depiction of non-normative sexual identities is perhaps most evident through the opposition of Ruth, who exudes maternal love for the "residents," and Evelyn, who embodies the sadomasochism that becomes standard in the later iterations of the genre.[11] Specifically, Ruth warns Marie that "no prison is a normal place," that she will "find all kinds of women" there, and that, while she will get lonely, she ought to find appropriate "outlets for affection." Yet Ruth's own sexual identity remains ambiguous. On the face of it, she is obviously heterosexual: she is Mrs. Benton, wears a ring on the fourth finger of her left hand, and keeps a prominent photo of a young man on her desk. All window dressing, according to Patricia White, is an "out-and-out charade" to create the illusion of heteronormativity.[12] Moreover, while Ruth provides maternal love to her charges, its expression is coded as a form of seduction. She seems to be heartsick at Marie's departure and speaks as though she is a jilted lover, with her voice cracking ("let's not lie to one another" and "if you need anything") in the final scene.

But the most explicit of the lesbian codes in the film lies in the role of Evelyn Harper, unforgettably portrayed by Hope Emerson. Emerson had a towering stature at six feet, two inches, and her training in Vaudeville meant that she was often cast in kitschy roles, such as the strongwoman in *Adam's Rib* (1949) who lifts Spencer Tracy in the air with one hand, and the radio voice of Borden Milk's Elsie the cow. The *Caged!* script describes Evelyn Harper as "semi-illiterate, wantonly cruel, mentally warped, cowardly," and she is played by Emerson as a parody of normative femininity and heterosexuality. We meet her reading *Midnight Romance* eating bonbons on a divan, resting on an embroidered pillow of Niagara Falls – gifts "from her girls" for "taking such good care of them." When she does explicitly adopt a feminine identity for a date on the outside, she becomes a grotesque expression of drag and attracts snickers from her charges. As one woman remarks: "I got news for ya: If that's what dames are wearin' now, I'm glad I'm in here." To which Evelyn replies with a malicious smirk: "The guy outside likes the way I look"; she channels Mae West at her peak: "Every time he kisses me goodnight, I just want to keep on leaving." Despite a narrative infused with heterosexuality, Hope Emerson's brilliant acting leaves little doubt that she is performing mainstream societal expectations of butch dykes. In keeping with the general trend in cinema at the time that characters who were non-gender conforming must "get it" in the end, Evelyn will die a particularly gruesome death.

The queer elements of the film did not attract scrutiny from the Production Code Administration (PCA), which seemed impervious to its implicit visual associations with lesbianism. Rather, it was the "question of dope addiction" with respect to one of the characters that caught the regulator's attention, and Warner Brothers promptly changed this issue to alcoholism.[13] The PCA would attempt to crack down on allusions to queerness in movies that came after *Caged!*, albeit unsuccessfully. For instance, the producer of *Girls in Prison* (1956) was told to eliminate the "suggestion of lesbianism either in mannerism or physical appearance" from the narrative. Given that its tagline was "what happens to women without men," that the *Monthly Film Bulletin* qualified the film as "an unpleasantly sensationalized story," and that one of the narrative axes involves the ongoing sexual advances by Melanee (Helen Gilbert) towards the innocent protagonist Anne Carson (Joan Taylor), it is clear that American International Pictures all but ignored the PCA's warning.[14] Despite such transgressions, most social problem

WIP movies of the mid-twentieth century still used the prison as a vehicle through which to develop a romantic heterosexual union between the protagonist and a man trying to save her.[15] In *Caged!*, however, it is the relationships between women that animate the narrative and, especially, the rivalry between Kitty and Elvira over Marie's body and the power struggle between Ruth and Evelyn over Marie's soul.

Troubling Feminist Reforms

The theatrical trailer for *Caged!* warns that the "first time loser" who is "exposed to the habitual criminal" will become "tomorrow's legion of the lost." While its protagonist's factual guilt is established in the first scene, any moral justification for her confinement is called into question throughout the film. *Caged!* is a feminist text that provides a critical lens on strategies and discourses aimed at improving the lives of criminalized women. It tells a deeper story than its trailer portends, making provocative statements about the binaries reproduced and reflected in the prison reform movement

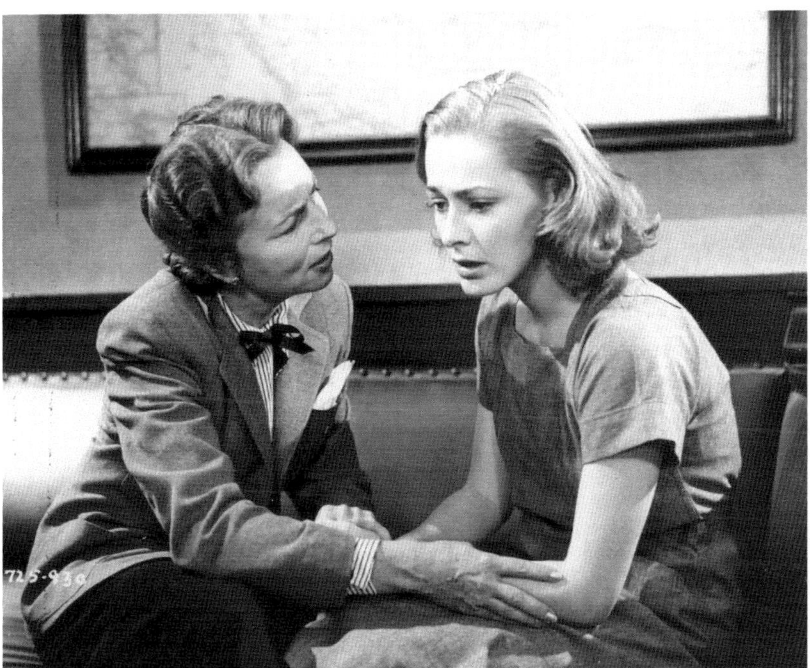

Figure 4 Ruth Benton (Agnes Moorehead) and Marie Allen (Eleanor Parker) in *Caged!* (1950). Licensed by Warner Brothers Entertainment (all rights reserved).

(first-timer or hardened con) as well as about those circulated in feminist discourses around prostitution (victim or entrepreneur). It is a compassionate inquiry into the limited options available to Ruth as she works within and against a repressive institution. It is also an intelligent exploration of Marie's decision to enter the sex trade that goes beyond simplistic understandings of choice.

In *Caged!*, Ruth questions the utility of warehousing women, but her energies are focused on changing existing conditions within prison and offering better opportunities to "help" women "leave the prison ... readjusted" and "worthwhile human beings." There is a bias here: moral frailties lead to her charges' coming into conflict with the law. In this regard, Ruth falls into a dichotomizing logic similar to that of other feminist prison reformers of her era. The feminist prison reform movement at the turn of the century sought more humane punishment and sex-specific institutions to shelter women from the violence inflicted by male guards or male prisoners. These women-only prisons permitted the next generation of feminist reformers to develop principles and practices to reform "fallen women" through spiritual guidance, education, and social services. Rather than furthering a punitive justice agenda that sought to sanction and discipline offenders, they believed that prisons could provide "maternal love" and restore women in conflict with the law, while simultaneously developing environmental and structural explanations for women's crime, which mainly included lack of education and intergenerational poverty.[16]

As Estelle Freedman has shown, the women-centred models of confinement and rehabilitation justified the reformation of some women while enabling others to become their "sisters' keepers" and, in the process, achieve greater emancipation.[17] The women who took up new positions as prison wardens, guards, and counsellors achieved a measure of social, political, and economic power. But while they believed in greater social and economic mobility for all women, they were also complicit with oppressive class structures insofar as these were integral to a system designed to transform "problem women" into a generation of domestic and domesticated labourers. "Correctional institutions" could thus instil self-sufficiency in convicted women and deter crime through training and opportunities for paid employment. Yet, in the new reformatories, women were primarily assigned clerical work and taught the basics of "home economics" (such as sewing, baking, and household maintenance) or offered "character building" through religion as well as refinement through classes in languages and art appreciation. Furthermore, in advocating for better treatment of women offenders, they drew on conflicting discourses of altruism and personal responsibility that were at cross purposes with the goal of achieving substantive equality for all women. *Caged!* captures this tension particularly well in the final interaction between Ruth and Marie. Ruth sits at her desk reading a file, which includes a photo of Marie the day she entered the prison: naive, wide-eyed, and terrified. On the day of her departure, Marie walks into Ruth's office without knocking; her metamorphosis is so complete that she is almost unrecognizable:

> RUTH: Now that you're leaving, let's not lie to each other ... The cashier job is a blind.
>
> MARIE: The parole officer okayed it, didn't she?
>
> RUTH: Elvira Powell has a lot of friends. [She pauses. Stands up, walks toward Marie and puts a hand on her shoulder.] In a couple of months, the parole officer could have found you work. You'd have made honest money. You'd have self-respect. Decency.
>
> MARIE: Where'd those things ever get me anyway?

Despite her training in feminized labour (the laundry), the reality is that with a criminal record Marie has little chance of finding gainful employment, recovering her baby, or even getting remarried. She no longer believes in Ruth's worldview or the promise that she will return to society whole and ready for a new life. Rather, taking in Kitty's warning that "most people in freeside won't hand you a job cleaning out a hogpen," she pursues what she perceives as the best possible option for herself: becoming one of Elvira's girls. This choice must have been particularly difficult, given the gendered social and legal regulation of sex work in the period when Marie is released from prison. In the early 1940s, the United States mounted propaganda campaigns urging women to take paid employment in war industries.[18] Women who were already employed in low-paid service sector work – as waitresses, cigarette girls, salesclerks, and housemaids – could now access positions previously held by men in factories. Moreover, women who had already secured industry jobs, whether clerical or otherwise, saw their wages increase considerably. At the same time, however, vice squads began to crack down on another form of remuneration for women: sex work.

The year Marie enters prison, the United States Congress passed the May Act, which made "vice activities" near military installations a federal offence.[19] Prostitution was the target because military authorities claimed that women who sold sex were the contaminating factor that led to lost "man power" as soldiers were treated for venereal diseases. These "victory girls" – a derogatory term used to depict women who had consensual sex with soldiers outside the confines of marriage – were the object of moral regulation through movies and Public Health Services' propaganda depicting syphilitic prostitutes using their wiles to lure soldiers into spilling military secrets. While only two states – Tennessee and North Carolina – implemented the federal law, over one thousand women would be charged under its provisions between 1941 and 1946. States were simultaneously enacting "morality" regulations, and, by 1948, each had its own prostitution law. The more repressive states built special detention facilities to house prostitutes; these quickly became overcrowded as the arrest and detention of women charged for selling sexual services near training camps reportedly increased (these women would have likely escaped criminalization had their sexual partners not been soldiers).[20] Simultaneously, the Federal Security Bureau created a special unit to work with municipalities, state governments, and private agencies such as the American Social Hygiene Association to eliminate prostitution and "rehabilitate" women through social hygiene education. The public health discourse bolstered existing anti-vice activists and purity crusaders, who lobbied local governments to regulate multiple forms of women's sexuality including adultery, fornication, female promiscuity, and, especially, commercialized sex.

It is in this repressive gendered legal and cultural context that Marie Allen determines that prostitution is her best and, indeed, her only option. While researchers, feminist reformers, and popular culture at the time either framed prostitution as part of the "white trade" or listed socialization (family dysfunction, poor socialization) and individual pathologies (feeble-mindedness and promiscuity) as factors leading women into prostitution, *Caged!* suggests more complicated reasons for women's entry into sex work. The movie acknowledges the relative agency that women exercise, meaning the ability, as Lois McNay puts it, to "manage ... discontinuous, overlapping or conflicting relations of power," to "act in an unexpected fashion," and even to "engender change within the socio-cultural order" when occupying various social locations and recognizing the daily negotiations that all women make within oppressive institutions.[21] Marie defies fetishistic and stereotypical cinematic representations about women engaging in sex work and does not fall into the dominant feminist discourses about commercialized sex that still prevail today. She does not embody the archetypal and stereotypical prostitute reproduced and reconfigured throughout mainstream cinema. Marie is not a "street angel," "suffering and degraded in life but spiritually transcendent."[22] Nor is she a "gold digger" who "exploits men's natural sexual desires to effect a redistribution of wealth in her favour." She is not the "gigolette" of French films made in the late 1940s and early 1950s that feature a utopic depiction of sex workers: as women who hold a kind of protected status among gangs and other criminal elements and exercise unbridled sexual freedom for economic gain. She is not the classic "femme fatale" who will seduce men to their downfall. And she is certainly not the "avenger" fighting against women's oppression in a sexist society. What is further unique about Marie is that she refuses to have her personhood reduced to one element of her identity. Women who engage in transactional sex have always been stock characters in the WIP genre; however, they are rarely depicted as such a fully-formed individual, and even more rarely are their pathways into sex work a pivotal narrative element.[23]

Caged! carefully depicts the experiences and social conditions that lead to, and, from Marie's perspective, justify, what for lack of better language can be called a decision to engage in prostitution. Thus, the film anticipates feminist analyses that highlight the fact that choice does not amount to agency when made in the face of unpalatable options. However, it also problematizes victimhood as the only feminist standpoint about prostitution. Contemporary feminist discussions on prostitution still seem locked in an ontological and epistemological debate about the nature of commercialized sex that circulates a binary understanding of women's subjectivity. To abolitionists, prostitution is the expression of male domination of women, and prostitutes are victims of coercion and other systems that objectify women. To rights advocates, sex work is a legitimate form of remuneration, and industry entrepreneurs are vulnerable because its criminalization renders their working conditions challenging, if not dangerous.[24] Both discourses reinforce dualistic views about women's agency (women's capacity to make individualized choices and to act in accordance with these choices) and their autonomy (women's ability to generate their own rules by which to live their lives).

Both perspectives elicit strong criticism. On the one hand, abolitionists use shaming tactics against buyers and deny that women who sell sex often transgress heteronormative femininity and sexuality and have access to a better income than available in other service sectors and that their preferred regulatory model (partial decriminalization) still forces transactions into more remote, poorly lit areas, thereby endangering lives. The sex workers' rights advocates, on the other hand, may dismiss the structural inequalities that render sex work one of the most lucrative options for some women and also fail to acknowledge that parts of the industry are embedded within, and reinforce, reductive standards of femininity and that regulation may require people who sell sex to register with municipal authorities, undergo invasive mandatory sanitary inspections, and carry identification cards, which may subject them to additional forms of discrimination. Furthermore, when sex work is framed as a pure choice rather than as an exercise in pragmatism, it is also infused with the discursive power of "liberation, freedom of empowerment"; it is correspondingly also within the discursive regime of "responsibility and blame."[25] A woman who chooses to sell sex will accordingly be held responsible for whatever dehumanizing treatment, violence, stigmatization, and marginalization she experiences by virtue of that choice.

Marie is neither victim nor entrepreneur. She is what Orit Kamir has called a "victimized subject," insofar as she has experienced oppression and abuse she is a capable and appropriate decision-maker who enacts her own judgment of those who have mistreated her and of those institutional practices that further her marginalization.[26] She inhabits the space between the binaries and manages to refuse inscription into either binary position. She makes what to her is the only reasonable choice and, in so doing, shifts the audience's judgment to the prison and the institutional mechanisms that have left her with a limited range of options. Marie's parting words to Ruth – "you can't lick the system" but "I hope you win" – and Ruth's awareness of the disconnect between her beliefs and the actual agency she has to effect change invite audiences to question one of the film's key jurisprudential conundrums: can prisons ever (re)form women?

Thus, the film foreshadows the transformative justice movement that will become an alternative to reform-based social change in the 1960s. Mainstream restorative justice is based on a series of beliefs: first, that people who commit crime should be brought to understand the harm they have caused to other individuals and to the broader community; second, that "offenders" should play an active role in repairing the harm to others and to society; third, that these reconstructive actions should also be part of a program to prevent future harm from occurring; and, fourth, that the mode and quality of reparation by the offender is to be determined collectively by their peers, the offender, the victim(s), and other members of the community. Whereas the ultimate aim of restorative justice is to rehabilitate the offender to enable her to return to her community,[27] the transformative justice movement's focus is on transforming oppressive institutions. Transformative justice moves away from early policies and practices of restorative justice (which aimed at reforming the existing institutions by infusing them with opportunities to develop empathy and community building) by promoting broader reparation of historical injustices and harm. It is a movement aimed at dismantling apparatuses of oppression to create space for better ways of addressing harm and conflict. Transformative justice opens the possibility of imagining better alternatives to the criminal system and its reliance on prisons.[28]

By asking whether prisons can ever reform women, *Caged!* goes beyond casting a critical lens on the institution and instead poses the prison abolitionist question: should prisons for women exist at all? Further, because *Caged!* does not blindly summon the misogynistic stereotype of fallen women who fall "on their backs," but, rather, challenges this stereotype through Marie's moments of self-affirmation, it is a critique of the law's authority to label her.[29] Marie refuses the legitimacy of the trial judge who puts her in prison ("I don't belong in here!") because it was desperate times and economic hardship that led to the commission of her husband's offence; she disputes the parole board's assessment of her ("I've paid my debt to society!"), and she confronts Ruth's assumption about her moral frailties ("where did [honour and decency] get me anyway?"). Yet to say that *Caged!* endorses prostitution or even makes arguments to decriminalize sex work might be an overstatement. The ambiguity that Marie expresses about her choice (she tells Ruth "I hope you win" and "for that forty bucks Tom and I heisted, I sure got myself an education") invites audiences to share her worldview and mourn her lack of alternatives. *Caged!* provides us with imaginary material on which to base a more just social safety net, one that is responsive to women rather than punitive towards them. The film's tensions introduce the possibility for myriad affective responses and perhaps even compel audiences to join forces with Marie in questioning the viability of feminist prison reform as well as any justification for her incarceration and, by extension, the existence of women's prisons in the first place. The next film to be discussed, *Caged Heat,* tackles issues at the forefront of critical criminology, including how particular women are labelled as dangerous, what the objectives of sentencing are, and how the false victim/perpetrator dichotomy plays out for already marginalized women.

4 Recuperating Exploitation: *Caged Heat*

The 1970s were a time of burgeoning social movements, political upheaval, and economic stagnation in the United States. The regulatory regime under the Motion Picture Production Code – whose significant censoring effects in Hollywood obliged filmmakers to communicate controversial material much more obliquely – was on its way out. By 1968, the Production Code had been replaced by the Motion Picture Association of America's film rating system, which is still applied today: "G" for general audiences; "PG" for parental guidance suggested; "PG 13" for parents cautioned; and "R," which requires anyone under the age of seventeen to be accompanied by an adult. With this shift, exploitation films gained popularity – that is, low-budget, "independent" features rated "R" (restricted) with cheap production values that were made for drive-ins or "grindhouse" viewings in late-night theatres.[1] These films "exploited" stylized and sensationalized violence and female nudity, and the audience's expectations of these elements, to commercial ends.[2] Variants of the exploitation feature include Blaxploitation, which attracted young Black audiences, and sexploitation, which catered to the "midnight movie" (soft-core) fans.[3]

In this context, Roger Corman – who started his career as a director for American International Pictures, where he capitalized on the popularity of exploitation films – moved to production and distribution. He founded New World Pictures (1970–83), whose business model consisted of the quick turnover of material catering to "male sexual fantasy" created by a cast, crew, and directors making poverty-level wages.[4] New World Pictures produced six movies, all featuring what Pam Grier has called "aggressive and bouncy" female protagonists, which would become, for fans, the canon of the women-in-prison (WIP) exploitation cycle.[5] These films, which, for the most part, do not fit into my critical taxonomy of WIP films, are sometimes referred to as "babes behind bars" movies. The first of this canon was *The Big Doll House* (1971), which showcased, according to its promotional poster, "Women Whose Bodies Were Caged." Four more movies came out between 1971 and 1973: *Women in Cages* (1971), with the tagline "White Skin on the Black Market"; *Big Bird Cage* (1972), with the tagline "Women So Hot with Desire They Melt the Chains That Enslave Them"; *The Hot Box* (1972), with the tagline "Their Guns Are Hot and Their Bodies Hard"; and *Black Mama White Mama* (1973), with the tagline "Chicks in Chains." The fifth film, directed by Stephanie Rothman, was the cult classic *Terminal Island* (1973). And the final feature of the New World Pictures's foray into women's imprisonment was *Caged Heat* (1974), which promised "Rape! Riot! and Revenge!"[6]

Rothman was the most explicit and direct of the New World directors in her feminist approach to WIP exploitation films.[7] In a recent interview, she explained that, when making a film within the exploitation formula, she

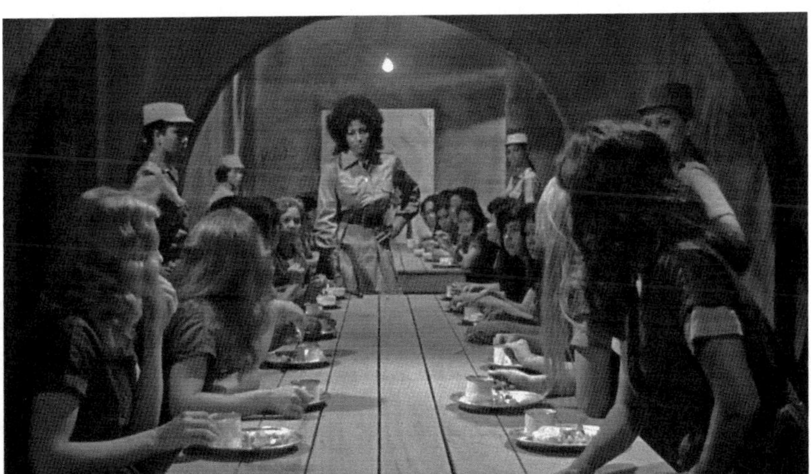

Figure 5 Pam Grier as the warden in *Women in Cages* (1971). Shout! Factory.

would try to "give it some meaning beyond the violence itself, or beyond the nudity itself" and in fact "tried very hard to not make it exploitative."[8] Yet Rothman's tenure with New World was brief. Citing poor pay and restrictive creative freedom, she and her husband later started their own production company. While her film *The Student Nurses* (1970) received some attention from WIP fans at the time of its release, it was Jonathan Demme's *Caged Heat* that has since been elevated to "the best sexploitation film of the era."[9] Regardless of one's view of such an honorific, no other WIP exploitation film has attracted as much scholarly attention. Furthermore, *Caged Heat* is the only film in the New World Pictures's roster that technically and strictly falls within my delineation of the WIP genre: most of the narrative takes place within a women's prison, and the prison is located in America (and not in an unnamed developing country). My definitional criteria of a WIP movie is likely irrelevant to the large pool of exploitation movie fans; however, their reviews, comments, and assessments of particular films do generate meanings for me about the appeal and expectations of the WIP genre.

Exploitation Fans' Constitutive Role in Developing the WIP Genre

The WIP movies of the 1970s – which are considered, according to one commentator, "the guiltiest of guilty pleasures for the cinema sleaze aficionado"[10] – are, generally speaking, exploitation films.[11] They are often categorized as vehicles providing "yards of masturbation fare for generations of boys," indulging fantasies about lesbian sexuality, powerful women (usually at least one of whom is Black), and domination/submission.[12] Given this premise, the exploitation WIP movies generated a cult-like following of (mostly) heterosexual men. Such fans are integral to the generation of meanings surrounding these movies because exploitation films, more than any other WIP cycle, had a clear intended audience – young urban heterosexual males – and therefore constructed tropes and imagery designed to maintain the loyalty of this community of viewers.

The devoted fan base of WIP films documents the cycle's appeal and constitutes audience expectations of the genre broadly in books, on websites, and through blogs.[13] As one *Variety* magazine contributor, in his review of *Big Bird Cage,* puts it, "audiences for this type of feature couldn't care less about histrionics as long as blouses are kept unbuttoned."[14] Similarly, an anonymous reviewer explains that "WIPs usually play on the common male fantasy of having power over a large number of beautiful women."[15] According to Jim Morton, the exploitation WIP films became prominent after the Second World War because women no longer wanted to "[submit] to the role of housewife, mother, inferior being" and men had "discovered that the bawdy, good-natured sexuality of the French was infinitely preferable to the puritanical guilt/shame prevalent in the States."[16] In his estimation, WIP movies are "not merely sexist": "women enjoy them as much as men do," he points out, noting that one of the hallmarks of these films is a cast of women who are "hard, mean and take no shit from anybody."[17] Roger Corman has admitted, however, that his studio's decision to have assertive women as protagonists was, first and foremost, an economic choice and that it was "simply reacting to the market."[18] As a surprisingly forthright fan surmises, much of the exploitation cycle's appeal is the possibility of neutralizing powerful women. "As long as men and women compete in the workplace," he writes, "the WIP genre will continue to be popular with males."[19] In contrast, reviewer Gary Morris believes that WIP exploitation movies actually draw their appeal from having strong women castigate violent men and thus resist at least one expression of male domination; in any event, he rightly notes, the political thrust of these narratives will "go largely unnoticed by its young male target audience, who are mesmerized by the sea of tits and ass that flows through the company's roster."[20]

Such fan commentary opens up the cycle to a feminist critique that draws on Laura Mulvey's work, lending support to a critical view of the WIP cycle as a form that circulates damaging stereotypes about women and prompts an objectifying male gaze.[21] Other feminists, however – starting with Pam Cook's early assessment of exploitation films and, later, work by scholars who adopt Carol Clover's opinions on identification – have confronted and challenged the concept of a fixed, intended WIP audience.[22]

Feminists Read and "Recuperate" the WIP Exploitation Film

Laura Mulvey makes political use of psychoanalysis to argue that "the unconscious of patriarchal society" has historically structured the cinematic form.[23] She hypothesizes that, in watching films, spectators objectify female characters and identify with the male character through voyeurism. The cameras are typically operated by men, which creates a particular point of view, and, thus, the ideal spectator will identify with the male protagonist, who is presumed to be a heterosexual man. But these processes are not necessarily gender specific because, as is often overlooked by these critics, Mulvey also believes that women derive pleasure by being engrossed in the action and motivation of the male characters and, importantly, by resisting the representation of the female characters.[24] While Mulvey has never addressed the WIP genre directly, it is difficult to see the WIP exploitation cycle as anything other than a product of a phallocentric culture (reflecting and reproducing a male viewpoint) or a genre that was intended to appeal to, and reproduce, a heterosexual male gaze upon the women it features, fetishizes, and objectifies. According to Nicole Rafter, the WIP exploitation cycle showcases young women "who tend to remove their bras before riots," and, thus, these films are "fixated on the sexual implications of all-female society, usually from the viewpoint of a heterosexual male who enjoys watching pin-ups in action."[25] It is interesting to note, however, that spectators are not as single-minded as some feminist theorists may assume: "Boris Lugosi," a fan who has written extensively on the genre, admits to an (albeit mild) ambivalence towards the conflicting messages that exploitation WIP films circulate about violence against women. Regarding *Women in Cages,* he explains: "Poor old Alabama [is] raped and drowned by the brutes. Sure, she's a villain, but I'm glad I didn't have any feminist friends watching this scene with me."[26]

Indeed, other feminists have been critical of the WIP exploitation cycle for reflecting and reproducing tired stereotypes about women. In one of the earliest socio-legal discussions of WIP films, criminologist Karlene Faith found that they generally exhibit "pornographic overtones" and "produce images of monster women bearing no resemblance to ... [the] women who are actually locked up."[27] It is hard to argue against this assessment given that *Caged Heat* was nominated for "Best Soft-Core Release" at the Adult Video News Awards in 1985. In her discussion of popular images of incarcerated women, Faith uses content analysis as a feminist methodology. Yet, as film theorist Pam Cook has pointed out in her critical engagement with exploitation films, the feminist impulse to replace fetishistic distortions with more accurate images is itself problematic:

> One of the symptoms of [the] desire to throw off the forms and language of the dominant ideology has led to the rejection of the stereotypes and codes of Hollywood cinema in favour of the alternative language of realism: that is, the representation of women in the "reality" of their oppression, replacing the manipulative, false patriarchal ideology with the "true" ideology of feminism in an attempt to rediscover the voice of women lost beneath the solidified surface of the stereotype.[28]

For Cook, the crucial site for feminist politics is production and distribution. Mainstream Hollywood naturalizes dominance through the use of stereotypes and generic conventions that "suppress contradictions."[29] But Cook finds that exploitation films hold subversive potential because of their use of exaggerated gender stereotypes (such as the aggressive revenge-obsessed heroine) and unnuanced narratives (the aggressive revenge-obsessed heroine enacts revenge). These "allo[w] us to see that language is at work" and take "a critical distance on the metalanguage of mainstream cinema."[30] Building on this insight, Judith Mayne has observed that the originally intended audience for WIP exploitation films could be discerned based on where these films were exhibited – that is, late-night cinemas that would not have been as accessible for women as for men.[31]

However, by the 1980s, when most of these films became directly available through video, mainstream television, or venues outside traditional theatres, any assumption of an intended audience becomes debatable. Indeed, the reality is that media consumption today, with emerging digital and streaming technologies, has changed profoundly. This observation bolsters the argument that WIP films have always appealed to a far broader constituency than heterosexual teenage males.[32] Certainly, one can surmise that Mai Zetterling and Cheryl Dunye had queer spectators in mind when they made *Scrubbers* (1982) and *Stranger Inside* (2001).[33] Further, the slate of television series that appeared during this era, beginning with Australia's *Prisoner* (1979–86), which was rebooted as the grittier *Wentworth* (2013–present), through to the United Kingdom's *Bad Girls* (1999–2006) and Canada's *Unité 9/Unit 9* (2012–19), all share to varying degrees an explicit educational impulse, endeavouring to sensitize a broad swath of the population to the lived realities of criminalized women. Finally, the women writers for both Fox Broadcasting Company's satire *Women in Prison* (1987–88) and Netflix's "dramedy" (dramatic comedy) *Orange Is the New Black* (*OITNB*) (2013–19), are strong and intentionally self-referential. Explicitly quoting WIP conventions, these programs attract a broad range of viewers, from sleaze aficionados to post-feminists.

Another critical intervention in feminist media, film, and cultural studies has been Carol Clover's work on American slasher and rape-revenge films.[34] She argues that, while spectators may generally align themselves with characters of their own sex, their identification is neither fixed nor inherently gender specific; rather, it is fluid and shifts across gender lines. Clover establishes how shot structures and narrative elements invite spectators, who are presumed to be primarily heterosexual men, to identify with the female victim/heroine ("final girl") rather than, or along with, her male tormentor. Drawing on Clover's critical intervention into psychoanalytic theory, it is possible, as Mayne proposes, that WIP exploitation films destabilize viewer identification because the cycle is "predicated on the possibility that women observe other women."[35] And while Mayne maintains that there is "much to love" about the WIP genre, there is also "much to hate," especially "the scenes of rape and torture" that "play on the helplessness and victimization of women."[36] Similarly, in her discussion of slasher films, Clover cautions that

> [she] is deeply reluctant to make progressive claims for a body of cinema as spectacularly nasty to women as the slasher film, but the fact is that the slasher does, in its own perverse way and for better or worse, constitute a visible adjustment in terms of genre representation. That it is an adjustment largely on the male side, appearing at the furthest possible remove from the quarters of theory and showing signs of trickling upward, is of no small interest.[37]

In my review of exploitation WIP movies – a body of cinema that has arguably been equally "nasty to women" and for which one of the conventions is that prisoners be forced into prostitution by the warden[38] – I would like to offer my aesthetic preference for the subtlety and understated subversions of the melodramas and the cheekiness of the newer televisual dramedies over much of the exploitative iteration. What is incontrovertible, however, is that exploitation movies have added conventions that draw attention to the everyday forms of humiliation that women prisoners experience – such as the invasive strip-search – and with a far richer palette in terms of protagonists' race and culture than earlier films.

Exploitation films also treat several feminist themes from different standpoints and thus hold the potential to attract a range of spectators.[39] First, unlike most mainstream cinema, in which male protagonists drive the narrative, or the early WIP movies, where secondary male characters are instrumental to the narrative as love interests, the male characters in the exploitation cycle are incidental to the general development of the plot. They are caricatured as horny buffoons or sadistic torturers who will inevitably be castrated, physically or figuratively, by the film's end.[40] Second, the female protagonists in the cycle are depicted with some dimension of character. For example, backstories provide insight into the crimes that the women committed. The women are shown to have political beliefs and motivations. And when they do enact violence, it is often of the righteous variety, in response to sexual violence and other forms of gendered oppression. A third, and final, feminist theme seen in many of the WIP exploitation features is that shared experiences of oppression within a corrupt institution can unify women rather than divide them.[41] In tackling these themes, the WIP exploitation cycle has attracted some feminist investment. Many of those undertaking the feminist recuperation of WIP exploitation films point to Jonathan Demme's film *Caged Heat* for its critical feminist potential.

Synopsis of *Caged Heat*

Jackie Wilson (Erica Gavin) is a white woman "from a good home" sentenced to forty years at the Connerville Federal Institution. She was found in possession of illicit drugs and tried as an accessory to an assault against a police officer. Upon arriving at the compound, she and the other "new fish" are groped by the male guard, then sent to the prison psychiatrist for processing. Dr. Randolph (Warren Miller) is a sadist who protests to the row of naked women that he does not like the "ritual" cavity searches any more than they do. Then, leering at them, he tells them to "do a few deep knee bends for openers." And so begins *Caged Heat*. Its ensemble cast of characters includes Pandora Williams (Ella Reid), a Black woman who has killed and castrated a man; her white lover Belle (Roberta Collins), a chronic shoplifter; Maggie (Juanita Brown), a sensible Black woman in for armed robbery; and Lavelle (Cheryl Smith), a white woman in for life for having murdered a rapist who happened to be politically connected. Gothic horror film star Barbara Steel plays Superintendent McQueen, a white woman who uses a wheelchair but has "disturbing but oddly gratifying" dreams in which she is a go-go dancer. McQueen is unmoved by the brutality enacted by her guards during "agricultural therapy" (gruelling manual labour) and by Dr. Randolph's "behavioural correction," which includes electroconvulsive treatments (ECT), and is instead obsessed with sexual propriety.

Pandora and Belle put on a campy cabaret show that McQueen finds offensive. Belle is forgiven, but Pandora, labelled the sexual instigator of the couple, is put in solitary confinement. Every night, Belle sneaks through the ventilation ducts to bring food to Pandora. On one of these trips, she accidentally kills a matron and is sent to Dr. Randolph, who convinces the superintendent to let him try out a new surgical procedure: excising the criminal elements from her brain. Meanwhile, Maggie and Jackie get into a fight, for which they are given kitchen duty. Maggie sees an opening for an escape, but her plan fails, and they also are sent to Dr. Randolph for a particularly brutal round of "corrective" therapy. When they are told that there will be a second round of ECT, they decide to escape again. Lavelle distracts the guards so that Maggie and Jackie can run. They safely make their way to the house of a friend, "Crazy" Alice (Crystin Sinclaire). Back on the compound, Lavelle witnesses Dr. Randolph sexually assaulting an anaesthetized Belle. She gets word to Pandora, and, together, they devise Belle's rescue just as Dr. Randolph is about to drill a hole into her prefrontal lobe. On the outside, Jackie feels remorse for having left behind the other women. She and Crazy Alice convince a reluctant Maggie to go back to the prison to get their friends. The three of them steal a car and break through the prison gate, while Pandora and her crew take McQueen and Dr. Randolph as hostages. In a final shoot-out, Dr. Randolph dies, and all of the principal characters tear off unscathed, accompanied by a blues music score.

The Production of *Caged Heat*

Caged Heat opened to a positive reception from exploitation fans. Since then, some reviewers have lauded its attempt to "take a genre that objectifies women as blatantly as any film in history" and turn it "into a story of female empowerment."[42] One critic applauded it for including a left-leaning perspective on social problems of the time, even though "comely damsels in jail being strip-searched and showering so that the audience can peep at tits and ass [is] what the movie is really about."[43] Indeed, *Caged Heat* seems to sit uncomfortably within the exploitation cycle's canon. It does meet all of the requirements of perversion and pleasure set out by New World Pictures – degenerate female sexuality, shower scenes, lurid guards, foul language, camp, and a revenge plot – but it also exhibits self-reflection that complicates viewers' expectations and provokes affective engagement with its characters. It showcases sufficient sleaze to meet fans' expectations while offering sufficient novelty to appeal to a wider audience.

Despite Roger Corman's belief that a film's voice comes from the producer rather than from the director or anyone else involved in the collaborative process, many of the qualities in *Caged Heat* may be attributed to screenwriter and director Jonathan Demme. He uses the language of cinema – sounds, light, shots – and makes stylistic choices, while giving sufficient artistic freedom to the actors to playfully engage with the script.[44] Admittedly, Demme operated within New World Pictures's framework. The film was billed as a spectacle of "crazed carnal confinement" with women "torn by penal passion." Demme cast a favourite of WIP movie fans, Roberta Collins, who also played in *The Big Doll House* and *Women in Cages*, in the role of the relative innocent. However, Demme's narrative choices reveal some ambivalence with Corman's formula. He incorporates intertextual references and parodies the melodramatic WIP movies, most obviously in the title (*Caged!* becomes *Caged Heat*) as well as through character interactions, such as when Pandora tells Jackie that she is really an undercover reporter trying to expose corruption. Moreover, while Demme relies on exaggerated stereotypes, he also moves away from them. For instance, while there are plenty of sex-hungry women, many of them lesbians, none of the principal characters is a lesbian predator. This is a significant departure for a genre that typically, like much of cinema, reproduces lazy stereotypes of lesbians and lesbian relationships.[45] Moreover, while the odd female guard may cast a longing glance, the lechery and sadistic inclinations are left to the white heterosexual male doctor, who, unlike the melodramatic cycle of WIP films, is neither a love interest nor a source of moral authority.

Finally, the film's editors, Johanna Demetrakas and Carolyn Hicks, use cinematic techniques to play with audience expectations. In one scene, for example, Pandora is shot from the waist up. Her eyes are closed. She moves her arms in a manner indicating that she is either masturbating or receiving cunnilingus. She moans: "Come on baby!" Then the camera pulls back to reveal that she is really just rolling the die, playing a convivial game of craps. A few short sequences also hint at the realist aesthetics also found in the social problem/melodrama WIP cycle.[46] A long tracking shot, taken on location at Lincoln Heights Jail, reveals women, who range in age, size, and race, smoking, talking, and, to accentuate the claustrophobia and lack of privacy, urinating in their cells. Then, to dispel any pretensions of realism, the camera pans up to a "No Laughing" sign, and the sequence is punctuated by a bizarre dream sequence in which a woman delights in the sexual fondling of her lover only to stab him with equal fervour. These features may have been the reason for Roger Corman's assertion that *Caged Heat* had "gone a little bit too far" in denaturalizing the male characters and the basic conventions of his studio's exploitation films.[47]

A Feminist Appropriation of *Caged Heat*

Three intertwining plot strands lend support not only to Corman's assertion that the film seems more preoccupied with women's motivations and choices but also to the argument that *Caged Heat* explores feminist themes. Each of these three plots underscores an aspect of female criminalization that the melodramatic WIP cycle of the 1930s–50s did not engage with as deeply: first, the policing of racialized lesbians; second, the blurring of the victim/offender dichotomy; and, third, the deployment of medical-legal apparatuses against women who are labelled unpredictable. These narrative features make an otherwise disjointed and at times poorly acted film into a movie worth writing about.

Policing Racialized Lesbians

Same-sex coupling has historically been prohibited in American prisons. However, with the appearance of women-only reformatories, lesbianism has been tacitly acknowledged. While "unnatural relationships" between female prisoners of the same race were tolerated, interracial couples were considered problematic. Racial segregation in women's prisons was instituted at the turn of the last century when reformers learned that Black and white women were developing sexual relationships.[48] Discourses around "deviant" sexualities and "dangerous" racialized groups were encrypted onto particular female bodies. Namely, women racialized as Black were identified as sexual aggressors, and women racialized as white were identified as "temporary partners." Around the same time, in literature and popular culture, the transgressive pairing of a Black woman with a white woman – in friendship – became a metonym for lesbianism. In actual prisons, however, Black women were often already coded as hyper-sexualized and violent and, thus, the source of "lesbian contagion."[49] This belief that the general population needed to be protected from female sexual predators was still strong in 1974 when *Caged Heat* was released. In fact, that year, a California appellate court held that the threat of lesbian attacks in a prison for women met the standard of a necessity defence to the felony of attempted escape.[50]

Caged Heat reproduces this stereotype, but the film also brings to light, through narrative and cinematic techniques, Pandora's experiences of injustice as a racialized queer woman. Pandora is a Black "lumberjack lesbian," incarcerated for having castrated a man. Her partner, Belle, is a quintessential "lipstick lesbian," a white woman convicted of a minor crime. They put on a burlesque show containing gender inversions and sexual puns, after which Superintendent McQueen tells Pandora and Belle that, "even for criminals," they are "a particularly poor reflection on womanhood." Pandora is blamed for the show in part because she resists McQueen's characterization of its content ("the others seemed to dig it," she tells the superintendent). McQueen claims that she has "strong ways of dealing" with any member of her "violent sorority" and that her goal is to "punish as well as correct," but Pandora is the only character put in isolated lockdown and permanently segregated from others. Pandora's status as both a Black woman and a lesbian is what makes her a candidate for punishment and containment rather than "correction."

The others, including Maggie (Black, heterosexual), Jackie (white, heterosexual), and, eventually, Belle, will all be sent for corrective treatment in the form of ECT. However, through narrative and cinematic choices, *Caged Heat* enacts what Orit Kamir calls "cinematic judgement" of the injustice experienced by Pandora, which invites critical engagement with the "fictional legal system" that McQueen constructs and presides over.[51] Pandora denounces the superintendent's sexual standards as hypocritical and unjust and refuses to display contrition or guilt. Her face is caught in a close-up, with the camera lingering on her quivering lip as she tells McQueen: "You've got real problems." In a later scene, her judgment is reaffirmed when Jackie challenges McQueen's penology: "Is putting Pandora in solitary supposed to correct her?"[52] Thus, adding nuance to bell hooks's accurate assessment that, for Black women in mainstream cinema, to be "sexually assertive will lead to rejection and punishment,"[53] Pandora is embraced by her peers, reunited with her partner, and vindicated; in contrast, Jackie discovers that being deemed correctable may not put her in a place of advantage.

Critiquing the Medical-Legal Regulation of Women

The inclusion of ECT as the tool of choice for male sadistic fantasies in *Caged Heat* can be dismissed as a "checking-off" of the exploitation cycle's required torture scene or it can be read as a subtle critique of the use of non-voluntary treatment on women in prison. As Michel Foucault points out, knowledge/power systems at the turn of the century produced experts who would "graft" psychiatric, social work, and other medical discourses onto existing legal structures in efforts to label and treat "offenders."[54] In the late 1940s and early 1950s, the American correctional system began to deploy a medical discourse that would replace the focus on reform. Under the new "treatment" model, corrections included medical interventions and behavioural modification techniques, during which experts administered aversion therapy. These treatments vary from the use of tranquilizers and the hallucinogenic drug LSD to experiments in sensory deprivation and the deployment of non-voluntary ECT.[55]

Since that time, the medical-legal professions (psychiatrists, capacity and consent tribunals, and mental health courts) have played a significant role in "treating" criminals to rid them of their predisposition towards criminality. In fact, the year *Caged Heat* was released, a psychology professor – whose starting assumption was that prisoners have "full-blown social neurosis" that "need[s] to be cured, not punished" – published an essay entitled "Criminals Can Be Brainwashed – Now." Among other things, the paper argued for combining the sensory deprivation of prisoners "with drugs, hypnosis, and astute manipulation of reward and punishment" in an effort to "restructure" personalities.[56] While a broad obligation to elicit prisoner consent before treatment has been legislatively achieved since the mid-1970s, the US Supreme Court determined as recently as 1996 that the forced treatment of prisoners was justifiable when "reasonably related to legitimate penological interests," including the maintenance of order in the prison environment.[57]

This treatment regime has had particular implications for women, who historically have come into contact with the law because their acts of violence, or even their retaliation to violence, are constructed as a medical pathology.[58] Moreover, case law reveals that, once in prison, women who exhibit an unorthodox expression of femininity risk being branded in need of medical (and often anti-psychotic) intervention, even in the absence of a diagnosis for mental illness.[59] Racialized women often bear the brunt of this labelling because of implicit racist biases on the part of corrections staff, who view "acute stress reactions" – which are entirely reasonable in a confinement setting – as "symptoms of mental disorder."[60] At the same time, women prisoners who are navigating mental illnesses, many of which emerge because of incarceration or are heightened by being in prison, are regularly denied access to appropriate healthcare.[61] In *Caged Heat,* Pandora, the Black lesbian who explicitly challenges Superintendent McQueen's authority, is put in isolated lockdown, stripped naked, and brutalized. However, her friends – all coded as heterosexual or "femme" – commit far more serious offences: Maggie and Jackie try to escape and, in the process, set fire to the prison kitchen, and Belle inadvertently kills a guard. But, unlike Pandora, they are sent for corrective therapy. When Jackie is dragged to the ECT table and restrained in a gurney with electrodes attached to her temples, she screams: "You're crazy! This is rape! You can't do this!" In a marked departure from other exploitation WIP films, which often explore graphic sexuality in the context of violence against women, Jackie remains fully clothed in this troubling and gruesome torture scene.[62]

Blurring the Victim/Offender Dichotomy

Before the film's culmination – in which Pandora and Belle are reunited, and the sadistic doctor is killed – the film problematizes many of its protagonists' engagements with the justice system in the first place. In so doing, *Caged Heat* also calls into question one of the foundational binaries of the criminal law – namely, the distinction between the legal subjectivities of victim and that of offender. The distinction between perpetrator (the person who causes harm) and victim (the person who experiences harm) is inadequate for capturing the diverse and multidimensional identities and experiences of women who come into contact with the criminal justice system. This is not to deny that women and girls are still far more frequently entangled in the criminal law as victims rather than as perpetrators of crime. Yet there are many women who deviate from the discursive construction and cultural expectation of a proper "victim" because of their race, class, ethnicity, and minority religious beliefs, or because they navigate mental health and substance use issues, or because they engage in marginalized labour, such as sex work. These women are more acutely policed while, simultaneously, not afforded the full protection of the criminal law when they experience violence or harm.[63]

To say that the distinction between perpetrator and victim fails to capture the experiences of most criminalized women is not to deny that women and girls are in fact engaging in crime. However, empirical research has shown that women who have committed an offence (violent or otherwise) have an overwhelming presence of past sexual, physical, and/or state-based violence or have lived lives otherwise marred by trauma, oppression, and abuse. Their past victimization is often inextricable from their conflict with the law.[64] Unlike formal legal regimes, the WIP genre has constantly called into question the clear division between those who commit crime and those who are victimized through a particular trope: in every WIP film, there is almost always at least one character who has killed an abusive partner out of self-defence and who is ultimately treated by staff and prisoners alike as though she should not be incarcerated.[65] *Caged Heat* expands this critique to include women who do not fall so easily within the legal and cultural construction of a proper "victim" – namely, women who engage in transactional sex.

When Maggie and Jackie find their way to Crazy Alice's, they find out that she has been recently laid off from the plant and is temporarily offering "satisfying private female wrestling" at the "Academy of Sexual Satisfaction," which she runs inside her flat. It turns out, however, that one of Alice's clients is actually an undercover police officer. In jurisdictions where prostitution is criminalized, sex workers are vulnerable to myriad abuses from their clients, ranging from breach of contract to sexual assault. They distrust the police and fear that, if they disclose their victimization, they will risk being arrested themselves, whether for solicitation or for another minor offence.[66] On another level, sex workers have been explicitly denied the full protection of the law. In New York State and other states, so-called prostitution evidence, which establishes that a complainant has engaged in the sale of commercialized sex, can be an admissible exception to "rape shield" provisions that would ordinarily protect a complainant from having their sexual past brought in as evidence. Prostitution evidence has been used successfully to discredit complainants in sexual assault trials by challenging their credibility or as a means of implying that they consented to the violence they endured.[67]

The scene in *Caged Heat* described above features an officer who, after his receipt of services, tries to arrest Alice for solicitation and prostitution. However, the three women jump the corrupt cop and tie him up before they head to the prison to free their friends. Alice is very aware that, as a sex worker, she could not turn to the formal law for entrapment, even in ordinary circumstances, and now that she is harbouring fugitives she is even more vulnerable. In addition to blurring the victim/offender boundary, this brief encounter raises other substantive law and jurisprudential questions, such as the nature of legal remedies that should be available for sex workers when a client refuses to pay and how the law around consensual sexual transactions for money might be reimagined.

Intertextual Dialogues

Like the film from which it gets its name, *Caged Heat*'s ending diverts from the WIP conventions at the time of its production. In *Caged!*, Marie Allen is not domesticated through the prison but, instead, resists the justice system's authority to label her a criminal. Similarly, the protagonists of *Caged Heat*, including, significantly, two Black women and a lesbian couple, escape the prison relatively unscathed – an ending quite unlike most WIP films in which the women attempt to escape.[68]

Caged Heat thus builds on the critique laid out in *Caged!* by incorporating other axes of disadvantage and inequality – namely, race and sexual orientation. Whereas *Caged!* includes moments of collective anger, which are directed against the brutish Evelyn Harper especially, it foregrounds the protagonist's individual act of defiance. By contrast, *Caged Heat* depicts women's personal disruptions – through sarcasm, creative expression, and acts of self-definition – while tending to the power of solidarity through race and class.

According to film reviewer Bruce Crowther, the WIP melodramas "soberly" depict women as "victim[s] of male dominated society" and have "a quality the later exploitation movies lack."[69] While the method may not be sobriety, several final narrative elements in *Caged Heat* tackle issues at the forefront of critical criminology, including how particular women are labelled dangerous, what the objectives of sentencing are, and how the false victim/offender dichotomy plays out for already marginalized women. Further, its parodic elements augur a number of feminist-leaning WIP satires in the 1980s. Often overseen by women writers, directors, and producers, a number of texts overtly mocked the exploitation genre in this period, such as the clever, but short-lived, Fox sitcom *Women in Prison.* More recently, Season 5, episode 7 ("Full Bush, Half Sinker") of *OITNB* is basically an inversion of the exploitation cycle's tropes, featuring all-male characters (guards who have been taken hostage during a riot), gratuitously shirtless, being subjected to hungry looks by a number of the incarcerated women. Their function seems little more than to provide a vehicle for Cindy Hayes (Adrienne C. Moore), who, in a guard uniform cinched tight with a belt, performs the role of the Warden of Bitchfield. Both (re)appropriate the lecherous matron character played by Pam Grier in *Women in Cages* and rearticulate the corrupt, but motherly, guard interpreted by Queen Latifah in *Chicago* (2002).[70] The music video *Telephone* (2009) is an homage to *Caged Heat,* depicting the jailbreak of an interracial couple (Beyoncé and Lady Gaga), and it shows irreverence towards the normative standards of female beauty and the dominant heteronormative narrative to which any New World Pictures film adhered. Finally, *Stuck!* (2009), shot in black and white, seems to be aiming for the feel of *Caged!* while maintaining the kitsch of the exploitation genre with an added layer of homonormative self-awareness.

Whatever one's view of *Caged Heat*'s merit as a cinematic text, it incontrovertibly set the tone for the often explicitly feminist, self-aware reworking of the genre in the 1980s, 1990s, and 2000s. Before those films emerged, however, American network television censors began to adapt to a changing cultural landscape and, during the mid-1970s, offered lurid stories about young women's incarceration. These films had pretensions of being socially relevant and important, but they often displayed sensationalized violence against women – sexual assault and sexual slavery especially. For instance, there is *Born Innocent* (1974), which stars Linda Blair – best known for playing Regan in *The Exorcist* (1973) and who became a staple in a string of exploitation WIP films – as fourteen-year-old Chris Parker.[71] Chris is sent to a reformatory for girls after having run away from foster care; while incarcerated, a lesbian gang sexually assaults her with a broom handle. That scene, which lasts almost two minutes, is said to have been the object of a copycat crime.[72] While the National Broadcasting Company intended to make an educational but titillating film, it ultimately produced a film that is derogatory in its treatment of queer youth and simplistic in its exploration of violence committed by girls.[73]

The two films I discuss next, *Stranger Inside* (2001), directed by Cheryl Dunye, and *Civil Brand* (2002), directed by Neema Barnette, distinguish themselves from these more sordid cautionary tales in no small part because both are directed by racialized women. Moreover, unlike Roger Corman's studio, these filmmakers aspired to provide critical commentary while deploying the tropes of exploitation films to launch a Black feminist critique of the over-representation of racialized women in prisons.

5 Representing Incarcerated Black Women: *Stranger Inside* and *Civil Brand*

Women-in-prison (WIP) movies, as a rare venue of entirely female casts, provide a unique creative space for women, giving them opportunities to write screenplays and, as I explore in this chapter, to take the helm as director. While the screenplays for two of the films discussed in other chapters, *Ann Vickers* (1993) and *Caged!* (1950), were written by women, both were directed by men.[1] In fact, *Within the Law* (1923) and *The Woman Condemned* (1934) are the only films during the first sixty years of the genre to be directed by women: Frances Marion and Dorothy Davenport, respectively.

The 1970s exploitation cycle, however, created new possibilities for women in front of the camera to take on action roles, especially for actors like Pam Grier, Tamara Dobson, Teresa Graves, and Jeanie Bell. But, in a few rare instances, women took up position behind the camera. Stephanie Rothman is credited as the driving force behind all of the feminist content surfacing in New World Pictures. In discussing the tight wire that she walked when directing exploitation films, Rothman explains: "As long as there was enough nudity and violence distributed throughout," directors could "have a dramatized discussion about issues that were then being ignored by big-budget major studio films."[2] Indeed, in her jungle WIP movie *Terminal Island* (1973), she explores formal equality, contradictory feminist discourses, and the possibility of solidarity between women and men engaged in social movements.

In the 1990s, a number of made-for-television movies featuring incarcerated women were directed by women. Linda Otto's *A Mother's Right: The Elizabeth Morgan Story* (1992) is a fictionalized account of Dr. Elizabeth Morgan's time in prison after refusing to reveal the whereabouts of her daughter, whom she feared had been abused by her ex-husband. Karen Arthur's *Against Their Will: Women in Prison* (1994) tells the story of lawlessness inside a women's maximum-security prison. Judith Light plays a woman falsely accused who is sexually assaulted, extorted, and threatened by the other prisoners. She survives her stint inside and, when released, becomes a prison reform activist.[3] Women, without a doubt, have produced thought-provoking, complex, compelling, and, especially recently, exceedingly popular television series. Kathleen Green created the clever, though short-lived, *Women in Prison* (1987–88).[4] Since then, Maureen Chadwich and Ann McManus (*Bad Girls* [1999–2006]), Lara Radulovich (*Wentworth* [2013–present]), and Jenji Kohan (*Orange Is the New Black* [*OITNB*] [2013–19]) have unquestionably altered and layered the popular cultural image of criminalized women.

Despite such advances, however, none of these groundbreaking creators are racialized women, and casting directors, screenwriters, producers, and filmmakers creating WIP stories are predominantly white. The absence of racialized women in positions of power in the film and television industries has translated into one-dimensional, often stereotypical roles for most racialized actors in WIP films. As Linda K. Fuller explains, it is only in the first half of the twentieth century that the roles available to Black actors "progressed from merely inhabiting the background to representing a servile and gratuitous stereotype."[5] Most WIP films of the melodramatic cycle pushed race to the margins by having entirely white casts. The few films that featured Black characters deployed racist strategies to further the plot's narrative. For instance, the only "Black" character in *Ann Vickers* is the uncredited "Lil – Black Woman," reportedly played by Sarah Padden, a white woman in black face. Lil appears only briefly, wailing in distress on her way to being hanged. When Black women with speaking roles were featured in films, they were generally embedded in antebellum racist stereotypes, especially the "Mammy" or "Aunt Jemima" – the caregiver and trusted adviser to a white protagonist. Always good natured, Mammy/Aunt Jemima stands as a counter to the belief that "slavery was hard and demeaning."[6] Working in the Jim Crow era, Louise Beavers appeared, quite remarkably, in well over a hundred movies. She took uncredited roles in two WIP movies, *Manslaughter* (1930) and *Paid* (1930), and later played a character named Ivory in both *Ladies of the Big House* (1931), in which she has killed her abusive husband, and *Women without Names* (1940). Madame Sul-Te-Wan, born Nellie Conley, the daughter of freed slaves, a respected stage actor, and the first Black American to sign a contract with a major film studio, took an uncredited speaking part in *Ladies They Talk About* (1933). She plays Mustard, a character who washes a white woman's undergarments in exchange for "bleaching cream and hair straightener." Off-camera, Sul-Te-Wan defended her pragmatism in taking such roles, as she preferred to "play a maid than [to] be one."[7] Finally, Academy Award nominee Juanita Moore appears as Polly Jones in *Women's Prison* (1955) and is introduced to viewers singing "Swing Low, Sweet Chariot" while scrubbing the floors.

In addition to carving out a space for themselves in mainstream white cinema, such performers found more meaningful parts in Black-cast films that were written, directed, and produced by African Americans. Between 1937 and 1944, for instance, Million Dollar Productions, founded by Black actor Ralph Cooper in collaboration with two white producers, made movies for racialized audiences in theatres owned and managed by African Americans.[8] *Reform School* (1939) was one such film.[9] In it, Louise Beavers plays "Mother Barton," a tough but devoted probation officer who discovers that one of her charges is being abused at the state reform school. The boys, played by the African American theatre troupe, the Harlem Tuff Kids, are neglected and beaten by the superintendent and his guards. Mother Barton becomes the "lone woman [standing] between them and a life of crime" and entreats the state to use education instead of repression to keep young Black men off the streets.[10]

As discussed earlier, it was not until the exploitation cycle that women racialized as Black were systematically offered roles that moved beyond what cultural historian Charlene B. Regester has qualified as their "strategic positioning ... to accentuate the prison landscape."[11] Not only did Black women take on more substantive speaking parts with the advent of exploitation WIP films in the 1970s, but also they were often central protagonists. One need only think of Pam Grier, who starred in a slate of "jungle" and prison-break movies and who has since been crowned queen of the WIP genre. She became one of the top-grossing female actors of the 1970s and went on to start her own production company.[12] In *The Big Doll House* (1971), Grier plays a sex worker jailed because she has too much information on her government clients, and, in *Big Bird Cage* (1972), she is a freedom fighter who has "committed crimes against the State," though she meets an untimely end in both films.[13] In these projects, Grier occupied a contradictory position, often embodying characters who espoused feminist values while fulfilling the dominant heterosexual fantasy of racialized women.[14] Yet she considered herself to be an action hero; she felt empowered by these characters and believed that she projected a strong image of Black femininity.[15] Grier was criticized by some of her peers, who wanted better parts for Black actors. She was also considered by some civil rights activists to be complicit with Hollywood in general, and with Blaxploitation films specifically, in perpetuating damaging stereotypes about Black women.[16] While it is true that exploitation WIP films circulated negative messages about Black women's experiences, one can adopt an oppositional stance towards these texts, as Yvonne Sims has argued, "reclaiming them, while discarding the negative attributes associated with [their] heroines."[17] The Black women in exploitation WIP movies were "no nonsense," had dimension and strength, and enacted "justifiable violence."[18]

Later WIP films that straddled the exploitation and realist drama cycles would offer a greater range to their Black principals, often positioning the racialized characters as the moral centre of the narrative.[19] In *Chained Heat* (1983), Duchess (Tamara Dobson), who was best known for her role as the titular character in *Cleopatra Jones* (1973), is a college graduate at the helm of the Black prisoners' cohort. She urges a white protagonist not to let the warden "pit Blacks against whites" and brings the two factions together to resist the sexual exploitation occurring within the prison. Similarly, in *The Naked Cage* (1986), the Black caucus advocates anti-violence, and their matriarch (Angela Gibbs) is trying to rid the prison of drugs. Finally, in the Fox Broadcasting Company's short-lived comedic series *Women in Prison,* C.C.H. Pounder plays Dawn Murphy, a level-headed solid con in for killing an abusive husband who makes pointed observations about racism and class privilege. Nevertheless, as bell hooks explains, Black women have historically been "adamant that they never [go] to the movies expecting to see compelling representations of black femaleness."[20] Her assessment may be different today given that "Shondaland" (the representational world constituted by Shonda Rhimes) has likely irrevocably shifted racialized women's expectations.[21] However, it is still rare for Black women to helm representations about women's incarceration and, consequently, rarer still to see images of criminalized Black women that resonate with racialized audiences.

There are two exceptions, however: Cheryl Dunye's *Stranger Inside* (2001) and Neema Barnette's *Civil Brand* (2002).[22] Long before *OITNB,* these films reflected Black and queer feminist discourses around gendered criminalization and, importantly, were stories told by Black women from the standpoint of racialized prisoners.[23]

Stranger Inside

Stranger Inside is the first WIP film to be written and directed by a Black woman, Cheryl Dunye.[24] From the outset of the Home Box Office (HBO) project, Dunye wanted to make a film that reflected the actual experiences of women in prison and to tell a story that would resonate with "people looking for more contemporary ... and [more] correct" depictions of "what's going on in the criminal justice system."[25] Consequently, she interviewed women at the Minnesota Shakopee Women's Correctional Facility; consulted with renowned Black feminist, prison activist, and educator Angela Y. Davis; and enlisted criminalized women to play small parts in the film. Dunye, an independent filmmaker, has always put race, sexual, and gender identities at the forefront of her projects. Dunye's first feature, *The Watermelon Woman* (1997), is an intertextual, self-reflexive account of a Black lesbian filmmaker, blending narrative fiction, experimental documentary practices, and autobiography.[26] With *Stranger Inside,* she relies on what Allison Perlman has called "the trifecta of HBO's innovation in television programming content" – violence, profanity, and nudity – while resisting the exploitation cycle's raison d'être of showing scantily clad women in a context of repression.[27] Instead, Dunye uses the WIP genre as a venue to explore family and motherhood from the standpoint of queer racialized women. In her words, she was interested in how incarcerated women "find that balance to being an inmate, being a mother, being a member of a family or a clan ... that they support or have to support."[28] Indeed, *Stranger Inside* does not follow the traditional WIP narrative of an innocent coming of age while incarcerated or discovering and successfully dismantling institutional corruption. Rather, the driving themes of the film is the prison as both "a home place, a place of family, and a domestic space" and an institution that functions to "deracinat[e]" and dismantle systems of "kinship."[29]

Synopsis of *Stranger Inside*

Treasure Lee (Yolonda Ross) is a young Black queer woman who was raised by her maternal grandmother and has since cycled in and out of youth reformatories for drug offences. On her twenty-first birthday, she stabs another prisoner to get herself transferred out of the Juvenile Authority Department of Corrections into an adult state facility. She's "going home," as she puts it, because she heard rumours that her mother, Margaret

"Brownie" Lee (Davenia McFadden), whom she thought was dead, has actually been serving a life sentence in the State Facility for Women. It turns out that Brownie is a tough and ruthless queen bee, but Treasure cannot be dissuaded from confronting her with an old family photo. While Brownie dismisses Treasure initially, her interest is peaked after she and Kit (Rain Phoenix), Brownie's white "prison daughter," devotee, and right hand, fight over who gets to sleep with Sugar (Patrice Fisher). Kit and Treasure are sent to the Security Housing Unit (solitary confinement). Impressed with Treasure's bravado, Brownie confesses to her in a rare moment of vulnerability that she is her mother. The state took Treasure away from her at birth, and she was raised by her maternal grandmother. Brownie vows to make up for lost time and takes Treasure in as part of her prison family.[30]

Given that the family happens to be the prison's main source for illicit drugs, Treasure is soon expected to pull her weight in sales. As she excels in her new position, Treasure slowly replaces Kit, who is eventually ostracized from the family and forced to find refuge with the white supremacist faction. Brownie insists that Kit is a liability and must be taken out; Treasure is charged with the task but ultimately is unable to kill Kit. When Kit realizes that she has been marked, she stabs Brownie in the neck. Treasure frantically offers her blood to be used in a transfusion, but tests show that their DNA does not match. It is revealed that Brownie is really Phyllis Stubbs, in for life without parole for the murder of Treasure's biological mother. The film ends with Warden Arnold (Lee Garlington) offering Treasure a deal: a transfer to a minimum-security institution if she becomes an informant and testifies against a corrupt guard. She takes the deal and, in the final scene, is shown smoking in the yard, having assumed her new identity: Brownie.

Criminalized Motherhood

Incarceration puts social and economic pressure on partners, families, and other kin relations of those individuals who are criminalized; it also has powerful and lasting effects on entire communities. Partners find themselves financially ruined with legal costs, additional childcare, and precarious housing. Children of incarcerated parents are more likely to use illegal drugs, face educational maladaptation, be underemployed, and navigate mental health strain.[31] Moreover, the caregivers of children whose parents are incarcerated tend to be their grandparents and, usually, their grandmother. The family or community members who assume guardianship of these children face economic hardship, health problems, and guilt. Incarcerated parents, especially women housed in rural areas several kilometres away and without adequate public transportation options, find themselves estranged from their children, despite theirs and their extended family's best efforts to stay connected.[32]

These negative social, economic, and emotional reverberations are heightened when it is mothers who find themselves incarcerated, and, in fact, mothers make up at least half of the prison population and over 80 percent of the jail population. The strains on extended families and the weakening of the parent-child bond are more acute when mothers are incarcerated because they are typically the primary caretakers of their children. With legislative frameworks that essentially default to termination of parental rights when a single mother is incarcerated for fifteen months or more, children of criminalized women are extremely vulnerable to being put into foster care and to suffering abuses while in the "care" of foster families. As a result, they are, as Gail Smith puts it, at a greater risk of coming into contact with the criminal law: "The path from foster care into delinquency and the juvenile justice system, and from juvenile detention into prison is all too familiar to service providers and advocates working with prisoners."[33]

Mothering, of course, is socially, historically, politically, and culturally construed and cannot be examined apart from intersecting power structures of gender, race, and class.[34] These negative impacts are exacerbated for impoverished racialized women and ethnic minorities – Black women and Latinas[35] especially – who navigate the complex process of scrutiny, surveillance, and social sanction characterized by the perception of some mothering as criminal and through legal and extralegal practices (formal and informal regulation) treating some women as deviant, dependent, and/or dangerous mothers.[36] For instance, while up to 25 percent of women – regardless of race or engagement with the law – have used illegal drugs or alcohol while pregnant, Black women are more likely to be reported to child and welfare authorities for doing so, punished by medical-legal apparatuses as a result, and imprisoned for the duration of their pregnancy.[37] The consequences of such regulation are extreme; depending on the state, a woman who consumes drugs or alcohol while pregnant may be charged with foetal abuse, child endangerment, delivery of a drug to a minor, and even manslaughter, attempted homicide, and murder.

Black and other women of racial/cultural minorities navigate varying material conditions, cultural landscapes, and community bonds that may result in mothering tactics and strategies that deviate from the white, middle-class, dominant norm. While adaptive, cooperative, and flexible modes of mothering facilitate resilience among racialized families, they also render Black mothers more vulnerable to surveillance and regulation by institutions that undermine and pathologize their mothering skills.[38] As a result, impoverished Black women are more likely to have their mothering highly scrutinized or devalued by child welfare agencies; they also risk being directly impacted by the cultural and racial stereotypes that give shape to their regulation as "bad mothers." That is, legal and regulatory apparatuses circulate and reinforce a myth of the "good" mother that is embedded in race, class, and gender biases: heterosexual, white, married, economically comfortable, and educated, though not necessarily a "working mom." Consequently, women who are racialized, who are members of cultural minorities, who are migrant, who do not have proper documentation, who are poor, who navigate addictions, and who are themselves survivors of the child welfare system are labelled as "bad" mothers and thus are more likely to find themselves in conflict with the law.[39]

Intertextual Dialogues

With the exception of the exploitation films of the 1970s – in which motherhood is explicitly absent as it might interfere with the sexual fantasy of young, unattached women resisting oppression one shower scene at a time – a key narrative element of the WIP genre is how mothers navigate the stigma and social consequences of criminalization. In the melodrama/social problem WIP cycle, motherhood is used as a pivotal narrative element insofar as it is the protagonist's separation from her child that sends her into a downward spiral. In *Caged!,* when Marie Allen (Eleanor Parker) is told that "inmates aren't allowed to go home to have their babies" and is then forced to hand her child over to the state because no other suitable guardian can be found, her physical and emotional transformation is stark. This is true for later iterations of the WIP genre in which a core dramatic element is the depiction of how mothers deal with separation from their children.[40] In Season 1, episode 8 ("Moscow Mule"), of *OITNB,* Maria Ruiz (Jessica Pimentel) goes into early labour, is sent away to give birth, and then returns to the prison without her newborn and slips into depression; by Season 4, she is hardened to the point of being one of the show's antagonists and, in a Dominican-led coup, takes over the leadership of "Spanish Harlem" from the Puerto Ricans.

A few WIP films feature a mother-infant program (prison nursery), where new mothers are given a finite time to bond and care for their children while serving out their sentences.[41] In *House of Women* (1962), Erica Hayden (Shirley Knight) is wrongfully convicted of robbery and sent to a women's institution for five years. According to the prison's rules, Erica, who is expecting her first child, is entitled to keep her baby with her for three years, after which she must hand it over to the state for adoption. A deadly uprising ensues when the warden decides to end the mother-infant program. In a few films, usually produced outside of the United States, criminalized mothers are depicted as mothers grappling with the stigmatization of being labelled "bad" while also finding new purpose and focus in their lives through the experience of giving birth in prison. In these films, motherhood becomes a catalyst for hope and personal transformation.[42] In the realist cycle, one's status as mother is often leveraged as a form of punishment. In *Nine Lives* (2005), for instance, Sandra (Elpidia Carrillo), who can only see her daughter once a month through a glass partition during visitation, is given a defective handset. She breaks down when her daughter cannot hear her and eventually lashes out at a guard; she is shackled and carried away to solitary in front of her child.

Motherhood permeates *Stranger Inside,* which contains chapter headings like "Mother and Daughter United" and "Anything for Mom's Love" and symbolism like Treasure's being more interested in a framed reprint of a Madonna and Child fresco than in the woman giving her oral sex.[43] Further, it is the first WIP film to explicitly feature a lesbian mother (through the character of Brownie).[44] It is also unique in that the emotional toll of mother-child separation is told from the child's perspective, through Treasure's quest to find her birth mother and through Kit's longing for recognition from her mother figure. However, while *Stranger Inside* revolves around such reconciliation plots, the film is really about kin relationships that do not conform to hegemonic sexual norms and roles. Despite the breakdown of familial bonds when a mother is incarcerated, new configurations of family are constituted in prison. Cheryl Dunye has stated that she wanted to explore "what it was like to wake up next to some woman who is a grandmother and her daughter is down the hall ... And who else becomes part of this family?"[45]

A key narrative element is the sibling rivalry between the two love-starved "sisters," Kit and Treasure. Kit's filial love for Brownie crosses race lines, and she confesses as much to Treasure: "I love her like a mother for real. I'd do anything for her." Her loyalty remains even after Brownie stabs her in the thigh for losing some money and tells her she is nothing more than a "yard dog." Yet Treasure quickly assumes a privileged status, as Brownie capitalizes on her fantasy. When Treasure tells Brownie of her childhood dream that she breaks out of prison and rescues her, she replies: "To find you now.

That's like a Miracle. My Blood." Finally, in a long tracking shot, another of the Black prisoners, Leisha (Medusa), leads the maintenance crew in a call-and-response work song that is reminiscent of those that arose out of slavery and endured during the reconstruction period (1865–77) and the era of industrialization:

> CALL: How many months do I love my Mama?
> ANSWER: Every month of the year.
> CALL: How many months do I love my Mama?
> ANSWER: Every month of the year.
> CALL: It's January
> ANSWER: January
> CALL: February
> ANSWER: February
> CALL: March. Everybody
> TOGETHER: April. May. June. July. August. September. October and November.
> TOGETHER: On the 25th day of December.
> TOGETHER: Every Month of the year.

This chant becomes the extra-diegetic score to a montage sequence showing Shadow (LaTonya "T" Hagans) "geeking with the library crowd," while Treasure starts dealing for Brownie out of the bathroom stalls. In other scenes like these, Dunye also encourages reflection upon the familial networks that exist beyond the mother-daughter dyad: Shadow, Treasure's long-time foster sister, takes on the role of the occasional "other mother."[46] Shadow initially gets word to Treasure about Brownie's existence, but seeing the lengths to which she will go to build connection and an affective relationship with a woman who turns out to be a sociopath, she endeavours to protect Treasure. Shadow encourages her to stay on a narrower path, learn a trade, get an education, and keep her head down.

Finally, the film grapples with the emotional strain on incarcerated mothers through unnamed characters, who reveal their life circumstances in group therapy sessions. These include a single mother who had two children by the time she was sixteen, a woman in her forties who has spent her entire adult life cycling in and out of institutions and never had a family, another who confesses in tears that she has "made mistakes" but "can never reverse the hatred in her [daughter's] face," and another who has a mental breakdown when she realizes her son will be sent back to their country of origin because of incarceration. These vignettes include improvised and deeply personal monologues:

> The biggest pain I've had to deal with is the feelings to do with my kids. I have three sons. My two oldest boys were taken from me when I was in the second term. My youngest boy I was pregnant with when I was in the federal pen. They didn't want a mom who was an ex-convict. They don't want a mom who is a prostitute. They don't want a mom that's a burglar.

In making motherhood the centre of its story about incarcerated women, *Stranger Inside* opens up the possibility of an even broader range of representations in later films. Indeed, in other realist dramas, the default assumption is that women in prison are mothers. In *Civil Brand,* a pregnant L'il Mama (Lark Voorhies) tells a "new fish": "Everybody got kids in here. Nikki got twin boys living with her mama. Wet got two kids too but they got taken away from her. Girl get ready, 'cause Mother's day is hard in here." In *Wentworth,* consider Doreen Anderson (Shareena Clanton), who is in for reckless endangerment for a drug-induced car accident in which she lost her unborn child; Bea Smith (Danielle Cormack), who will murder to avenge the death of her daughter; and Liz Birdsworth (Celia Ireland), who is a recovering alcoholic who longs to be reunited with her daughter Sophie and will be when Sophie finds her way into prison for a crime almost identical to her mother's. Similarly, *OITNB* showcases different modalities of motherhood: Cindy Haye's (Adrienne C. Moore) repressed guilt and secretiveness about being a teenage mom whose daughter is now being raised as her sister; Sophia (Laverne Cox), a transgender woman will be shown to have a strained relationship with her son in part because of her decision to transition; Yvonne "Vee" Parker's (Lorraine Touassaint) manipulation of foster children whom she recruits in her drug ring; Dayanara "Daya" Diaz's (Dascha Polanco) shift from the primary and attentive caretaker of her siblings to an ambivalent mother unsure about being a suitable parent; and Alieda Diaz (Elizabeth Rodriguez) and Daya's tortured mother-daughter relationship and the former's unorthodox expressions of devotion and love.

Civil Brand

Civil Brand also touches upon motherhood; however, it does so through sensationalized accounts: L'il Mama will miscarry and die during a violent outbreak, and Frances Shepard (LisaRaye McCoy) will have a psychiatric break when she discovers her daughter has died while in foster care. This film is more concerned with, and thus more effective in, its exploration of the overrepresentation of Black women under the control of the corrections system, their use as cheap labour for corporate interests, and what Black feminist scholar and activist Michelle Alexander has coined the "new Jim Crow."[47] Filmmaker Neema Barnette chose the title *Civil Brand* not only as a nod to the Sybil Brand Institute in East Los Angeles, named after a feminist prison reformer, but also as a play on the labelling and stigma that criminalized women experience. The premise of the film, in which women organize a peaceful work stoppage to get better wages and fair labour conditions, was in part inspired by real events. In addition to interviewing incarcerated women in two states, Barnette incited her actors to engage in ethnographic explorations of their own: "[We] made all the actresses go to prison. They were inside and they saw what it was like. We did homework."[48] Suspending the ethical issues that critical anthropologists, sociologists, or criminologists might have with the possible exploitative nature of prisons and prisoners as objects of inquiry, Barnette's intention seems to genuinely have been to provide a serious exposé of prison life.[49]

Like *Stranger Inside, Civil Brand* relies on the more lascivious tropes of earlier cycles, especially the one-dimensional evil warden.[50] However, the fact that the film was directed by a racialized woman with the intention of centring the experiences of criminalized Black women sets it apart from any Roger Corman-like film of the 1970s. In fact, Black feminist cultural critic Jacqueline Bobo has qualified the film as part of a "corrective narrative" that "counterbalances" the stranglehold of the pervasive heroic images of law enforcement agencies fighting valiantly against those who are routinely portrayed as demonic lawbreakers."[51] Indeed, Barnette's cast, which is almost entirely Black, consists of hip-hop pioneer and feminist M.C. Lyte, playing Sargent Cervantes; the politically provocative Mos Def, playing Michael "Mike" Meadows; and Monica Colhoun, playing political activist Wet, a savvy political agitator who stands in for Black feminist, activist, and educator Angela Y. Davis. While Wet is a secondary character, the story revolves around her fight to expose unfair and illegal labour practices in prison. Through Wet, Barnette expresses her vision for the film as "a work of passion ... about slave labor in the prison system."[52] It is Barnette's desire to denounce the supremely unfair working conditions for incarcerated women that sets *Civil Brand* apart from any other WIP film made before it.

***Synopsis of* Civil Brand**

The film opens with shots of Whitehead Correctional Institute's facade and Sabrina (Da Brat) in voiceover telling us how "winning" was "a real victory." It then cuts to her reading the newspaper headline: "Twenty-five Women Win Abuse Case." The rest of the film is a long flashback, beginning with a bus ride to the institution in which a meek, cuffed Frances, a nurse in for killing her abusive husband, meets the seasoned but kind Sabrina. The cycle of abuse repeats itself in a new iteration as she and the other women with whom she is incarcerated, all Black, are subjected to sexual, emotional, and financial violence at the hands of the African American men who wield power within the institution. The "new fish" are initiated into the prison rules by Captain Alan Dease (Clifton Powell), who lets them know in no uncertain terms that they "are now the property of Whitehead Correctional Institute." The other prisoners – in for crimes ranging from possession with intent to sell to murdering a sexually abusive stepfather – welcome Frances to "the Plantation" and give her a breakdown of a day in the life of the prison: six hours of sewing factory work for $1.50 a day, one hour of yard time, a meal, prison maintenance labour (cleaning, meal preparation, shipping and receiving), a final meal, then one hour of personal time before lights out.

Frances's arrival coincides with the arrival of a new guard, Michael "Mike" Meadows, a compassionate university student who took the job to cover his tuition and pay off his loans. His "real education," however, "began when he started working at the prison," and his orientation includes Captain Dease, an uneducated, pro-gun degenerate who extorts sexual favours from the women, who offers him this nugget of corrections philosophy: "Women are animals in need of discipline." Warden Nelson (Reed McCants) is little better, bragging to a representative of Wall Corporation, who owns and manages private prisons, about the cost-effectiveness of prison labour: "The workers can't quit!" He has no aspirations to rehabilitate women, his only objective is to attract corporate sponsors and generate even more profits. In fact, when faced with a potential riot, he refuses to put the unit in lockdown to avoid losing valuable factory time. In a sequence set to the extra-diegetic a cappella rendition of "There Were No Mirrors in My Nana's House," which tells the story of a child seeing the beauty of the world through the loving eyes of her grandmother, the prison is shown as having contaminated food, poor ventilation, a rat infestation, little to no access to basic health services, a demoralized staff, and sweat-shop working conditions. Meanwhile, Frances discovers that her daughter has been killed by a stray bullet during a drug deal. She breaks down, but Wet, an aspiring lawyer, Nikki Barnes (N'Bushe

Wright), the queen bee and hardened lifer who wants desperately to regain custody of her child, and Rose "Lil' Mama" gather around her, and her agony becomes a purpose: to expose these breaches of fundamental human rights and create better living conditions for incarcerated women.

Despite initial infighting between the easily vexed Nikki and Aisha (Tichina Arnold) – who formerly wielded some power in the prison because she was Captain Dease's favourite – Wet and Frances convince the other women to organize a work stoppage. They draft a petition demanding "fair treatment for inmates, better living conditions, better work conditions, better heat, and an end to the vicious beatings and sexual abuse we face every day." Wet and Frances are put in the hole for their part in the peaceful protest. Increasingly troubled by what he sees in the prison, Mike further discovers the magnitude of the for-profit corrections model through a simple Internet search, which reveals headlines like "Today's Prison Parallels the Plantation of the Early South" and "Cashing In on Criminality: Private Prisons, Corporate Power and the Color of Crime." He becomes the women's ally but is too late: Captain Dease's rape of Lil' Mama has forced her to miscarry, and she ultimately haemorrhages to death. There is an uprising. The women take hostages and murder Dease. Unlike *Caged Heat* (1974), in which the women head off together into the sunset, *Civil Brand*'s entire ensemble cast, with the exception of the narrator, will be killed. Nevertheless, the media

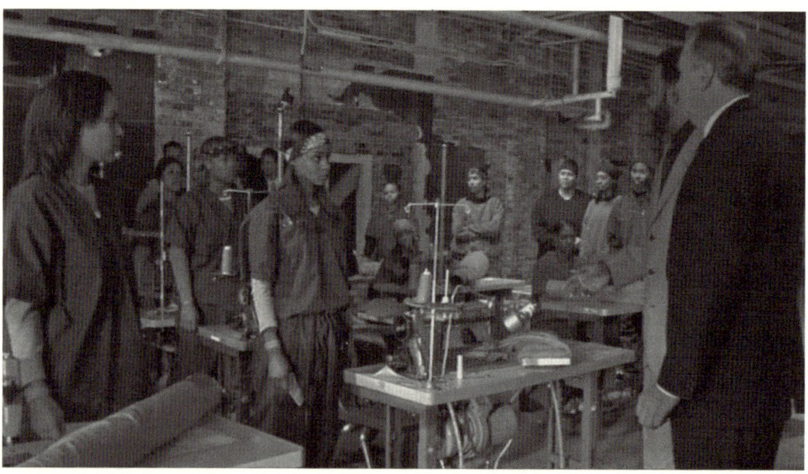

Figure 6 Leading a peaceful protest, Frances (LisaRaye McCoye) [*left*] and Wet (Monica Calhoun), next to her, confront the warden in *Civil Brand* (2002). Courtesy of Lions Gate Films (all rights reserved).

attention is sufficient to expose the warden's corruption and the other abuses suffered by the incarcerated women.

Exposing the Prison Industrial Complex

In an interview about her film, Neema Barnette states that her primary motivation was to expose the prison industrial complex:

> There was one line in the old script that said a corporation came to visit a prison and so I asked my husband, why would a corporation come to visit a prison? I had no idea so I went online and I typed in "prison as business" and when I [did] ... I found out that Angela Davis had a movement called Critical Resistance, which was totally about the prison-industrial complex. All these major companies are doing business with prisons – they're closing down their companies and Americans of all colors are losing their pensions, their medical because they're getting fired. There's no need for them because [companies] are getting such cheap labor in jail. And so that became the lead story in "Civil Brand." It's a major reason why there is a three strikes law, why young people are kept in jail after their time is up. You know, the fuller the prison the larger the contracts.[53]

The concept of the prison industrial complex has been deployed by scholars to help explain America's carceral boom in the 1980s as a consequence of the rise of neoliberal industrialization and policies of privatization, austerity, and deregulation, which resulted in a decrease in industrial sector labour and a large swath of precarious workers.[54] It refers to the myriad ways that government and private industry intersect, such as in the official embedding of corporations in prisons since the passing of the Prison Industry Enhancement Act in 1979 and the use of surveillance practices, aggressive policing, and mass imprisonment to further those interests.[55] Since then, prison industrial complex scholars have shown that mass incarceration occurred in tandem with economic deindustrialization, a discursive and actual shift towards "tough-on-crime" policies to address deeply entrenched social inequalities and racial stratification, and an expansion of incarceration beyond "prison" in the form of immigration facilities, county and military jails, youth detention centres, and psychiatric institutions. Black feminist scholar and activist Beth E. Richie refers to this new social, political, historical, and economic context as the prison nation.[56]

While the overrepresentation of Black Americans in the prison nation is one of the lingering impacts of the slavery system[57] as well as of the legislated discrimination and racial segregation in the Jim Crow South, its persistence is attributable to the prison industrial complex, as expressed through white supremacist ideology embedded in ostensibly neutral legislative enactments,[58] racist discursive constructions of Black bodies as dangerous and/or dependent in mainstream media and popular culture,[59] and the deliberate or tacit unwillingness of policy-makers and other people wielding power to further racialized Americans' civil, political, and social rights.[60] Feminist researchers have underscored how Black women are uniquely impacted by the prison industrial complex: specifically, they are at greater risk of coming into conflict with the criminal law because they are, whether through unconscious bias or racist animus on the part of individual officers, disproportionately impacted by aggressive policing strategies. Even when controlling for criminal history, Black women will receive harsher sentences than their white counterparts.[61] Moreover, mandatory sentencing strips judges of the ability to take into consideration whether incarceration is the appropriate sentence for a mother with primary childcare responsibilities, a situation in which close to 30 percent of incarcerated Black women find themselves.[62] This reality has a devastating impact on families under the purview of the Adoption and Safe Families Act, which includes default provisions of termination of parental rights when children are placed in foster care for fifteen months.[63]

Mandatory minimum sentences also directly impact Black women insofar as they overwhelmingly enter prison for relatively minor drug offences. Specifically, women acting as drug mules for men who they are romantically attached to, economically dependent on, or have a filial bond with and who are more substantially engaged as dealers or traffickers may be labelled as conspirators and handed the same sentence.[64] These practices are specific historically, but they can be traced back to slavery, which systematically separated mothers and daughters and began the cycle of intergenerational incarcerations. That cycle is further reinforced through the backlash against civil rights activists and an ongoing legacy of being simultaneously over-policed and under-protected by the criminal apparatus.[65]

Specifically, as Beth E. Richie has shown, Black women who live in low-income communities are the "most stigmatized [and] the least protected" by virtue of their experiences of structural racism and economic exploitation, their political disenfranchisement, and the direct incursion of conservative public policy into their lives. Consequently, they are more likely to experience state violence (for example, police brutality or excessive use of force), street violence (for example, random acts of violence by strangers, public aggression if they defy hegemonic gender norms, and physical harm when they inadvertently witness a crime), and interpersonal violence (for example, economic, emotional, physical, and/or sexual abuse inflicted by someone they know or someone in their households).[66] This segment of the Black community is also less likely to report experiences of violence because of what Richie has called the "trap of loyalty": a matrix of personal and communal expectations that Black women ought not to be complicit in bringing more racilized men into the criminal justice system, combined with the sociocultural construction of Black women as strong and impervious to mistreatment and accepted truths within the community that Black women are in a privileged position in relation to Black men.[67]

Importantly, as Angela Y. Davis, the scholar and activist that Barnette refers to earlier in this chapter, has made clear, "the exploitation of prison labor by private corporations is [only] *one aspect among an array of relationships linking corporations, governments, correctional communities,* and media." Furthermore, the "drive to fill these new structures with human bodies [has] been driven by ideologies of racism and the pursuit of profit."[68] *Civil Brand* tackles prison privatization and labour practices that amount to involuntary servitude. In so doing, the film opened the door for further explorations of prison labour, most notably in *OITNB,* in which one interaction between Janae Watson (Vicky Jeudy), who is characteristically insightful about systemic racism, and Joel Luschek (Matt Peters), a white male guard, repeats *Civil Brand*'s central motif:

> JOEL: [Tosses a massive book on the table.] Read this. [Slams an old lamp on the table.] Fix this. That's your job.
> JANAE: [Tsks] Jobs pay. This is bullshit.
> JOEL: You're making 11 cents an hour.
> JANAE: Right. So I could like, save up and buy a 6$ Pepsi at the company store? It's bullshit. I ain't pickin' cotton.

Expanding beyond *Civil Brand*'s commentary, *OITNB*'s narrative is also organized around women's everyday unpaid work, which, beyond generating profits for administrators, actually sustains the prison itself: women are shown doing janitorial work, laundering uniforms, acting as administrative assistants, managing the library, transporting prisoners in and out of the institution, providing extracurricular programs,[69] and running the commissary.[70] *OITNB* also explores the other side of the prison industrial complex, including the individuals who staff the prisons and are given little training and low wages for emotionally difficult and physically dangerous work; who are victims of union busting; who have lost employment security, health insurance, and retirement plans with privatization; and who have seen their work progressively contracted out to former military personnel (many of whom are themselves dealing with post-traumatic stress, depression, addiction, or other trauma).[71]

Further, *Civil Brand* falls short of getting at how incarceration in the prison industrial complex has become the solution to dealing with compounding social problems (racial disparities, poverty, mental illness, and non-conformism). The women in Neema Barnette's prison are all violent offenders who have committed crimes out of jealousy (Wet) or who have murdered abusive men (Lil' Mama and Frances). That these women also happen to be Black and make claims that, on the surface, justify their resistance in terms of race (Wet, for instance, rallies the women by saying: "We have to do something instead of going out to work like some docile field [workers]") tells us little about what broader life circumstances led them to crime. The film, for instance, does not interrogate the overused and institutionalized disciplinary protocols in schools (around normatively appropriate clothing) and zero-tolerance policies (around non-normative expressions of resisting authority) that effectively push Black girls out of the school system through suspensions and removals and into the juvenile justice system.[72]

In the end, *Civil Brand*'s moral stance is best encapsulated in its narrator's final monologue, which is reminiscent of *Scared Straight* (1978), a cultural phenomenon/documentary. She admonishes Aisha, who, while instrumental in exposing the corruption and abuses, was ultimately killed in a fight for "not being able to shake that prison mentality." Her parting words are: "We did the crime. And we had to do the time. But ain't nobody said abuse and exploitation was part of the sentence." That being said, the film does prefigure the success that some imprisoned women or their families have had in bringing lawsuits against private corporations in cases of sexual misconduct, sexual assault, and wrongful death occurring in privatized prisons.[73]

Black Women Directing/Representing Incarcerated Black Women

According to Jacqueline Bobo, *Civil Brand* opened in Black neighbourhoods to "turn-away crowds" at several film festivals.[74] Despite her positive assessment of its reception and impact, I believe that *Civil Brand* suffers from budgetary restrictions and production issues. Barnette claims to have been forced to remove controversial aspects of the original script in order to appease correctional administrators of the Tennessee State facility where the film was shot. The shooting schedule was cut by half subsequently, resulting in the loss of additional scenes and several continuity issues.[75] Although the character of Sabrina morphed into a narrator in order to fill in lacunas in the plot,[76] the result is a story that, as one *New York Times* critic notes, "erupts into over-the-top melodrama" and essentially "short-circuits almost as soon as it begins."[77] Similarly, *Stranger Inside* won a number of awards and was showcased in a *Feminist Studies* special issue on incarcerated women as a noteworthy depiction of the bonds that form in prison.[78] Without doubt, there is some strong acting, and the scenes depicting the vulnerability and strength of actual incarcerated women are compelling. But, ultimately, the film generally feels hyper-dramatic and somewhat superficial in its exploration of criminalization. As one commentator writes, the film is "over the top" and occasionally "cartoonish" in its depiction of prison life.[79]

Despite these minor weaknesses, we cannot overstate the importance of *Stranger Inside* and *Civil Brand* as WIP movies directed by Black women with the view to centring the experiences of criminalized Black women. Without delving into, or reducing, these texts to their directors' intention, it is worth mentioning that both Cheryl Dunye and Neema Barnette had bold aspirations for their films. For Dunye, the aim was to get "some of these middle-of-the-road or Republican or far-right people [to] relate [and] see a bit of themselves in the film" and perhaps even "want to vote differently."[80] For Barnette, her greatest pride was "the opportunity to show Black women resisting abuse," which is something "we are never shown ... in movies."[81] What I find most interesting about both films is how they deploy and challenge the exploitation cycle's use of female nudity and queer identification as a trope. First, in *Stranger Inside,* the female body is almost de-eroticized through strategic editing choices. Cavity searches are alluded to through a close-up of a nurse putting on surgical gloves and a cut to a guard spreading lubricant on an unsterilized metal speculum. Further, the intake sequence, with women lined up and being told to open their mouths to have their teeth inspected, is reminiscent of slave auctions.[82] There is no nudity in *Civil Brand,* although there are plenty of insinuations of sex and scenes of women in their underwear. Second, all three main characters in *Stranger Inside* – Treasure, Brownie, and Kit – are lesbians. *Civil Brand* tells a heteronormative story about women's incarceration, but while none of its protagonists presents as queer, several of its cast may be coded as butch. There is no monstrous lesbian in either film. Brownie is both the villain and a lesbian, but it is not her sexual identity that makes her deviant; rather, her monogamous union and clear delineation of "family" may even help to humanize her. Moreover, the stereotypical fantasy of lesbian sex of the exploitation cycles is absent in these films. In fact, in both films, the sexual identity labels and gender expressions performed and deployed by queer women are affirming and empowering.

Dunye claims that she was motivated by a desire to tell the stories of incarcerated women of colour because "nobody is telling that story at all." This claim may have had resonance when she completed her film. Since then, however, we have seen compelling images of diverse criminalized women – notably, complex Indigenous characters in *Wentworth* and queer women in *Bad Girls* (1999–2006). The palette of personalities and identities, as well as the audiences for stories about incarcerated women, has continued to expand with the arrival of *OITNB*. This series and its recalibration of the WIP genre through its fusion of comedic and dramatic elements in telling complex stories about women's incarceration over time has helped generate empathy for women in prison and outrage over their incarceration in the first place.

6 Representation and Recalibrating the WIP Genre: *Orange Is the New Black*

Orange Is the New Black (*OITNB*) (2013–19), an adaptation and extension of Piper Kerman's memoir by the same name, is set in the fictional Litchfield Correctional Facility for Women.[1] The Netflix series, which follows a diverse ensemble of women prisoners, has witnessed overwhelming commercial and popular success.[2] I began writing this book well before the show's debut in 2013 and, consequently, before the dramatic shift in viewing practices that Netflix and other streaming sites have ushered in. Much of my thinking about the women-in-prison (WIP) genre precedes the mountain of monographs, scholarly work, blogs, and other user-created content now devoted to *OITNB*.

Several feminist scholars have criticized the show. They accuse it of circulating heteronormative and ableist narratives about women in conflict with the law, presenting dangerous stereotypes about racialized women and tacitly contributing to the acceptance of post-industrial neoliberal capitalism, including its dominant expression of the privatized prison.[3] I confess that I was also sceptical of *OITNB*'s white middle-class solipsism, seen through Piper Chapman's (Taylor Schilling) privileged worldview in its first season, as well as the show's depiction of mental illness through the caricature of "Crazy Eyes" and its prototype of poor rural white women as ignorant, religious fanatics, embodied in the much-maligned and practically toothless "Pennsatucky." I was equally uneasy about the sociopathic villain in its second season in the form of the Black drug dealer Yvonne "Vee" Parker

(Lorraine Touassaint).[4] Perhaps even worse for a WIP film devotee, I felt that the show offered nothing interesting or remarkable to the genre.

By Season 3, however, I had undergone, for lack of a better expression, a one-eighty in my assessment of *OITNB*.[5] I now believe that, over the course of its first five seasons, the show tells intelligent and humanizing stories about incarcerated women. The series is quintessentially queer, critical of race dynamics in the United States, and a third-wave feminist oeuvre. I also know it to be exceedingly entertaining. In fact, it has taken what I most love about the WIP genre – large ensemble casts of women resisting oppression – and contests and renews the occasional troubling elements of the earlier cycles: the caricatured depictions of women of colour, denigration of non-normative gender, and fetishized sexual violence against girls and women.

Through self-conscious intertextual dialogue with the familiar tropes of WIP films, *OITNB* recasts the genre as part of an arsenal to be deployed by prison abolitionists, critical race theorists, and feminist activists in their critique of the institution and the neoliberal discourses in which it is embedded. Its power to evoke a prison abolitionist worldview stems from its form as a serialized show unfolding over seven seasons, slowly drawing in a broad and diverse audience whose loyalty and interest is maintained through the use of narrative conventions. These include flashbacks that invite introspection (about lost time, the relativity of freedom, and how privilege is often cast as luck), the strategic deployment of dark humour and self-reflexive dysphemism to comment on historical and contemporary social inequities, and the affection the performers so obviously exhibit for the characters they perform.

The Politics of Representation in *OITNB:* Race and Ethnicity

Creator Jenji Kohan's choice to use an entitled, white, middle-class protagonist as the show's anchor, she maintains, was always meant as a "Trojan horse." According to Kohan, Piper's social location as a normatively attractive, Anglo-Saxon, suburban woman appeased Netflix executives while also offering an entry point for mainstream audiences – assumed to also be white and middle-class – into the more interesting experiences of the show's real object – that is, marginalized women who are far more likely to be incarcerated than the purported protagonist.[6] Indeed, the show has elicited more praise than critique for Jennifer Euston's casting direction and her desire "to populate the TV landscape with reflections of what she sees on the streets and stages of New York."[7] The expression of that desire is evident through the active solicitation of actors to embody a mosaic of characters who are located along multiple and intersecting axes of differentiation in terms of race, citizenship/ethnicity, and sexualities/genders.

First, *OITNB* offers the most complex and nuanced fictional representation of criminalized Black women that I have found in the genre.[8] Early depictions of incarcerated Black women in the WIP genre were either uncredited, such as "Lil – Black Woman" in *Ann Vickers* (1933). The exploitation cycle of WIP films fleshed out Black women's roles a bit further. *The Big Doll House* (1971) featured a Black lesbian holding a position of power within the institution, albeit as a villain, and *Big Bird Cage* (1972) featured a Black political activist, though always in an ensemble cast of white women. The work of two independent racialized filmmakers, Cheryl Dunye and Neema Barnette, has since laid the groundwork for greater diversity in the WIP genre. These filmmakers have created stories from the standpoint of diverse Black women and given racialized audiences more characters in which to invest. *OITNB* is a direct legacy of their work, more explicitly exploring diverse Black women's experiences of structural disenfranchisement and interpersonal challenges as well as their strength, resilience, and leadership in carving out better conditions for themselves and for others.

The Black women of Litchfield – Alison Abdullah (Amanda Stephen), Sophia Burset (Laverne Cox), Cindy Hayes (Adrienne C. Moore), Tasha "Taystee" Jefferson (Danielle Brooks), Suzanne Warren (Uzo Aduba), Poussey Washington (Samira Wiley), and Janae Watson (Vicki Jeudy) – inhabit different locations along axes of disadvantage before entering prison. Consequently, they navigate unique forms of discrimination because of their gender expression (Sophia is a transgender woman), sexual orientation (Poussey is a lesbian), mental health (Suzanne is a person with schizophrenia and intellectual disabilities), religion (Alison is a devout Muslim who dons the hijab, and Janae is the daughter of conservative followers of the Nation of Islam), and class (Cindy was raised by a single mother, Janae grew up middle class in a neighbourhood marred by the drug trade, and Taystee cycled in and out of foster care and other juvenile institutions). They also exhibit relative autonomy and power within the prison because of their unique markers of privilege, whether educational accomplishments (Poussey is a college graduate who speaks several languages and becomes a librarian; Janae was admitted to college on a full scholarship and becomes one of the few trained skilled workers), cultural capital (Suzanne's white middle-class adoptive parents are afforded more regular visits than other prisoners' families), entrepreneurial skills (Sophia is a former firefighter and runs a successful salon in the prison), and intelligence (Taystee will parley an otherwise unhelpful mock interview exercise into a position as Warden Joe Caputo's (Nick Sandow) administrative assistant).[9]

At the same time, these characters share experiences of everyday intersecting forms of gender and racial discrimination, both subtle and overt, that play a central role in the lives of all Black women. Yet the show also carefully explores the multiple expressions of Black women's resilience and resistance to such oppression. Sophia, in her candidacy for the Women's Advisory Committee (WAC), endeavours to use institutional means to advance substantial change through recognizing basic human rights. Poussey and Taystee use humour in the form of their running joke between two white rich alter egos, Mackenzie and Amanda, to challenge the conflation of whiteness and refinement. Taystee also deploys comedic rhetoric to dismantle racist discourse in the prison. When Tiffany Doggett (Taryn Manning) runs on a "whites only" platform to seek election to the WAC, Taystee warns her: "This ain't *The* fuckin' *Help* bitch. But you will eat my shit."[10] Janae's lifelong experiences of micro-degradation and explicit discrimination make her a strong and effective spokesperson against the multiple forms of everyday violence Black women experience within the prison.[11] In her interactions with well-meaning or condescending white characters, Janae also speaks directly to privileged audience members. As Erica "Yoga" Jones (Constance Shulman) plans a hunger strike, Janae says: "I'm not here to make you feel good about yourself, alright?"[12] When Piper compares the wages that the women make in the lingerie factory to "slave labour," Janae corrects her with: "Technically, it's more like indentured servitude."

OITNB also consistently features nuanced portrayals of women with brown/tanned skin who are coded as Brown (Latina).[13] Historically, Latina characters in mainstream representations have been one-dimensional and confined to reductive stereotypes, often linked to unbridled sexuality.[14] Indeed, actor Jessica Pimentel (mixed heritage Taino/Arawak, Western European, and Malian) – whose character Maria Ruiz is marked, and self-identifies, as Dominican – recently pointed out that, even though she is trained professionally to be an actor, most of the roles she landed before *OITNB* were some variation of a one-dimensional "sex worker."[15] There are a few minor Latina characters in earlier WIP movie cycles prior to this series, but they often tend to fall into another stereotype associated with unbridled sexuality – the unwed mother who will inevitably be punished for having transgressed the boundaries of respectability. In *Ladies of the Big House* (1931), Maria (Miriam Goldina) is pregnant and plans to break out so that her child is not born in prison but then is shot and killed cutting through the barbed wire fence while the other women escape. In *Blonde Bait* (1956), Marguerite Chavez (April Olrich) is also pregnant, gives birth in prison, and is instrumental in helping the protagonist get out, but she is captured and brought back to justice.

In *Cage without A Key* (1975), one of the main characters is Angelita Perez (Edith Diaz), a mother and occasional sex worker, who "made a vow before God to never get into no more trouble." Sadly for her, "God doesn't hear so good in the Barrio," and, to put a finer point on it, she adds: "All my friends are either dead or in jail. A birth in my neighbourhood isn't a birth, it's a sentence." Equally troubling, she vows to stay away from her daughter once released because she is "nothing but a whore." Despite the reproduction of easy stereotypes of poverty in Latin American communities in other WIP films, Angelita is one of the few Latinas that I have found in the entire canon who is in a normalized, interracial, same-sex couple. She is the "mama" of a family that she heads with Tommy (Jonelle Allen), the "papa," a Black woman who will ultimately die saving one of their "daughters."[16] In the exploitation flick *The Concrete Jungle* (1982), Latina characters are limited to their role as drug dealers and are coded as such by their thick accents and their cholas and bandanas; whereas in *Nine Lives* (2005), a short film that appears later in the same collection, Sandra (Elpidia Carrillo) is a Mexican American in for an unnamed crime. She is simply trying to "mind her own business" and serve out her sentence as quickly as possible. But her prospects of an early dispense are shattered when she attacks a guard who shows complete indifference to the trauma she is suffering by not having regular contact with her daughter. American Peruvian actress Jenny Gago plays Angie in *Convicted: A Mother's Story,* and is one of the few racialized queen bees of the WIP canon. Finally, in the short-lived syndicated soap opera *Dangerous Women* (1991), Maria Rangel plays one of the leads, Maria Trent, a stoic anti-drug advocate doing time for the murder of her abusive husband.

In *OITNB,* the women of "Spanish Harlem" are some of the show's main protagonists. They continue to dominate the narrative in Season 4, which is largely organized around a power struggle between factions within the Latina cell block. The Spanish Harlem is a heterogeneous network of Colombians, Cubans, Dominicans, and Puerto Ricans, communities that exhibit divergences beyond the prison walls in terms of language, race, and experiences of colonialism while sharing a common history of discrimination.[17] Each of these characters carries the markers of her unique relationship with law enforcement as a woman coded as Latina, but each of them is also given the space to express her individual normative commitments, to develop her own understanding of familial responsibilities, and to live a matrix of competing desires, expectations, habits, and values. Matriarch Gloria Mendoza (Selenis Leyva), who was previously the owner of a small bodega, is serving time for committing fraud (selling ineligible food stamp items) when she was trying to raise enough money to get herself and her son away from an abusive domestic partner. Dayanara "Daya" Diaz (Dascha Polanco), who is of Puerto Rican decent, is referred to by outsiders as the "Spanish girl who don't speak Spanish" and occasionally ostracized by her own community for having refused to learn her mother's first language. Marisol "Flaca" Gonzales (Jackie Cruz) grew up in a working-class Colombian community and is serving time for fraud and endangerment. The unfilled teardrops she paints on her face suggest Mexican drug cartel membership but are actually the expression of teenage emo/goth sensibilities. The fact that these teardrops are fake is pointed out by Carmen "Ouija" Aziza (Rosal Colon), a Dominican woman who dons the real markers for each of her hits but is later revealed as being incarcerated for having committed fraud, specifically, falsely receiving WIC (Women, Children and Infant) benefits. Zircona Carbrera (Danielle De Jesus), with cropped hair and golden grills, presents as a gangster while circulating radical, ecofeminist discourse and demanding roll-on deodorant because of the environmental impact of using aerosol.[18]

As effective as the series has been in breaking down one-dimensional racial and ethnic archetypes of Latinas in the WIP genre, it has shown less retrospection in how it represents criminalized Indigenous women.[19] In fact, there are few Indigenous characters in any of the North American iterations of the WIP film. In the Columbia Broadcasting System's made-for-television feature *Girl Called Hatter Fox* (1977), Hatter Fox (Joanelle Nadine Romero, who is of mixed ancestry: Mescalero Apache/Cheyenne/Sephardic Jew) is a seventeen-year-old Navajo Native American. She is charged with addiction-related crimes – namely, prostitution and theft – and labelled "incorrigible" by the reformatory's administrators. The staff subject her to cruel and humiliating treatment, putting her in a doghouse and tying her to a bed during a physical examination. Hatter is eventually released into the custody of the film's protagonist: a well-meaning white doctor. Thanks to his tireless efforts, her disciplinary issues are revealed as her way of navigating the sexual assault she experienced at a mission school. It is difficult not to read this film as a leveraging of Indigenous women's pain and trauma to advance a white saviour narrative. Moreover, while the film and the novel from which it was adapted tackled questions of assimilation, cultural appropriation, and institutional violence,[20] both are the artefacts and interpretations of white settlers and, thus, as cultural theorist Maureen Trudelle Schwarz explains, may well rely on codes that stand in "as signs or fetishes for ... contradictory concepts as primitiveness, nature, spirituality, unbridled sexuality, violence, nobility or heathenness."[21] Nevertheless, Joanelle Romero defends the role since it was, at the time, the first-ever cinematic depiction of a contemporary American Indigenous woman.[22] More recently, however, Indigenous Chilean Canadian filmmaker Jorge Manzano brings audiences into the world of an incarcerated two-spirited Cree woman in *Johnny Greyeyes* (2001). Its titular character is played by Metis actor Gail Maurice. This film began as a documentary, however, becoming a distaff and more in-depth version of Manzano's earlier film about incarcerated Indigenous men.[23]

Indigenous girls currently make up 3.5 percent of the detained youth population in the United States. Accounting for variations according to jurisdiction, the national trend is that 179 of every 100,000 Native American girls will end up in residential placement.[24] The actual number of incarcerated Indigenous women is likely much higher because official statistics are derived from flawed government accounting of racial and ethnic composition that drastically underestimates the number of Native American women housed in correctional facilities and does not accurately account for women who self-identify as Indigenous.[25] This over-representation is a vestige of cultural assimilation and ethnic cleansing from America's racist colonial past, including forced removal from their ancestral territory, the systematic destitution of Aboriginal communities, and intergenerational trauma that has resulted from the removal of children from their families into the "boarding school" system.[26] Moreover, despite recognition of Indigenous legal systems and Indigenous protocols for conflict resolution for criminal matters, Indigenous peoples' pathways to incarceration may attach to them by virtue of their Indigeneity. For instance, activists organizing peaceful protests over their ancestral land's use have been charged with trespass and incitement to riot.[27]

While *OITNB* unfolds in New York, a state with approximately twenty-five thousand Native Americans from nine recognized nations,[28] only one character identifies as mixed race –Native Hawaiian/Aboriginal Polynesian – Stephanie Hapakuka (Jolene Aiko Purdy, of mixed Japanese and white European descent).[29] The first iteration of the Australian series *Prisoner* (1979–86), on the other hand, featured two ancillary Indigenous characters: prison psychologist Pamela Madigan (Justine Saunders, who is Woppaburra) and her patient Sarah West (Kylie Belling, who is Yorta Yorta/Bangarang/Wiradjurri). They are shown navigating institutional discrimination and experiencing direct racism.[30] The series' reboot, *Wentworth* (2013–present), includes several Indigenous characters with commanding presence and complicated story arcs – for example, Doreen Anderson (Shareena Clanton, of mixed ancestry: Wongatha/Yamatji/Noongar/Gitja, African American, and Etowah Cherokee/Blackfoot), who is in for reckless endangerment but becomes a peer worker and is eventually let out on parole, and Officer Will Jackson (Robbie Joseph Magasiva, a Samoan New Zealander), a trusted and competent guard with a background in social work. More recently, the series has included Ruby Mitchell (Rarriwuy Hick, of mixed ancestry: Yolngu and white European), a boxing champ forced to put her career on hold while she serves a sentence for assault and resisting arrest, and Rita "the Beater" Connors (Leah Purcell, of mixed ancestry), a sharp, independent woman with affiliations to and influence within the biker community.

The Politics of Representation in *OITNB:* Gender and Sexuality

The WIP genre, predicated on large numbers of women being confined together in a repressive institution, has long been associated with the Sapphic. Sometimes, as with the trope of the butch lesbian predator, the depiction of non-normative sexualities and gender expressions has been reductive. More cavalier depictions of queer women are frequent: in *Born Innocent* (1975), we witness one character's violent rape with a broom handle by a ruthless lesbian gang; *Cage without a Key* shows a character being forcibly kissed by a white lesbian who is depicted as emotionally unstable with a low IQ, as well as a Black woman confessing that she became a lesbian after her drug-addicted foster mother molested her; and in *Vendetta* (1986), a white woman is murdered by a queen bee after turning down the latter's advances. However, from its earliest films, the WIP genre more often than not has provided a space for the subtle exploration of non-normative sexualities and subversive gender identities.

In fact, Joseph Breen's office forced the producers of *Ann Vickers* to eliminate the existing lesbian cues from the prison scenes.[31] Despite this directive, however, the Motion Picture Production Code regulators seem to have missed Linda (Lillian Roth) – an attractive and popular short-haired woman with swagger who smokes cigars and "likes to wrestle" – in *Ladies They Talk About* (1933). Of course, Hope Emerson's unforgettable parody of normative femininity and heterosexuality in her portrayal of Evelyn Harper in *Caged!* (1950) became the standard for the caricatural masochistic lesbian in the later iterations of the genre, especially Ida Lupino's performance as Amelia Van Zant in *Women's Prison* (1955), the sadistic matron decades later in *Women in Chains* (1972), and even Pam Grier as Alabama in *Women in Cages* (1971). Furthermore, both *Caged Heat* (1974) and *Cage without a Key* feature normalized same-sex unions and biracial lesbian couples. Antionette Byron plays a sex worker in the comedic television series *Women in Prison* (1987–88); her clients are men, but she only dates women. Moreover, even in films that reinforce reductive views about sexuality and gender, the scripts handed to the actors invite campy, pro-queer interpretations. In *False Arrest* (1991), which is based on Joyce Lukezic's memoir of her wrongful imprisonment for murder, a character who is meant to elicit fear propositions the protagonist with the words "I'm gonna treat you so good, I'm gonna wish I was you."[32] A similar character in *Reform School Girls* (1986), played by punk legend Wendy O. Williams, tells an innocent: "I'm all the stud that you need."

Building on the WIP genre's existing tropes, *OITNB*'s writers have also offered unrelentingly queer narratives, committed to telling stories from transgender and gender non-conforming standpoints. For instance, the fact that Sophia Burset (Laverne Cox), one of the show's most popular characters, is played by a Black transgender woman is itself noteworthy. In fact, the only other openly transgender woman offender on television is from the Australian series *Wentworth*. Maxine (Socratis Otto), played by a cisgender man, is a henchwoman with a soft heart and is presented in a sympathetic light, revealing increasing layers as the show unfolds. She is in prison for having stabbed her boyfriend when he rejected her after her sex reassignment surgery. Despite various interventions, Maxine remains, in the words of Otto, "unambiguously male." And while the show initially came under fire for that very reason, it has since been applauded for showing Maxine struggling with how to perform her own femininity in spite of the narrow and still idealized (heteronormative, imperialist, white supremacist) standards imposed on, or internalized as, a transwoman. Of course, these are the very standards that Sophia – and her "diamond pussy" – unambiguously meet. Both women are criminalized for reasons that are inextricably linked to their gender identity. However, Maxine's situation speaks to an interpersonal conflict and a moment of explicit transphobia by a man she loves, whereas Sophia's speaks to the more invisible, but just as present, everyday forms of intersecting and systemic discrimination that transgender individuals face in accessing gender-affirming healthcare and maintaining employment. Specifically, she is doing time for credit card fraud because, even with a middle-class income and a supportive partner, she could not afford the associated costs of her transition. Yet she is not reduced to that singular identity but, instead, is shown to occupy a range of subjectivities, whether as a struggling parent, a loyal friend, a savvy entrepreneur, or an activist.

Finally, when *OITNB* does make explicit the queer- or transphobia, the characters who hold such animus are used for comic effect. Officer Sam Healy (Michael Harney), for instance, warns Piper (incarcerated incidentally for having committed a crime with her then girlfriend) that she in no way "[has] to have lesbian sex."[33] Moreover, in place of the one-note stereotypes of early iterations of butches in the genre, *OITNB* features a broad and amorphous array of gender performances and sexual identities, including any number of the lesbian and bisexual characters. Carrie "Big Boo" Black (Lea DeLaria), a butch, while having shown herself to be capable of violence, is more often deeply sentimental, caring, and protective of the vulnerable. And Brook Soso (Kimiko Glenn) is a pansexual who "like[s] people not genders."[34]

Recalibrating the WIP Genre

Using smaller plot elements, *OITNB* explores otherwise absent themes from the WIP genre. For instance, the series tackles stereotypes about women and aging in Season 2, when Galina "Red" Reznikov (Kate Mulgrew) and a diverse assemblage of characters making up the "Golden Girls" develop a complex drug-smuggling business. It also reproduces the familiar representation of the prison as a breeding ground for incompetent or sadistic staff and administrators.[35] Nevertheless, like most other dramatic WIP films, the show also advances stories about the impossibility of well-intentioned people being able to reform these poisoned institutions. For instance, one of the few Black women in a position of authority at Litchfield is suspended when her arts program results in the production and circulation of erotic science fiction.[36] Similarly, an empathetic and well-liked female guard resigns after being violently attacked by a prisoner in distress.[37] The show also refines earlier depictions in the WIP genre of women's resistance to oppression through momentary acts (including sexual enjoyment,[38] spirituality,[39] and creativity),[40] by constituting family and friendships that transcend vectors of race, culture, class, sexuality, and age[41] and by showing more collective organizing through the peaceful protests and inevitable riot that unfold in Season 5.[42]

However, *OITNB* is most provocative in how it recalibrates two of the genre's core themes – that is, the unique modes through which women resist interpersonal violence and the gendered nature of criminalization. *OITNB* makes these themes more relevant to the economic and social context of the present-day United States.

Intertextual Dialogues

In earlier iterations of the genre, women's victimization was primarily imagined in terms of domestic abuse. Generally, violence against women would either be alluded to superficially or used for comedic effect. The former can be seen, for example, in *Ladies They Talk About,* where there is a brief mention of the crime committed by Ivory, a Black woman with a one-hundred-year sentence for having killed her husband. The latter is apparent in the treatment of Emma Barber (Ellen Corby) in *Caged!,* who bemoans the inefficacy of the justice system, which had multiple opportunities to stop her from killing her man:

> When Joe first beats me up, I grab his gun and just wing him in the shoulder. Do they arrest me? No! Then a year later, I fires at Joe again and miss. Do they give me a rap for attempted assault? No! Then last year, I defends myself again with a gun, and the police still treats me like I was poison ivy. And then finally I finish Joe off for good. Well, it's that judge. If he had nabbed me the first three times while I was just practicing, I wouldn't be here now for murder.

In these social problem WIP films, sexual violence, if addressed at all, is imagined as something enacted by caricatured predatory lesbians – essentially, a situational risk when large numbers of women are incarcerated together.

By the 1970s, the exploitation cycle largely abandoned the theme of domestic violence and, instead, focused on women's sexual victimization, usually by guards and occasionally by other prisoners. In the exploitation cycle, rape became the driver for a protagonist's radicalization and her enactment of violent retribution. *OITNB* departs from earlier depictions of sexual violence against women in two ways: unlike the exploitation cycle, rape is entirely desexualized and, unlike the social problem films, rape is an act committed by men in positions of power. Moreover, rather than using rape as a plot device to drive a more important storyline, as is the case in so many depictions of sexual assault in popular culture, or using rape only as a way to draw sympathy for an otherwise unlikeable female character, as is also the case in many depictions of sexual violence in popular culture, the rape by Charlie Coates (James McMenamin) of Tiffany Doggett and its consequences take up the lion's share of an entire episode and is used as a legitimate theme and core plot element in its own right.[43]

Charlie is an equable and generally compliant correctional officer who takes a keen interest in Tiffany. The friendship quickly turns abusive, beginning with an uninvited kiss and culminating in Charlie raping Tiffany in the back of a service vehicle. Tiffany is a complex character. In Season 1, she is reviled for her racism and homophobia and easily dismissed as a caricature of poor, uneducated, rural America. In Season 2, she becomes an object of derision for her earnest spiritual awakening. In Season 3, however, Tiffany's character is drawn with greater care, most notably through her interaction with Big Boo. This relationship begins as a series of practical jokes – namely, that Tiffany has the power to heal sexual deviants and that she needs to ward off a "secret lesbian agenda."[44] However, given that both of them have had their membership to their respective clans unceremoniously revoked – Big Boo has double-crossed Red and Tiffany is abandoned by her Christian followers, Leanne Taylor (Emma Myles) and Angie Rice (Julie Lake) – a genuine friendship develops.[45] It is, after all, Big Boo who notices signs of distress in Tiffany's demeanour and who sees the bruising on her arms. It is also Big Boo who unequivocally characterizes what has transpired as violence and who wants to enact retributive justice. And it is Big Boo who ultimately shepherds Tiffany through the difficult process of making meaning of her experience.

Glimpses into Tiffany's past, through a sequence of flashbacks, offers insight into why Tiffany's instinct is to normalize her victimization and avoid Charlie rather than confront him. At a young age, Tiffany learned from her mother that female sexuality is about submission and emotional detachment. As her mother told her: "Now that you're a-tittin' and a-hairin', boys are gonna see you different, and pretty soon, they're gonna do you different. Best thing is do go on and let 'em do their business, baby. If you're real lucky, most of 'em be quick, like your daddy." Tiffany is shown a few years later trading sexual favours with a boy for soda; they are interrupted, but he comes back to claim what he says is rightfully his.[46] These scenes give texture to Tiffany's ambivalence as she tries to make sense of what has happened in a deeply stigmatizing social context that encourages victims to self-blame. Finally, because the rape is explored from different vantage points – not only Tiffany's but also Big Boo's and, eventually, Charlie's – the show asks hard questions about consent, intimacy, and how some male perpetrators of sexual violence, by virtue of their privilege and socialization, may well be impervious to the trauma they inflict.

When Tiffany eventually puts a name to Charlie's action – rape – he is genuinely distraught. Rather than showing anger or deflection, he is shown to experience confusion and sorrow: "But I love you." This admission from a young man raised in a society that gives him an entitled sense of privilege over women's bodies is followed by justifications indicating that he may still be ignorant to the harm he has done: "And I said it when [pause] When I said it. So that makes it different." The scene in no way exonerates Charlie, and the later interaction between Big Boo and Tiffany confirms the show's moral stance regarding him as a violent assailant in that moment.[47]

Women in Conflict with the Law

In many ways, *OITNB* gives life to the empirical evidence that the vast majority of women incarcerated in the United States have committed minor crimes – often theft or drug and property related. Only a minority of the women of Litchfield can be considered "career criminals": Alex Vause (Laura Prepon) is a high-level drug smuggler; Red was a racketeering consultant to the Russian mafia; and Mei Chang (Lori Tan Chinn) was herself the boss of an organized crime syndicate. Yet an even-smaller minority of those incarcerated are dangerous enough to warrant more permanent separation from society. Vee, Taystee's dysfunctional mother figure, for instance, killed her former foster child and lover because he was skimming funds from her heroin-trafficking ring. Throughout, she exploits those under her care and even convinces Suzanne to beat Poussey into submission. However, Vee is an outlier in the series, and she meets an untimely end. Furthermore, with the exception of Vee, the truly senseless acts of violence are the purview of white women: specifically, Tiffany has murdered an abortion provider; Frieda (Dale Soules) has cut her husband's penis off with a dull knife; and Brandy Epps (Asia Kate Dillon) has poisoned Jewish and racialized customers when working as a barista.[48] Furthermore, other characters who are confined for having committed white supremacist violence or who perform outwardly racist acts in the prison are used to mock ignorance and prejudice.[49]

Consequently, very few of the women in Litchfield have committed truly violent crimes. Those that have, in keeping with one of the genre's dominant tropes, have killed men who are sexual or physical predators. Miss Claudette (Michelle Hurst) reproduces the WIP standard that women who murder kill men who have been sexually or physically violent. She is a Haitian woman who ran a cleaning service. She killed a man who sexually assaulted one of her charges. Another woman, Norma Romano (Annie Golden), is doing time for voluntary manslaughter for having pushed her emotionally abusive guru/husband off a cliff. The pathway to crime for most of these women cannot be extricated from their economic vulnerability, social immobility, addiction, or other forms of marginality. The women housed in Litchfield largely come from neighbourhoods that are entrenched in poverty. Many have pre-existing histories of trauma, systemic racism, violence, and time in foster care. Several have had their own children taken by the state. It is true that there are a few white-collar criminals and political dissidents, but they tend to be some variation of middle class, educated, and white.[50] Of these, some have engaged in calculated acts to achieve social and economic means that were otherwise unattainable. Cindy, who is shown to be a bit rash and irresponsible, is handed a sentence of felony theft for having abused her position as an airport security agent, extorting gifts for her family from unwitting passengers. Maritza Ramos (Diane Guerrero), a shrewd and confident woman, lands a prison sentence for carjacking.

But even these characters are not reduced to easy rational actor theories because their choices are already embedded in their social and economic circumstances as racialized women living in America. Cindy represses her distress by pretending to be a sister to her daughter, who was the result of a teenage pregnancy. Maritza is also a single mother who is supplementing her income as a cocktail waitress. Moreover, while none of the women are the perfect innocents of melodrama, a few particularly unfortunate cases stand out. Suzanne, who suffers from long-standing psychiatric issues, unintentionally kidnaps a boy she thought wanted to play with her. Lolly Whitehill (Lori Petty) cycles between mental health facilities, carceral institutions, and a life on the street because her hallucinations and paranoia inhibit her from being able to hold onto a job. Yoga Jones accidentally shot and killed a boy in a drunken haze. Flaca, who is entrepreneurial, ambitious, and, in her own words, "too complex for mainstream academics," developed and sold fake high-end LSD at her high school, which had a placebo effect on an already fragile student, who ended up taking his own life.[51]

However, it is Poussey Washington's story that is pure tragedy, written as a direct indictment of how deeply the criminal justice system infiltrates the lives of Black women in America, regardless of their class or other markers of privilege. Poussey is a first offender who is serving time for possession of marijuana with intent to distribute. Despite the presumption by some of those closest to her, Poussey did not live in a low-income neighbourhood keyed in by law enforcement and is not the product of a broken home.[52] She is educated, multilingual, and the daughter of a high-ranking military officer. Whether as a result of the implicit bias that permeates the criminal justice system or the racist animus of an individual officer, she is handed the harshest penalty available. Like the morally innocent (though factually guilty) protagonists who preceded her in the WIP genre, Poussey's mental health slowly deteriorates over the course of her incarceration: her mother dies during the second year of her six-year sentence; she is betrayed by her clan and beaten by Suzanne; and she self-medicates her depression with alcohol. Poussey is eventually redeemed through her close relationships, which transcend race and class differences: Soso's love, Taystee's friendship regained, and Judith "Judy" King's (Blair Brown) mentorship. This redemption is fleeting, however, as she faces an untimely demise at the hands of a white guard, Baxter Bayley (Alan Aisenberg).

Paradoxically, Baxter has also committed an almost identical minor offence in his youth: possession and trespass. He is let go after a night in the drunk tank and a stern warning by a white member of the small-town police force.[53] The juxtaposition of Poussey and Baxter calls explicit attention to systemic racism and white privilege that runs through the criminal justice system, from the discretionary measures taken by police in their day-to-day management of insignificant offences to the sentencing guidelines applied by judges. In direct reference to the #BlackLivesMatter movement, Poussey's last words are: "I can't breathe."[54] In the wake of Poussey's death, Warden Caputo, in disaster-management mode and trying to spin the death of a non-violent, non-threatening prisoner as an unfortunate accident, omits Poussey's name altogether. Taystee, Cindy, Alison, and Janae fight to achieve justice for their friend, more explicitly in line with the #SayHerName project that documents and disseminates the often unrecorded and untold stories of Black women being killed at the hands of police.[55] While the other women loot and take hostages, Taystee, Cindy, Alison, and Janae take to social media.

In a scene that is recounted in different iterations, Taystee makes an impassionate plea to keep Poussey's death at the hands of the law enforcement agent in the public imaginary.[56] In the first of these scenes, Warden Caputo is captured through the camera of a tablet. Cindy is also in the frame standing over him as he says: "Her name was Poussey Washington." When Warden Caputo refuses to continue with the script written for him by the women, Taystee turns the tablet to face herself and speaks directly into the camera: "She was murdered. C.O. Bayley murdered her. And we [pause]

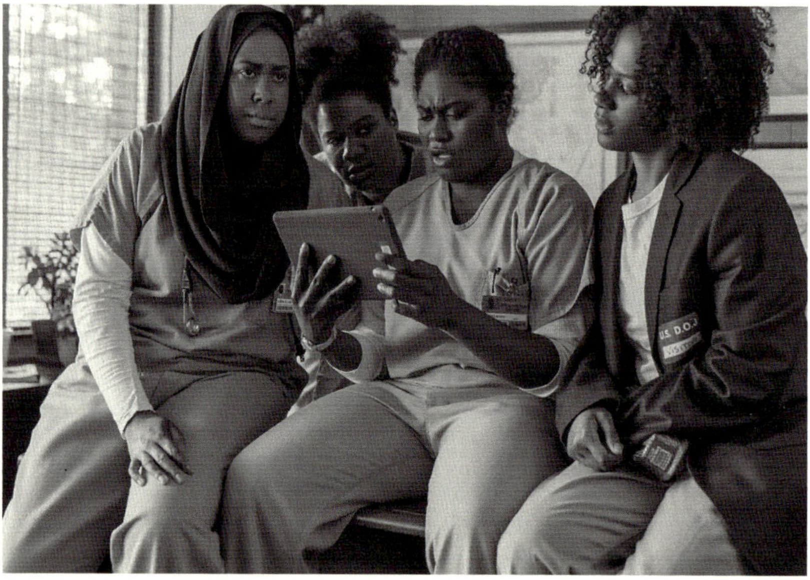

Figure 7 [*left to right*] Abdullah (Amanda Stephen, Cindy (Adrienne C. Moore), Taystee (Danielle Brooks), and Watson (Vicki Jeudy) in *Orange Is the New Black,* Season 4, episode 12, "The Animals" (2016). Courtesy of Lions Gate Films (all rights reserved).

want [pause] justice." As Taystee turns the camera on herself, the effect is a selfie in extreme close-up, reminiscent of Carl-Theodor Dreyer's depiction of Joan of Arc. In this one moment, Taystee engages in a direct indictment of the prison, of racist American society, and of neoliberal capitalism. By reluctantly, but effectively, engaging with social media activism, she offers a meta-commentary on the commodification of imprisoned women in undeniably profound ways.

Visualizing the Abolitionist Critique of the Prison

According to prisoner activist Victoria Law, who has applauded *OITNB* when it "reflects the real-life situation" of incarcerated women, this series has "catapulted women's incarceration into popular culture consciousness." She adds, however, that the show simply "isn't going to revolutionize the prison system."[57] With all respect to Law, I think she may be asking too much of one cultural artefact. I have found that by pushing the already fluid boundaries of the WIP genre, *OITNB* is not trying to revolutionize the prison system; it is, however, telling different stories about incarcerated women to people who might otherwise not care about the lived experiences of marginalized women. In this way, the series is subtly mainstreaming a prison abolitionist agenda.

Specifically, in its exploration of women's pathways to incarceration, *OITNB* presents a critique of the rational actor theory of crime. The rational actor theory is premised on the belief that people commit crime as free and autonomous beings making clear, measured, and rational choices. Consequently, people can be deterred from deviance by the threat of punishment. A related element of the rational actor model is that some people have a criminal disposition by virtue of biological, genetic, environmental, or psychological factors, and these factors, without intervention, will remain undeterred by the threat of punishment. This theory translates into practice through zero-tolerance disciplinary measures in schools, "tough-on-crime" political agendas, and the curtailment of judicial discretion in sentencing. Prison abolitionists oppose the rehabilitation/deterrence/punitive models of regulation, whereby incarceration has become the symbol and embodiment of how the United States addresses entrenched economic, political, cultural, and social problems. Yet statistics have shown that, once a woman has come into conflict with the criminal law, her chances of being involved with the criminal justice system again in the form of a new arrest are about 25 percent within the first six months, about 33 percent within the first year, and almost 70 percent within five years of her release.

The illogical premise that prisons rehabilitate women is exposed throughout the series. The carceral apparatus is shown to set formerly incarcerated women up to fail at reintegrating because of the stigma, social exclusion, and other barriers they face upon dispense. This fact is bleakly pointed out by Taystee when she is granted parole during the first season. She returns to Litchfield a few weeks later, partly demoralized, partly relieved. Lacking the benefit of meaningful ameliorative social programs within the prison, her assessment of her life options on the outside – with little education, few employment prospects, and unstable housing, coupled with being away from her primary support system – is grim:

> Minimum wage is some kind of joke. I got part-time working at Pizza Hut and I still owe the prison 900 dollars in fees I gotta pay back. I ain't got no place to stay. I was sleeping on the floor at my second cousin's like a dog and she got six people in two rooms. One of the bitches stole my check. I got lice. Everyone I know is poor, in jail or gone. I know how to play it here … what rules to follow. I got a bed. And I got you.[58]

Throughout the series, few women are able to finally disentangle themselves from the tentacles of the criminal justice apparatus. These include those who have escaped (Miss Rosa [Barbara Rosenblatt], Mei, and Tiffany); those who already had, and maintained, the capital and resources needed to reintegrate (Judy); and those who have been killed (Vee and Poussey). The show cannot be read as an endorsement of prison; rather, it shows us that the entire carceral/justice system is broken. Far from being a method of eradicating economic, political, social, and cultural inequalities and conflict, incarceration exacerbates them.

Conclusion

Genre films appeal to a broad and shifting audience because their elements – conventions, themes, characters, narratives, and recurring symbols – are familiar but varied enough that the stories they tell feel both known and brand new. The differentiation or variation, as film theorist Christine Gledhill has pointed out, ensures "the pleasure of recognition" of recurring tropes, in addition to the "frisson" of new ways of exploring particular themes.[1] In Jessica Silbey's excellent delineation of trial films, she argues that the genre operates in ways that may help sustain "the power and legitimacy of the legal institution."[2] Throughout this book, I have argued that the women-in-prison (WIP) genre has the potential to do the opposite: it reveals that prisons are archaic, violent, totalizing institutions without justification that set up the women they warehouse to fail. Whereas the movies that make up the WIP genre have historically been dismissed as trite or offensive and, thus, largely ignored or under-read by feminist socio-legal and film scholars, the cultural conversation around these representations has dramatically shifted with the arrival of television series such as *Bad Girls* (1999–2006), *Unit 9* (2012–19), *Wentworth* (2013–present), and of course, *Orange Is the New Black* (*OITNB*) (2013–19). These have attracted positive critical appraisals, a broad, faithful, and expanding fan base, and a plethora of feminist scholarship.

I have argued throughout this book that the familiarity and newness afforded by the WIP genre allowed it to become a platform for audiences to see and feel the criminalization of women navigating entrenched inequalities. Yet one question has animated my discussion: what are the ethical dimensions of creating, consuming, and circulating images of incarcerated women? In a self-reflective piece on her effort to document the injustices of women's incarceration, filmmaker and scholar Alexandra Juhasz asks:

> Given that female inmates of American prisons are victims of state, social, and ideological systems (such as prison, welfare, racism, sexism, and physical, emotional or drug abuse) that punish them for their usually victimless crimes; and given that a special condition of their punishment is a near black out of representations of their pain and suffering in and out of prison; and given that the most common response to such a predicament is the unleashing of that too-familiar form, the victim documentary; and given that the victim documentary must perform the work of re-victimizing ... can the crisis of women's victimization in prison be represented in ways that challenge this harm without its self-perpetuation?[3]

The same may be asked of all fictional representations of incarceration: they risk being sanitized and safe venues for exploring the lives and experiences of some of the most marginalized members of our society. To address this issue, I have situated six artefacts – *Ann Vickers* (1933), *Caged!* (1950), *Caged Heat* (1974), *Stranger Inside* (2002), *Civil Brand* (2002), and *OITNB* – in their unique legal, social, and cultural contexts as well as within the structural and semiotic universe of the genre they constitute. I have argued that they reveal the process of dehumanization that occurs within total institutions in a way that may actually have material consequences: specifically, they gesture towards a prison abolitionist worldview.

The fictional stories I have focused on are not first-person accounts from women who have experienced criminalization and incarceration, nor are they documentaries intended as visual evidence of the atrocity of mass incarceration. Nevertheless, the majority of WIP films from the melodramatic, realist, and dramatic-comedy cycles are grounded, at least in part, in empirical data. *Ladies They Talk About* (1933) is an adaption of a play written by Dorothy Mackaye about the twenty-five months she spent in San Quentin for her part in the death of her husband. *Caged!* is based on reporter Virginia Kellogg's ethnographic work when she went undercover into a women's prison and spent several weeks informally interviewing imprisoned women. Jean Rouverol conducted research in women's reformatories before writing the script for *So Young, So Bad* (1950). Joyce Lukezic's memoir from her time in jail was the basis for *False Arrest* (1991). Ann McManus and Maureen Chadwick, the creators of *Bad Girls*, interviewed and consulted with incarcerated women and engaged in participant observation at an institution for several years during pre-production of the series. Cheryl Dunye's *Stranger Inside* began as a collaborative art project in a women's prison. And, finally, *OITNB* was inspired by the memoir of the same name, which details Piper Kerman's thirteen months in detention. While I applaud these writers and producers who endeavoured to use self-reflexive narrative inquiry to tell meaningful stories about criminalized women, my aesthetic preference for their films and shows does not stem from them being perfectly accurate depictions of women's lived experience in prison. Instead, I selected these films because they deploy the strategies and tools of fictional visual storytelling in such compelling ways and suggest truths about the lived realities of criminalized and incarcerated women without being entirely accurate or "factual."

It is undeniable that WIP films and television series are sometimes inaccurate. However, this fact seems insignificant given that most people do not watch WIP films out of a genuine desire to become well informed about the policies and practices that leave some women more vulnerable to criminalization than others. And, yet, it is also true that the mediated prison has always been, to some extent, a way for people who occupy spaces of privilege to imagine and grapple with punishment. Earlier social problem films and the later realist cycle provided some of the few ways to bring the inner world of the prison and the general inhumanity of incarceration to light. Later films revealed the population of women that overwhelmingly make up the bodies we warehouse in these institutions. And with these films, most notably those created and produced by independent racialized filmmakers, the WIP genre has become a venue that brings marginalized experiences to the fore. Since the early 2000s, WIP films usually combine some of the cinematic techniques of early social problem films – the titillation and intentional campiness of the exploitation cycle with a comedic narrative and soap operatic form – to explore the current social crisis of mass incarceration. *OITNB* has expanded the WIP genre's exploitation of the oppression of particular women even further to include types of women originally not considered in earlier theorizing on the prison industrial complex, such as trans women. These shifts in the representation of incarcerated women have expanded the audience and fan base of the genre. That alone is worthy of notice, given that, as Black feminist, educator, and prison abolitionist Angela Y. Davis has written, "the realities of imprisonment are hidden from almost all who have not had the misfortune of doing time."[4]

Since I began writing this book almost a decade ago, the number of women and girls incarcerated in the United States – whether in local jails, confinement facilities operated by American Indian Tribal authorities, youth and immigration detention centres, or territorial, military, state, and federal prisons – has steadily increased. In America today, there are over 219,000 women and girls warehoused in these kinds of correctional facilities, and the conditions for these women and girls are dire. For instance, in Maryland, a woman was sentenced to twenty-one years in prison after she bought and shared heroin with a friend who fatally overdosed. In New York, a woman was denied the opportunity to provide breast milk to her infant. In Florida, a pregnant woman navigating mental illness was forced to give birth alone and without medical assistance in an isolation cell. In fact, throughout the country, pregnant women still regularly give birth while shackled. In some cases, women who have had a caesarean section will be transported back to prison with a chain around their freshly sutured belly. In Michigan, after a woman's request for a suicide prevention vest was ignored by guards, she hanged herself in the shower. A transgender woman in Texas was forced to expose her genitals to prison guards so they could determine which prison she should be assigned to, only for them to place her in a holding area with men and have her shower with incarcerated men. A transgender woman in a Kansas military prison was denied hormone therapy. Women in San Francisco have been forced to be strip-searched while being watched by male deputies. Women and children detained by Customs and Border Protection agents are routinely held for several nights in bitterly cold cells, commonly called "freezers," and are denied the opportunity to bathe or access menstrual hygiene products. Sixty percent of women currently held in jails across the country have not even been convicted of an offence and are awaiting a hearing. Moreover, women and girls who have pled guilty to minor offences and have been handed a parole sentence find themselves in perpetual breach of their parole because they are unable to pay the associated fines in addition to the administrative, public defender, and supervision fees.

Given the continued dire living conditions for incarcerated women, careful and self-reflexive popular representation of these women's lives matters, regardless of the flaws, inaccuracies, or contradictions in these shows. We need to embrace WIP movies and television series as part of an arsenal, along with grassroots activism, critical theory, political mobilization, and empirical research. These films play different, but not less relevant, roles in the struggle to end the ongoing mass incarceration of women.

Notes

Introduction

1 Approximately two hundred thousand women are incarcerated in the United States, and an additional million women are on probation or parole. E. Ann Carson, "Prisoners in 2016," Bureau of Justice Statistics, Office of Justice Programs, US Department of Justice, https://www.bjs.gov/content/pub/pdf/p16.pdf; Zhen Zeng, "Jail Inmates in 2016," Bureau of Justice Statistics, Office of Justice Programs, US Department of Justice, https://www.bjs.gov/content/pub/pdf/ji16.pdf.

2 Correctional institutions include prison, jail, detention centres, immigration detention centres, and other forms of coerced state custody. Women overwhelmingly enter correctional facilities for relatively minor offences, especially those associated with drug use, such as shoplifting, prostitution, theft, and property crime. "Incarcerated Women and Girls," *Sentencing Project,* http://www.sentencingproject.org/wp-content/uploads/2016/02/Incarcerated-Women-and-Girls.pdf.

3 Alarming numbers of undocumented migrant women are being detained, many of whom are racialized as Latina. Martha Escobar, *Captivity beyond Prisons: Criminalization Experiences of Latina (Im)migrants* (Austin: University of Texas Press, 2016).

4 My use of the terms "racial/cultural/ethnic minority" includes mainly people who identify not only as African Americans and Latinx Americans but also as Asian Americans, Pacific Islanders, and Indigenous/Native Americans. I use Latina rather than Hispanic or Chicana. The term Hispanic more accurately refers to people from geographical locations that have been colonized by Spain or where Spanish is spoken (including all the countries where Spanish is the official language, such as Argentina, Cuba, and the Dominican Republic, as well as those where English is now the official language, such as Jamaica, the Philippines, and the Republic of Trinidad and Tobago). The term Chicana refers to a North American person who is a native of Mexico or a descendent of one. The term Latinx (the gender neutral form of Latino/a)

refers to individuals from Latin American countries (where Spanish as well as Portuguese are spoken) who are the product of a racial mix of Indigenous, African, and white European. According to Jack Forbes, the word "Indigenous" should include peoples from Latin America; in this view, the creation of the sociocultural group "Hispanic" has weakened the potential solidarity among Indigenous peoples. Jack Forbes, "The Hispanic Spin: Party Politics and Governmental Manipulation of Ethnic Identity," *Latin American Perspectives* 19, no. 4 (1992): 59–78.

5 Manuel Villa, "The Mental Health Crisis Facing Women in Prison," *Marshall Project*, June 22, 2017, https://www.themarshallproject.org/2017/06/22/the-mental-health-crisis-facing-women-in-prison; Stephen J. Tripodi, Eyitayo Onifade, and Carrie Pettus-Davis, "Nonfatal Suicidal Behavior among Women Prisoners: The Predictive Roles of Childhood Victimization, Childhood Neglect, and Childhood Positive Support," *International Journal of Offender Therapy and Comparative Criminology* 58, no. 4 (2014): 394–411; Doris J. James and Lauren E. Glaze, "Mental Health Problems of Prison and Jail Inmates," Bureau of Justice Statistics, Office of Justice Programs, US Department of Justice, https://www.bjs.gov/content/pub/pdf/mhppji.pdf.

6 Approximately 4 percent of women begin their sentences pregnant; nearly two-thirds of women in prison have childcare responsibilities; the overwhelming majority of incarcerated women are the only caregivers for their children. Lauren E. Glaze and Laura M. Maruschak, "Parents in Prison and Their Minor Children," Bureau of Justice Statistics, Office of Justice Programs, US Department of Justice, 5, last updated March 30, 2010, https://www.bjs.gov/content/pub/pdf/pptmc.pdf.

7 *O'Lone v Estate of Shabazz*, 482 US 342 (1987).

8 Angela Y. Davis, *Are Prisons Obsolete?* (New York: Seven Stories Press Open Media Series, 2003), 17.

9 See Paula C. Johnson, *Inner Lives: Voices of African American Women in Prison* (New York: New York University Press, 2003); Victoria Law, *Resistance behind Bars: The Struggles of Incarcerated Women* (Oakland: PM Press, 2009); Venezia Michalsen and Jeanne Flavin, "Not All Women Are Mothers: Addressing the Invisibility of Women under the Control of the Criminal Justice System Who Do Not Have Children," *Prison Journal* 94, no. 3 (2014): 328.

10 Gilles Deleuze, *Cinema One: The Movement-Image*, trans. Hugh Tomlinson and Barbara Habberjam (Minneapolis: University of Minnesota Press, 1986); Laura U. Marks, *The Skin of the Film: Intercultural Cinema, Embodiment, and the Senses* (Durham, NC: Duke University Press, 2000); Jacques Rancière, *Film Fables*, trans. Emiliano Battista (Oxford: Berg Publishers, 2006).

11 Please refer to the Selected Filmography at the end of this book.

12 Nicole Hahn Rafter, *Shots in the Mirror: Crime Films and Society* (Oxford: Oxford University Press, 2006), 175.

13 I am grateful to Ann McGillivray for making the connection between this film and the WIP genre.

14 The transcript of Joan of Arc's trial begins in March 1491, halfway through the testimony that began on January 9, and is reproduced in its entirety in *The Trial of Jeanne d'Arc*, trans. W.P. Barrett (New York: Gotham House, 1932), reprinted in Paul Halsall, ed., *Internet Medieval Sourcebook* (New York: Fordham University, 1999). Joan was captured in Bishop Pierre Cauchon's (1371–1442) diocese and posthumously

declared innocent at the conclusion of the 1456 nullification trial. She was canonized in 1920. Regarding the cinematic Joan, see Gerda Lerner, "Joan of Arc: Three Films," in *Past Imperfect: History According to the Movies,* ed. Mark C. Carnes et al. (New York: Henry Holt and Company, 1995), 54–59.

15 There has long been critical engagement with genre in film studies. My argument that women-in-prison (WIP) movies constitute a genre is informed by Stephen Neale, *Genre* (London: British Film Institute, 1980); Rick Altman, *The American Film Musical* (Bloomington: Indiana University Press, 1987); Christine Gledhill, "Genre," in *The Cinema Book,* 3rd ed., ed. Pam Cook (London: British Film Institute, 2007), 252–59. Jessica Silbey's constitution of the "trial film" genre's "identifiable patterns of narrative structure, cinematic features, and character development" was also particularly enlightening. Jessica Silbey, "Patterns of Courtroom Justice," *Journal of Law and Society* 28, no. 1 (2001): 97. Finally, Steve Greenfield, Guy Osborn, and Peter Robson also grapple with the law, film, and genre in Steve Greenfield, Guy Osborn, and Peter Robson, *Film and the Law: The Cinema of Justice,* 2nd ed. (Oxford: Hart Publishing, 2010).

16 Marie Allen (Eleanor Parker) in *Caged!* (1950) and Red Reznikov (Kate Mulgrew) in Season 5 of *Orange Is the New Black* (*OITNB*) (2013–19).

17 Of course, excellent scholars have written on WIP movies, especially (in chronological order) Anne Morey, "'The Judge Called Me an Accessory': Women's Prison Films, 1950–1962," *Journal of Popular Film and Television* 23, no. 2 (1995): 8–87 (argues that WIP movies constitute a pastiche of multiple genres); Beverley Zalcock and Jocelyn Robinson, "Inside Cell Block H: Hard Steel and Soft Soap," *Continuum: Journal of Media and Cultural Studies* 9, no. 1 (1996): 88–97 (argues that some WIP films are proto-feminist); Judith Halberstam, *Female Masculinity* (Durham, NC: Duke University Press, 1998) (argues that WIP movies may constitute a critique of orthodox masculinities and femininities); Judith Mayne, "Caged and Framed: The Women-in-Prison Film," in *Framed: Lesbians, Feminists, and Media Culture* (Minneapolis: University of Minnesota Press, 2000) (argues that the interracial relationships in WIP films facilitate the representation of same-sex partnership and vice versa); Suzanna Danuta Walters, "Caged Heat: The (R)evolution of Women-in-Prison Films," in *Reel Knockouts: Violent Women in the Movies,* ed. Martha McCaughey and Neal King (Austin: University of Texas Press, 2001) (argues that WIP exploitation movies extol the power of female solidarity in response to oppression); Melanie Williams, "Women in Prison and Women in Dressing Gowns: Rediscovering the 1950s Films of J. Lee Thompson," *Journal of Gender Studies* 11, no. 1 (2002): 5–15 (studies two British representations in the 1950s that, at the time of their release, were a rare vehicle for strong female protagonists); Didi Herman, "'*Bad Girls* Changed My Life': Homonormativity in a Women's Prison Drama," *Critical Studies in Media Communication* 20, no. 2 (2003): 141–59 (examines how one dramatic series normalizes and validates lesbian relationships); Jenni Millbank, "It's About *This:* Lesbians, Prison, Desire," in *Law and Popular Culture,* vol. 7, ed. Michael Freeman (Oxford: Oxford University Press, 2005) (explores the disruptive and counter-hegemonic themes in *Bad Girls*); David Gonthier, *American Prison Films since 1930: From the Big House to the Shawshank Redemption* (Lewiston, NY: Edwin Mellen Press, 2006) (explores prison films through a queer theory lens and includes a chapter devoted to WIP

films); Suzanne Bouclin, "Women in Prison Movies as Feminist Jurisprudence," *Canadian Journal of Women and the Law* 21, no. 1 (2009): 19–34 (argues that women in prison movies constitute a genre of their own that reveals truths about the criminal justice system); Janet Stewart Adamson, "The Subjectivities of the Female Lawbreaker in Visual Culture: Cinematic Trajectories of Representation in the Exploitation, Hollywood, and Independent Film in Depictions of the Carceral World" (PhD diss., Simon Fraser University, 2014) (offers a critical taxonomy of various cultural representations of criminalized women). There is also considerable academic conversation around *OITNB* in Chapter 6 of this book.

18 Mariana Valverde, *Law and Order: Images, Meanings, Myths* (New Brunswick, NJ: Rutgers University Press, 2006).

19 Karlene Faith, *Unruly Women: The Politics of Confinement and Resistance,* rev. ed. (New York: Seven Stories Press, 2011), 255–73; Dawn K. Cecil, *Prison Life in Popular Culture: From "The Big House" to "Orange Is the New Black"* (Boulder, CO: Lynne Rienner Publishers, 2015).

20 Christine Gledhill, "Recent Developments in Feminist Criticism," in *Film Theory and Criticism: Introductory Readings,* 5th ed., ed. Leo Braudy and Marshall Cohen. (New York: Oxford University Press, 1999), 251–72.

21 Sally Engle Merry, "Legal Pluralism," *Law and Society Review* 22, no. 5 (1988): 870.

22 James A. Holstein and Jaber F. Gubrium, *The Self We Live By: Narrative Identity in a Postmodern World* (New York: Oxford University Press, 2000), 215; see also Hanne Petersen and Henrik Zahle, eds., *Legal Polycentricity: Consequences of Pluralism in Law* (Aldershot, UK: Dartmouth Publishing, 1995). Compare Roderick Macdonald, who acknowledges that a polycentric theory of law underpins radical legal pluralism, but who concedes that radical legal pluralism "cannot even be polycentrist" because that metaphor implies a centre (and, therefore, a periphery) to a legal regime. Roderick A. Macdonald, "Here, There ... and Everywhere: Theorizing Legal Pluralism; Theorizing Jacques Vanderlinden" in *Étudier et Enseigner le Droit: Hier, Aujourd'hui et Demain – Études Offertes à Jacques Vanderlinden,* ed. Lynne Castonguay and Nicholas Kasirer (Cowansville, QC: Éditions Yvon Blais, 2006), 406; see also Martha-Marie Kleinhans and Roderick A. Macdonald, "What Is a Critical Legal Pluralism," *Canadian Journal of Law and Society* 12, no. 2 (1997): 25–46.

23 Stewart Macaulay offered one of the first treatises regarding the powerful socializing and pedagogical effects of visual media on the legal profession. Stewart Macaulay, "Images of Law in Everyday Life: The Lessons of School, Entertainment, and Spectator Sports," *Law and Society Review* 21, no. 2 (1987): 197. According to Kathy Laster and colleagues, film and television remain "the main source[s] of common knowledge about 'the law.'" Kathy Laster et al., *The Drama of the Courtroom* (Sydney: Federation Press, 2000), 10.

24 Rosemary J. Coombe, "Contingent Articulations: A Critical Cultural Studies of Law," in *Law in the Domains of Culture,* ed. Austin Sarat and Thomas R. Kearns (Ann Arbor: University of Michigan Press, 2000), 21. It is still rare for law and film academics to ask what law transposes to film, with the exception of Jane Gaines's rich discussion on the reproducibility of film and its implications for law. Jane Gaines, *Contested Culture: The Image, the Voice, and the Law* (Chapel Hill: University of North Carolina Press, 1991).

25 The Motion Picture Production Code, also called the "Production Code" or the "Hays Code," was a voluntary regulatory mechanism used to govern film content from 1930 to the 1960s. The entire text of the Production Code is reproduced online at "'Complete Nudity Is Never Permitted': The Motion Picture Production Code of 1930," *History Matters: The US Survey Course on the Web,* http://www.historymatters.gmu.edu/d/5099. "Jim Crow" refers to the matrix of laws and customs deployed to maintain segregation in public spaces, including movie theatres, which implicitly governed the cultural construction of blackness in post-Reconstruction America (1870s–1960s).

26 Robert A. Rosenstone, "The Reel Joan of Arc: Reflections on the Theory and Practice of the Historical Film," *The Public Historian* 25, no. 3 (2003): 65.

27 Rebecca Johnson and Ruth Buchanan, "Getting the Insider's Story Out: What Popular Film Can Tell Us about Legal Method's Dirty Secrets," *Windsor Yearbook of Access to Justice* 20 (2001): 90.

28 I refer to a "shift" or "a move toward" an alternative "law and film." I do believe, however, that there has been a cavalcade of thinking in this field. Law in film scholarship weaves through law and film, asking questions about how film can be descriptive and normative simultaneously, how it shapes and reflects law, and how the law and film entanglement is one of mutual resistance, adaptation, and interdependence. See, for instance, one of the earliest law and film scholarly works that explores how, despite the fact that formal legal structures often discourage empathy for lawbreakers, a viewer's response to protagonists like Thelma and Louise will vary depending on one's social location and how one navigates law's authority. Elizabeth Spelman and Martha Minow, "Outlaw Women: Thelma and Louise," *New England Law Review* 26 (1992): 1281–96, reprinted in *Legal Reelism: Movies as Legal Texts,* ed. John Denver (Chicago: University of Illinois Press, 1995).

29 According to Richard Sherwin, these differences are "vanishing" as law becomes increasingly cinematic. Richard K. Sherwin, *When Law Goes Pop: The Vanishing Line between Law and Popular Culture* (Chicago: University of Chicago Press, 2000).

30 David Black argues that films about law are always already intertextual because they are "at one and the same time, both film (one narrative regime) and about law (another)." David Black, *Law in Film: Resonance and Representation* (Urbana: University of Illinois Press, 1999), 1.

31 Ruth Buchanan and Rebecca Johnson, "Strange Encounters: Exploring Law and Film in the Affective Register," *Studies in Law, Politics, and Society* 46 (2008): 37. Much of the socio-legal research on the prison genre uses content analysis, measuring the veracity of stock characters and the crimes they commit. Ruth Buchanan and Rebecca Johnson encourage law and film scholars to move beyond narrative deconstruction to consider the affective dimensions of film. Scholarship, they explain, should develop a "more robust vocabulary for discussing how films work on us," which can include attention to the cognitive, affective, and embodied dimensions of thought and constitution of subjectivities.

32 Gérard Genette, *Palimpsests: Literature in the Second Degree,* trans. Channa Newman and Claude Doubinsky (Lincoln: University of Nebraska Press, 1997), 1.

33 Mikhail Bakhtin, *Speech Genres and Other Late Essays,* trans. Vern W. McGee (Austin: University of Texas Press, 1986), 92.

34 Julia Kristeva, "Word, Dialogue and Novel," in *The Kristeva Reader,* ed. Toril Moi (New York: Columbia University Press, 1986), 37.

35 Michael Worton and Judith Still, eds., *Intertextuality: Theories and Practices* (Manchester: Manchester University Press, 1990), 1; Kristeva, "Word, Dialogue and Novel," 37; Julia Kristeva, "Towards a Semiology of Paragrams," in *The Tel Quel Reader,* ed. Patrick French and Roland-François Lack (London: Routledge, 1998), 30; see also Genette, *Palimpsests;* Robert Stam, *Subversive Pleasures: Bakhtin, Cultural Criticism, and Film* (Baltimore: Johns Hopkins University Press, 1989).

36 Gérard Genette, *The Architext: An Introduction* (Berkeley: University of California Press, 1992).

37 Koenraad Claes, "Supplements and Paratext: The Rhetoric of Space," *Victorian Periodicals Review* 43, no. 2 (2010): 200, referring to Genette, *Palimpsests.*

38 Christine Gledhill, "Pleasurable Negotiations," in *Female Spectators: Looking at Film and Television,* ed. E. Deidre Pribram (London: Verso, 1988), 74.

39 Genette, *Palimpsests,* 4–7.

40 Amanda Ann Klein distinguishes a cycle from a genre: both are a series of films that share themes, images, characters, narrative structures, and settings, but "film genres are primarily defined by the repetition of key images (their semantics) and themes (their syntax)," while "cycles are primarily defined by how they are used (their pragmatics)." Moreover, a "cycle will form only if its originary film – the film that establishes the images, plot formulas, and themes for the entire cycle – is financially or critically successful." Amanda Ann Klein, *American Film Cycles: Reframing Genres, Screening Social Problems, and Defining Subcultures* (Austin: University of Texas Press, 2011), 4.

41 Michelle Alexander, *The New Jim Crow: Mass Incarceration in the Age of Colorblindness* (New York: New Press, 2012).

42 Black women comprise approximately 13 percent of women in America but make up about 30 percent of all women incarcerated. They are also disproportionately represented in violence against women statistics: approximately 25 percent have experienced intimate partner violence. Further, homicide by an intimate partner is the second most frequent cause of death for Black women under the age of twenty-five. Beth E. Richie, *Arrested Justice: Black Women, Violence, and America's Prison Nation* (New York: New York University Press, 2012), 26.

43 Susan Sontag, *Against Interpretation: And Other Essays* (New York: Anchor Books, 1990), 9.

44 George Toles, "Luxury and Largesse in Film," *Movie: A Journal of Film Criticism* 4 (2013): 7.

Chapter 1: A Genre of One's Own

1 Christine Gledhill, "Genre and Gender: The Case of Soap Opera," in *Representation: Cultural Representations and Signifying Practices,* ed. Stuart Hall (London: Sage Publications, 1997), 356.

2 Jacques Derrida, "The Law of Genre," trans. Avital Ronell, *Critical Inquiry* 7, no. 1 (1980): 56.

3 Andrew Tudor, "Genre," in *Film Genre Reader IV,* ed. Barry K Grant (Austin: University of Texas Press, 2012), 3.

4 Virginia Woolf, *A Room of One's Own* (New York: Harcourt, Brace and Company, 1929).
5 Pat Carlen, ed., *Women and Punishment: The Struggle for Justice* (Cullompton, UK: Willan Publishing, 2002), 3.
6 Currently, over seven hundred thousand women are held in penal institutions worldwide. These numbers do not include all jurisdictions, especially those that tend to not publish official statistics (such as China, Cuba, Eritrea, North Korea, Rwanda, and Somalia) and those not recognized as states in international law. Elizabeth Swavola, Kristine Riley, and Ram Subramanian, *Overlooked: Women and Jails in an Era of Reform* (New York: Vera Institute of Justice, 2016); Roy Walmsley, *World Female Imprisonment List: Women and Girls in Penal Institutions, Including Pre-trial Detainees/Remand Prisoners*, University of London, Birkbeck, World Prison Brief, 4th ed. (London: Institute for Criminal Policy Research, 2017).
7 I use Richard Altman's methodology while drawing extensively on Christine Gledhill's understanding of genre. Richard Altman, *The American Film Musical* (Bloomington: Indiana University Press, 1987); Christine Gledhill, "Genre and Gender" (1997) and "Genre," in *The Cinema Book*, 3rd ed., ed. Pam Cook (London: British Film Institute, 2007).
8 Franco Moretti, *Distant Reading* (London: Verso, 2013). I am grateful to Will Straw (McGill University) for bringing Moretti's work to my attention.
9 Suzanne Bouclin, "Punishment in Film," in *The Social History of Crime and Punishment in America: An Encyclopedia*, ed. Wilbur Miller (London: Sage Publications, 2012).
10 Brian Jarvis, *Cruel and Unusual: Punishment and U.S. Culture* (London: Pluto Press, 2004), 174. These themes are not usually the subject of the whimsical variation of the prison film, including, for example, *Convict 13* (1920), *The Hoose-Gow* (1929), *Up the River* (1930), *Jailhouse Rock* (1957), and, more recently, *Big Stan* (2007). On the male prison genre, see Ronald B. Querry, "Prison Movies: An Annotated Filmography 1921–Present," *Journal of Popular Film* 2, no. 2 (1973): 181–97; Christopher Hale, "Punishment and the Visible," in *The Prison Film*, ed. Mike Nellis and Christopher Hale (London: Radical Alternatives to Prison, 1982); James Robert Parish, *Prison Pictures from Hollywood: Plots, Critiques, Casts and Credits for 293 Theatrical and Made-for-Television Releases* (Jefferson, NC: McFarland and Company, 1991); Derral Cheatwood, "Prison Movies: Films about Adult, Male, Civilian Prisons: 1929–1995," in *Popular Culture, Crime, and Justice*, ed. Frankie Y. Bailey and Donna C. Hale (Belmont, CA: Wadsworth Publishing, 1998); David Wilson and Sean O'Sullivan, *Images of Incarceration: Representations of Prison in Film and Television Drama* (Winchester, UK: Waterside Press, 2004).
11 Many of the first prison films were produced by Edison Studios (1894–1918); see for instance *The Ex-Convict* (1904), in which the protagonist is poor and did what he had to do to support his family. The studio marketed a number of pieces used to "enact the proper, or improper, terms of individual citizenship and state responsibility" as authentic evidence of key historical moments. Bill Nichols, *Speaking Truths with Film: Evidence, Ethics, Politics in Documentary* (Oakland: University of California Press, 2016), 15. While some filmmakers used the prison metaphor to explore the transformative potential of treating people with decency, the more explicit and guiding theme of the action/drama prison film has generally been the scope, nature, and

purpose of punishment. Joe Wlodarz, however, maintains that voyeurism and homoeroticism are constitutive of the prison genre. Joe Wlodarz, "Maximum Insecurity: Genre Trouble and Closet Erotics in and out of HBO's *Oz*," *Camera Obscura* 20, no. 1 (2005): 59–105. See also, Suzanne Bouclin, "Punishment in Film." Regarding the "Convict Code," see Donald Clemmer, *The Prison Community* (New York: Holt, Rinehart and Winston, 1966).

12 Respectively, *Convict's Code* (1930); *Oz* (1997–2003); *The Shawshank Redemption* (1994); *Prison Break* (2005–17).

13 For bank robbery, counterfeiting, and embezzlement, see respectively *Convict's Code; Numbered Men* (1930); *The Outer Gate* (1937). For murder, see *Each Dawn I Die* (1939); *Prison Break.*

14 David Wilson and Sean O'Sullivan deploy a functional analysis to explore how prison films actually serve *five* such purposes. They may be revelatory, act as a benchmark, work in defense of gains, serve as collective memory, or humanize incarcerated people. Wilson and O'Sullivan, *Images of Incarceration,* 98.

15 A rape-revenge movie, according to Alexandra Heller-Nicholas, "is one whereby a rape that is central to the narrative is punished by an act of vengeance." Alexandra Heller-Nicholas, *Rape-Revenge Films: A Critical Study* (Jefferson, NC: McFarland and Company, 2011), 3. To be female-centred, Sarah Projansky explains, "revenge is taken by women who have faced rape themselves" and "can be understood as feminist narratives in which women ... recognize that the law will neither protect nor avenge them, and then take the law into their own hands." Sarah Projansky, *Watching Rape: Film and Television in Postfeminist Culture* (New York: New York University Press, 2001), 60.

16 Stanley Cavell, *Pursuits of Happiness: The Hollywood Comedy of Remarriage* (Cambridge, MA: Harvard University Press, 1981), 24.

17 *Caged!* (1950) falls more naturally within the social purpose/melodrama women-in-prison (WIP) cycle than within film noir because it does not have two staples of the latter genre – namely, the "investigative narrative structure" or the "femme fatal." Christine Gledhill, "*Klute* 2: Feminism and *Klute,*" in *Women in Film Noir,* ed. E. Ann Kaplan (London: British Film Institute, 1998), 102, 106.

18 See, for instance, the National Broadcasting Corporation's made-for-television movie *Born Innocent* (1974).

19 The show was also unique in the crimes for which women found themselves incarcerated. Bonnie Harper (Antoinette Byron) is a lesbian and a sex worker; Pam Norwell (Wendie Jo Sperber) is a tech genius, in for embezzlement. *Second City Television* (1976–84), a Canadian sketch comedy show, also aired a spoof of the genre in 1977 entitled *Broads Behind Bars* (1977).

20 *Orange Is the New Black* (*OITNB*) (2013–19), Season 1, episode 8 ("Moscow Mule").

21 Christine Gledhill found that in the nineteenth century "melodrama" referred to a broad range of dramatic and fictional ("male") stories, including cape-and-sword, nautical, and frontier productions that were "conceived as viewing reality in moral and emotional terms" and were judged by their "authenticity and labour-intensive technical realization on stage." Gledhill, "Genre and Gender," 350. Annette Kuhn argues that one defining characteristic of "women's pictures" is "their" construction of narratives motivated by female desire and processes of spectator identification

governed by female point-of-view." Annette Kuhn, "Women's Genres," *Screen* 25, no. 1 (1984): 18; see also Mary Ann Doane, *The Desire to Desire: The Woman's Film of the 1940s* (Bloomington: Indiana University Press, 1987); Sandy Flitterman-Lewis, "The Blossom and the Bole: Narrative and Visual Spectacle in Early Film Melodrama," *Cinema Journal* 33, no. 3 (1994): 3–15.

22 See Annette Kuhn, *Cinema, Censorship and Sexuality 1909–1925* (New York: Routledge, 1988); Peter Roffman and Jim Purdy, *The Hollywood Social Problem Film: Madness, Despair, and Politics from the Depression to the Fifties* (Bloomington: Indiana University Press, 1981); for a definition of the "social problem film (social cinema, social consciousness cinema)," see Annette Kuhn and Guy Westwell, *Dictionary of Film Studies* (Oxford: Oxford University Press, 2012), 383.

23 Tagline for *Caged!*.

24 Tagline for *Caged Heat* (1974).

25 Kuhn and Westwell provide a definition of a "woman's picture" as one that is "aimed at and/or enjoyed particularly by women." Kuhn and Westwell, *Dictionary*, 157. On the emergence of the exploitation WIP movies, see Henry Jenkins, "Exploiting Feminism in Stephanie Rothman's *Terminal Island*," in *The Wow Climax: Tracing the Emotional Impact of Popular Culture* (New York: New York University Press, 2007), 102–24.

26 In 1991, Home Box Office also released a dramatic trilogy: *Prison Stories: Women on the Inside* (1991).

27 Didi Herman, "'*Bad Girls* Changed My Life': Homonormativity in a Women's Prison Drama," *Critical Studies in Media Communication* 20, no. 2 (2003): 143. The show's website states: "Bad Girls has set out since its first series to raise awareness of what happens in women's prisons and to highlight the issues women in prison face. Those involved in its production have gone to great lengths to try to make it as accurate as possible, but it is a drama series and life in prison is not always so exciting, so it would not be fair to think that everything Bad Girls shows us actually happens on a regular basis." Quoted in Andrea Mayr and David Machin, *The Language of Crime and Deviance: An Introduction to Critical Linguistic Analysis in Media and Popular Culture* (London: Continuum International, 2012), 187–88.

28 Quoted in Maria St. John, "Making Home/Making 'Stranger': An Interview with Cheryl Dunye," *Feminist Studies* 30, no. 2 (2004): 332.

29 Beth E. Richie, "Queering Antiprison Work: African American Lesbians in the Juvenile Justice System," in *Global Lockdown: Race, Gender, and the Prison-Industrial Complex*, ed. Julia Sudbury (New York: Routledge, 2013), 76.

30 The made-for-television movie *Cage without a Key* (1975) was produced at the height of the exploitation cycle. Given its original distribution by a television network, its content and its aesthetic fall squarely within the realist cycle. The film ends with statistics on the resources available to young offenders and a plea to reform carceral institutions for girls. It is also the only American WIP film I have found that features an Asian American queen bee who is also one of the main characters.

31 Leah R. Ekdom Vande Berg, "Dramedy: *Moonlighting* as an Emergent Generic Hybrid," in *Television Criticism: Approaches and Applications*, ed. Leah R. Vande Berg and Lawrence A. Wenner (New York: Longman, 1991), 95.

32 Marta Fernández-Morales and María Isabel Menéndez-Menéndez, "'When in Rome, Use What You've Got': A Discussion of Female Agency through *Orange Is the New Black*," *Television and New Media* 17, no. 6 (2016): 538.

33 Altman, *American Film Musical*, 13.

34 American documentaries include *Angela Davis: Portrait of a Revolutionary* (1972); *What I Want My Words to Do to You: Voices from Inside a Women's Maximum Security Prison* (2003); *13th* (2016); and *Conviction* (2019) and the television series *Bad Girls behind Bars* (2019–present). In other jurisdictions, see, for instance, *O Cárcere e a Rua* (2005); *Girls behind Bars* (2008); *Holloway: Women behind Bars* (2009). On the political possibilities of the documentary tradition, see Jane M. Gaines and Michael Renov, eds., *Collecting Visible Evidence* (Minneapolis: University of Minnesota Press, 1999).

35 Alexandra Juhasz, "Victim Stories: Documenting Pain, Punishment, Prison and Power," *Studies in Law, Politics, and Society* 30 (2004): 247. She is self-reflexive regarding her own film, *Released: 5 Short Videos about Women and Prison* (2001): "To speak, even as a victim, is better than to be silenced. To speak as a victim creates the possibility of collaboration with others to work against such conditions; to hear a victim speak allows for witnessing, which affirms and marks publicly that the victimization occurred" (251).

36 Jessica Silbey argues that, in legal proceedings, to assume documentary films as "truth-revealing" is not only a mistake, but it may also undercut the justice system. Jessica Silbey, "Filmmaking in the Precinct House and the Genre of Documentary Film," *Columbia Journal of Law and the Arts* 29, no. 2 (2005): 107; see also Charles Musser, "Cinema Verité and the New Documentary," in *The Oxford History of World Cinema: The Definitive History of Cinema Worldwide*, ed. Geoffrey Nowell-Smith (Oxford: Oxford University Press, 1996); Lee Grieveson, *Policing Cinema: Movies and Censorship in Early-Twentieth-Century America* (Berkeley: University of California Press, 2004).

37 Piper Kerman wrote *Orange Is the New Black: My Year in a Women's Prison: A Memoir* (New York: Random House, 2011) after serving her sentence at the Danbury Women's Prison in Connecticut. See also, *Ladies They Talk About* (1933), based on screenwriter and playwright Dorothy Mackaye's time served at the San Quentin prison; and *Love, Mary* (1985), *False Arrest* (1991), *Conviction: The Kitty Dodds Story* (1993), *Within These Walls* (2001), and *Guilt by Association* (2002), which are all based on factual events.

38 Gledhill, "Genre and Gender," 343. Television series also prolong scenes to maintain audience interest and loyalty and may have episodic interruptions by way of advertisements or news.

39 Julia Sudbury, "Introduction: Feminist Critiques, Transnational Landscapes, Abolitionist Visions," in *Global Lockdown: Race, Gender, and the Prison-Industrial Complex*, ed. Julia Sudbury (New York: Routledge, 2013), xiv.

40 The basement: *The Collector* (1965); the psychiatric institution: *The Snake Pit* (1948), *Lilith* (1964), *Girl, Interrupted* (1999); the prisoner-of-war camp: *Three Came Home* (1950); *Sophie's Choice* (1982); the convent: *Girls Town* (1959), and *The Magdalene Sisters* (2002).

41 On the cinematic representation of boarding schools, see Grace Chailler (Sicangu Lakota), "Boarding and Residential School Experiences in Film," in *American Indians*

and Popular Culture, ed. Elizabeth DeLaney Hoffman (Santa Barbara, CA: Praeger, 2012), 117–34. With the exceptions of *The Only Good Indian* (2009) directed by Kevin Wilmott, and *Older Than America* (2008) directed by Georgina Lightening (Samson Cree Nation), mainstream fictional films that deal with boarding schools have, Chailler argues, told "shallow and sanitized" stories about the forced removal of Indigenous children from their communities (118).

42 I could have chosen any number of excellent films from other jurisdictions, including Manijeh Hekmat's gripping *Zendan-e zanan* (*Women's Prison*) (2002), which is based in an Iranian prison; Maeve Murphy's *Silent Grace* (Ireland, 2002), which explores the protests at Armagh Women's Prison in Northern Ireland; Kang Dae-kuès *Hamoni* (*Harmony*) (2010), in which a pregnant woman is sent to prison for killing her abusive husband; and Mai Masri's *3000 Layla* (*3000 Nights*) (2015), which follows a Palestinian political prisoner. I will leave to future research the intertextual dialogue between American movies about incarcerated women and those from other jurisdictions that may have similar or incompatible approaches to penology.

43 Dimension Pictures also released *Sweet Sugar* (1972), in which a white sex worker is diverted to a prison labour camp in Costa Rica.

44 *The Sin of Nora Moran* (1933); *Swamp Women* (1956).

45 David A. Black, *Law in Film: Resonance and Representation* (Urbana: University of Illinois Press, 1999), 164.

46 Between 1915 and 1948, Hollywood developed a mode of film-making production, distribution, and exhibition known as the "studio system," which favoured narratives that met four criteria: clarity, unity, goal-oriented characters, and closure. Maria Pramaggiore and Tom Wallis, *Film: A Critical Introduction* (London: Laurence King Publishing, 2005), 38–46.

47 *Manslaughter* (1922) and (1930); for a more recent variation, see *Love, Mary* (1985).

48 *Godless Girl* (1929); *Manslaughter; Ladies of the Big House* (1931); *Hold Your Man* (1933) *Condemned Women* (1938); *Convicted Woman* (1940); *Women without Names* (1940); *Gallant Lady* (1942); *Lady Gangster* (1942); *Roxie Hart* (1942); *Girls in Chains* (1943); *Girls of the Big House* (1945); *Betrayed Women* (1955). Compare *Ladies They Talk About* (1933) in which the ending is ambiguous regarding the protagonist's genuine desire to marry.

49 *Paid* (1930); *The Bridge of Sighs* (1936); *Women in Prison* (1938); *Convicted Woman*; *Betrayed Women.* This feature is a standard of many of the more recent films, whether satires or dramas, such as *Girls in Prison* (1994) and *Convicted* (2004).

50 *Acquitted* (1929); *Condemned Women*; *Convicted Woman; Ladies of the Big House; Lady Gangster; Girls of the Big House;Women without Names.* This trope recurs in later iterations: *The Concrete Jungle* (1982); *Cage without a Key.* In *OITNB,* Janae Watson (Vicky Jeudy) and Aleida Diaz (Elizabeth Rodriguez) are serving time in place of their boyfriends.

51 *Caged!; Ladies They Talk About; The Lullaby* (1924).

52 *Caged!.*

53 *Caged!; Girls of the Big House; Hold Your Man; The Lullaby.* More recently, see *Ombline* (2012); Daya in *OITNB* (except that her pregnancy is the result of an affair with a guard while imprisoned).

54 *Convicted Woman* and *Girls in Chains*. This trope is much more frequent in later iterations of the genre, across cycles. See *Chained Heat* (1983); *Bad Girls Dormitory* (1986); *Naked Cage* (1986); *Against their Will* (1994).
55 *Ladies of the Big House; Condemned Women; Lady Gangster; Girls of the Big House; Good-Time Girl* (1948); *Blonde Bait* (1956). More recently, in *Condition Red* (1995) a corrections officer helps an innocent prisoner, with whom he has fallen in love, escape.
56 Chaplain/minister: *The Midnight Flower* (1923), *Ladies They Talk About, Girls in Prison* (1956); prison doctor/psychiatrist: *Acquitted, Condemned Women, Prison Without Bars* (1938), *So Young, So Bad* (1950), *Reform School Girl* (1957), *Girl Called Hatter Fox* (1977), *Reform School Girls* (1986); reporter/journalist: *The Woman Condemned* (1934), *Convicted Woman, Lady Gangster, Slammer Girls* (1987), *Civil Brand* (2002); lawyer/district attorney: *Manslaughter, Woman Against the World* (1937), *Girls of the Big House.*
57 *OITNB,* Season 1, episode 6 ("WAC Pack").
58 *The Godless Girl; Red Hot Tires* (1925); *Good-Time Girl; Yield to the Night* (1956); *The Green-Eyed Blonde* (1957).
59 Brenda (Jan Sterling) in *Women's Prison* (1955) cycles in and out of prison for writing bad cheques. The same performer is a "common prostitute" in *Caged!*.
60 *Manslaughter; The Godless Girl; Hold Your Man; Condemned Women; The Story of Molly X* (1949). More recently, *Love, Mary; Ombline.*
61 On situated readings of films, see Annette Kuhn, *Women's Pictures: Feminism and Cinema* (London: Verso, 1994).
62 For a sample of Stanwyck's incarnation of the femme fatale, see *Babyface* (1933), in which she plays a sex worker who uses her feminine wiles to attain power; *Double Indemnity* (1944), in which she plays Phyllis Dietrichson, a frustrated homemaker who plots her husband's death; and *The File on Thelma Jordon* (1950), in which she commits a murder but is acquitted after she seduces the district attorney.
63 Tagline for *Caged Heat.*
64 Jenkins, "Exploiting Feminism," 102–24.
65 Further, *OITNB,* Season 1, episode 1 ("I Wasn't Ready") begins with Piper taking a shower. Violent cavity searches: *The Big Doll House* (1971), *Caged Heat;* electro-shock therapy: *Caged Heat;* torture: *Women in Cages* (1971); sexual assaults by male or female guards, the warden, or other prisoners: *The Big Doll House, Jackson County Jail* (1976), *The Concrete Jungle, The Naked Cage, Civil Brand, OITNB,* Season 3, episode 10 ("Tongue Tied").
66 *The Big Doll House; Caged Heat; The Concrete Jungle; The Naked Cage; Girls in Prison* (1994).
67 *The Naked Cage.*
68 *The Concrete Jungle; Chained Heat.*
69 *Women in Cages; The Big Doll House; Big Bird Cage* (1972); *Caged Heat; Chained Heat; The Naked Cage; The Concrete Jungle; Bad Girls Dormitory* (1986).
70 With a few key exceptions, women who incite riot or escape often meet a bitter end in every WIP movie cycle; see *Condemned Women; Violent Women* (1960); *The Naked Cage;* and *Civil Brand.*

71 "Women in Prison," accessed August 2015, http://www.prisonflicks.com, quoted in Suzanne Bouclin, "Caging Women: Punishment, Judgment, Reform, and Resistance in Women in Prison Films" (Master's thesis, University of Manitoba, 2007), 62.

72 Rikke Schubart, "Hold It! Use It! Abuse It!: Ilsa, She-Wolf of the SS and Male Castration," in *Femme Fatalities: Representations of Strong Women in the Media,* ed. Rikke Schubart and Anne Gjelsvik (Gothenburg: Nordicom, 2004), 195.

73 Kuhn and Westwell distinguish soft-core pornography, "in which sex is simulated and there is some level of plot and characterization," from hard-core pornography, which displays "a series of unsimulated sexual 'numbers,' with little or no attempt at a story." Kuhn and Westwell, *Dictionary,* accessed online at https://www.oxfordreference.com/view/10.1093/acref/9780199587261.001.0001/acref-9780199587261-e-0540?rskey=ABor8M&result=542. Accordingly, the films that I discuss in the exploitation cycle are probably soft-core pornography, though there certainly are hard-core versions of the babes-behind-bars films. Films excluded from my data set because the prison was incidental to the overarching plot: *99 Women* (1969), *Escape from Women's Prison* (1978), *Caged Fury* (1990); films taking place in "jungle prisons": *Terminal Island* (1973), *Escape from Hell* (1980), *The Concrete Jungle;* films taking place in Nazi camps: *Ilsa: She Wolf of the SS* (1975); *Deported Women of the SS Special Section* (1976); *Ilsa, the Wicked Warden* (1977). It is noteworthy that, in the Ilsa series, Isla was originally played by Phyllis Davis, who also starred in *Sweet Sugar,* a prison-like film that takes place on a plantation, and *Terminal Island.* Davis ultimately lost the role to Dyanne Thorne because Davis refused to urinate on a co-star. Thorne has qualified Isla – who castrates men and terrorizes women – as a feminist. Regarding the tensions and feminist possibilities of Isla's particular mode of domination, see Schubart, "Hold It! Use It! Abuse It!"

74 In film studies, see Carol J. Clover's exploration of male masochism and cross-gender identification in rape and horror films. Carol J. Clover, *Men, Women, and Chain Saws: Gender in the Modern Horror Film* (Princeton, NJ: Princeton University Press, 1992). Elizabeth Cowie grapples with the cinematic apparatus as fetishistic and voyeuristic masculine pleasure; she develops a theory of feminine identification that validates the pleasures that male and female spectators may experience, confront, or disavow. Elizabeth Cowie, *Representing the Woman: Cinema and Psychoanalysis* (Minneapolis: University of Minnesota Press, 1997). For Kaja Silverman, fetishistic representation may be capitulation to heteronormativity; it may also subvert this order insofar as it "crosses the boundary separating food from excrement (coprophilia); human from animal (bestiality); life from death (necrophilia); adult from child (pederasty); and pleasure from pain (masochism)." Kaja Silverman, *Male Subjectivity at the Margins* (New York: Routledge, 1992), 187. In law, Ummni Khan explores how the judicial/legal treatment of erotic practices and role playing ("BDSM") reflects and is constituted through medical discourse, including psychiatric definitions, knowledge claims advanced by feminist scholars and activists, and cultural sites of meaning, including cinema. Ummni Khan, *Vicarious Kinks: S/M in the Socio-Legal Imaginary* (Toronto: University of Toronto Press, 2014).

75 See also Linda Williams, *Hard Core: Power, Pleasure, and the "Frenzy of the Visible"* (Berkeley: University of California Press, 1999).

76 See Anne McGillivray's work on law and literature. Anne McGillivray, "*Recherche Sublime:* An Introduction to Law and Literature," *Mosaic: An Interdisciplinary Critical Journal* 27, no. 4 (1994): i–x.

77 *Blonde Sinner* (1956); *Yield to the Night; I Want To Live!* (1958) (for which Susan Hayward won an Academy Award for her portrayal of Barbara Graham); *Why Must I Die?* (1960); *I Want to Live* (1983), a made-for-television remake of the original film by the same name, starring Lindsay Wagner; *Dance with a Stranger* (1985); *Too Young to Die?* (1990); *Better Off Dead* (1993); *Last Dance* (1996); *Dancer in the Dark* (2000); *Convicted.* See also Brian Jarvis, *Cruel and Unusual: Punishment and U.S. Culture* (London: Pluto Press, 2004), who considers the specificities and shared plot structures in *The Last Mile* (1932); *Monster's Ball* (2001); *The Execution of Solomon Harris* (2007); *Dead Man Walking* (1995). Arguably, *Condemned* (2010) is a death row film, even though the protagonist's executioner is not a state agent (but another prisoner).

78 Regarding the affirmative potential, as well as the stereotypical usage of labels such as "butch"/"femme," see generally Ja'nina J. Walker et al., "Butch Bottom–Femme Top? An Exploration of Lesbian Stereotypes," *Journal of Lesbian Studies* 16, no. 1 (2012): 90–107; Alix Genter, "Appearances Can Be Deceiving: Butch-Femme Fashion and Queer Legibility in New York City, 1945–1969," *Feminist Studies* 42, no. 3 (2016): 604–31.

79 See especially *Caged Heat.*

80 Pat Carlen, "Introduction: Women and Punishment," in Carlen, *Women and Punishment,* 4.

81 Women engaging in sex work to subvert economic dependence on men: *Caged!, Caged Heat, The Big Doll House;* addiction-related petty offences: *Ann Vickers, Caged!, OITNB;* bigamy: *Gallant Lady, Blonde Bait* (1956); political prisoners: *Iron Jawed Angels* (2004), *OITNB*; assisted suicide: *Gallant Lady*; labour activists: *Hold Your Man, Ladies They Talk About, Civil Brand;* environmental activist: *OITNB;* infanticide or maternal filicide: *Five Bold Women* (1960), *The Big Doll House, Caged Fear* (1991). Others are in for "accidental" crimes: Helene Jensen in *Women's Prison,* for instance, ran over a child when passing a car.

82 Ivory (Louise Beavers) in *Ladies of the Big House;* Emma (Ellen Corby) in *Caged!;* Bonnie (Michelle Newkirk) in *Vendetta* (1986); Dawn (C.C.H. Pounder) in *Women in Prison* (1987–88); Maria (Maria Rangel) in *Dangerous Women* (1991); Roxie Hart (Renée Zellweger) in *Chicago* (2002); Frances (LisaRaye McCoy) and Lil' Mama (Lark Voorhies) in *Civil Brand;* Bea (Danielle Cormack) in *Wentworth* (2013–present).

83 Consider Matron "Mama" (played by Queen Latifah) in *Chicago* or any of *OITNB*'s matriarchs – for example, Galina "Red" Reznikov (Kate Mulgrew), Gloria (Selenis Leyva), and "Vee" (Lorraine Toussaint), all of whom present as heterosexual.

84 In *Girls in Prison* (1956), Dorothy (Phyllis Coates) attacks the protagonist whom she images to be having an affair with her husband. In *OITNB,* Lolly, Suzanne, and Morello all navigate serious mental illness.

85 Andrea Weiss, *Vampires and Violets: Lesbians in Film* (New York: Penguin Books, 1993).

86 *Ladies of the Big House; Convicted Woman; Girls of the Big House.*

87 *Caged Heat; The Big Doll House; Black Mama White Mama.*
88 Whereas in *Caged Heat,* the main character has killed a rapist, in *Ombline* and *OITNB,* most, if not all, of the characters are marked with a history of poverty.
89 In *Big Bird Cage,* Pam Grier's character is a political revolutionary (and possible homage to Angela Davis) who is arrested for civil disobedience.
90 On the significance of, and contradictions within, Blaxploitation, see Yvonne D. Sims, *Women of Blaxploitation: How the Black Action Film Heroine Changed American Popular Culture* (Jefferson, NC: McFarland and Company, 2006); Eithne Quinn and Peter Krämer, "Blaxploitation," in *Contemporary American Cinema,* ed. Linda Ruth Williams and Michael Hammond (Berkshire, UK: McGraw-Hill Education, 2006); Linda Williams, *Playing the Race Card: Melodramas of Black and White from Uncle Tom to O.J. Simpson* (Princeton, NJ: Princeton University Press, 2001). Regarding some of the stereotypical representations of African American women in cinema, see Paula J. Massood, *Black City Cinema: African American Urban Experiences in Film* (Philadelphia: Temple University Press, 2003); Adria Y. Goldman et al., eds., *Black Women and Popular Culture: The Conversation Continues* (Lanham, MD: Lexington Books, 2014).

Chapter 2: Reforming Prisons, Transforming Women

1 *Ann Vickers* (1933). Dir. John Cromwell. Screenplay: Jane Murfin, based on the novel by Sinclair Lewis. RKO Radio Pictures.
2 Sinclair Lewis, *Ann Vickers* (Garden City, NY: Doubleday, Doran & Company, 1933).
3 In the late 1920s and early 1930s, women held over 60 percent of social worker positions but few managerial positions. Alice Kessler-Harris, *Out to Work: A History of Wage-Earning Women in the United States* (New York: Oxford University Press, 1982), 224–36.
4 Lawrence W. Levine, "The Folklore of Industrial Society: Popular Culture and Its Audiences," *American Historical Review* 97, no. 5 (1992): 1392, referring to Umberto Eco, *The Role of the Reader: Explorations in the Semiotics of Texts* (Bloomington: Indiana University Press, 1979), 4, 9–10, 22–23.
5 Sally E. Parry, "The Changing Fictional Faces of Sinclair Lewis' Wives," *Studies in American Fiction* 17 (1989): 65. Sinclair Lewis's three books – *The Job* (New York: Harper and Brothers, 1917), *Main Street* (San Diego: Harcourt, Brace and Howe, 1920), and *Ann Vickers* – are generally considered to have explicitly feminist protagonists and themes and are actually a "caricature of feminism rather than a tribute to the sisterhood to which his [second] wife [Dorothy Thompson] had profoundly belonged and in which she still claimed membership." Marion K. Sanders, *Dorothy Thompson: A Legend in Her Time* (Boston: Houghton Mifflin, 1973), 173.
6 Quoted in Nan Bauer Maglin and Donna Marie Perrie, eds., *"Bad Girls"/"Good Girls": Women, Sex, and Power in the Nineties* (New Brunswick, NJ: Rutgers University Press, 1994).
7 The book treats the subject of Ann's participation in the suffrage movement satirically: feminist organizers are a "piratical crew" of "young devils who made miserable the lives" of politicians, who aggressively rioted and "pestered" senators. Lewis, *Ann Vickers,* 103.

8 Joan Henry's novels were adapted and include *Weak and the Wicked* (1954) and *Yield to the Night* (1956).

9 She plays Sabra in *Cimarron* (1931), which was based on Edna Ferber's novel and encouraged respectful, nation-to-nation engagement between white settlers and the Cherokee people.

10 Wes D. Gehring, *Irene Dunne: First Lady of Hollywood* (Lanham, MD: Scarecrow Press, 2006), 40.

11 Kate Cameron, "Irene Dunne Shines as Lewis's Heroine," *New York Daily News*, September 29, 1933, 48.

12 Gehring, *Irene Dunne*, 153.

13 Gehring, *Irene Dunne*, 137. John Cromwell's three films about women's incarceration – *Ann Vickers* (1933); *Caged!* (1950); *The Company She Keeps* (1956) – reflect and reproduce discourses about social reform while never amounting to didactic yarns. Cromwell was eventually barred from Hollywood during the House Un-American Activities Committee for allegedly holding communist beliefs.

14 Several film scholars have traced the genealogy of self-regulation in the film industry. See Paul W. Facey, *The Legion of Decency: A Sociological Analysis of the Emergence and Development of a Social Pressure Group* (New York: Amo Press, 1974); Lea Jacobs, *The Wages of Sin: Censorship and the Fallen Woman Film, 1928–1942* (Madison: University of Wisconsin Press, 1991); Gregory D. Black, *Hollywood Censored: Morality Codes, Catholics and the Movies* (Cambridge: Cambridge University Press, 1994); Richard Maltby, "The Production Code and the Hays Office," in *Grand Design: Hollywood as a Modern Business Enterprise, 1930–1939*, ed. Tino Balio (New York: Scribner, 1993), 37–72; Thomas Doherty, *Pre-Code Hollywood: Sex, Immorality, and Insurrection in American Cinema, 1930–1934* (New York: Columbia University Press, 1999).

15 The Women's Christian Temperance Union of America voiced strong concerns about cinema's impact on women's mental health, morality, and well-being and lobbied for governmental regulation. Their lobbying was effective, and, at the turn of the twentieth century, some municipalities (Chicago in 1907) issued censorship ordinances, and some states (Pennsylvania in 1911, Ohio in 1913, and Kansas in 1913) introduced censorship legislation to regulate film content. In 1915, the US Supreme Court upheld the legality of state censorship laws, finding that films did not constitute protected speech. *Mutual Film Corporation v Industrial Commission of Ontario et al*, 236 US 230 (1915). The federal government did not have jurisdiction over film content; however, it did retain authority over the importation and traffic of obscene materials.

16 Alexander McGregor, *The Catholic Church and Hollywood: Censorship and Morality in 1930s Cinema* (New York: I.B. Tauris & Company, 2013), 64.

17 The International Federation of Catholic Alumnae categorized and ranked movies according to their moral content: Class A1 (morally unobjectionable for children); Class A2 (morally unobjectionable for adults); Class B (objectionable in part); and Class C (condemned).

18 Martin Quigley, *Decency in Motion Pictures* (New York: Macmillan Company, 1937), 31.

19 Quigley, *Decency in Motion Pictures*, 31. See also Stephen Vaughn, "Morality and Entertainment: The Origins of the the Motion Picture Production Code," *The Journal of American History* 77, no. 1 (1990): 39.

20 The entire text of the Motion Picture Production Code is reproduced online at "'Complete Nudity Is Never Permitted': The Motion Picture Production Code of 1930," *History Matters: The US Survey Course on the Web*, http://www.historymatters.gmu.edu/d/5099.

21 John T. McNicholas, "The Episcopal Committee and the Problem of Evil Motion Pictures," *Ecclesiastical Review* 91 (1934): 118.

22 Compare "More Than 100,000 in Brooklyn Alone Promise to Refrain from Attending Objectionable Pictures: Exhibitors Score 'Cancellation' Order," *Catholic News Service,* August 4, 1934, with James M. Connolly, "Boycott Not Legislation: Another View of Legion of Decency's Aims toward Movies," *New York Times,* July 11, 1934.

23 Gregory D. Black, *Hollywood Censored: Morality Codes, Catholics, and the Movies* (Cambridge: Cambridge University Press, 1994); Gregory D. Black, *The Catholic Crusade against the Movies, 1940–1975* (Cambridge: Cambridge University Press, 1997).

24 According to at least one commentator, the battle between Radio-Keith-Orpheum (RKO) and the Hays Office over Ann Vickers, "almost single handedly brought in the tougher controls of the Hollywood Production Code." Peter J. Patrick, "Oscar Profile #142: John Cromwell," *Cinema Sight*, July 11, 2013.

25 Letter from Joseph Breen to James Wingate, May 5, 1933, *Ann Vickers,* Production Code Administration Archives, Academy of Motion Pictures Arts and Sciences Library, Los Angeles, California. Around the same time, other companies also put out films that elicited scrutiny from the Hays Office for depicting strong, sexual women. Paramount pictures produced Mae West's *She Done Him Wrong* (1933) and *I'm No Angel* (1933), and Metro-Goldwyn-Mayer Studios released *Bombshell* (1933), starring Jean Harlow.

26 Motion Picture Production Code, Chapter 2, "Sex"; Breen to Wingate, May 5, 1933; Letter from James Wingate to Merian Cooper, May 8, 1933, *Ann Vickers,* Production Code Administration Archives, Academy of Motion Pictures Arts and Sciences Library, Los Angeles, California.

27 Black, *Hollywood Censored,* 103.

28 Cromwell would actually direct the adaption of Maugham's novel a year later. William Somerset Maugham, *Of Human Bondage* (New York: George Doran, 1915).

29 But, according to Richard Maltby, the concessions made by RKO left the film's characters "ritually denounced and burdened with a conventional morality" and its "thematic and narrative coherence muddied to a point of internal contradiction." Richard Maltby, "'To Prevent the Prevalent Type of Book': Censorship and Adaptation in Hollywood, 1924–1934," *American Quarterly* 44, no. 4 (1992): 564.

30 In this regard, despite its critical gaze on the prison, the film does not reflect the novel's more overt prison abolitionist stance. As one reviewer writes, "thousands of persons will see a prison-building differently if they meet one while riding or walking, just because they read about Copperhead Gap Prison in Lewis's book; it will be impossible for them to do otherwise, for Lewis just twists the sickeningly cruel prison into you, in a way that words can, and the motion-picture ... can't." Eli Siegel, "Ann Vickers. By Sinclair Lewis. Doubleday, Doran. $2.50," Book Reviews by Eli Siegel, 1931–1934, *Scribner's Magazine,* March 1933.

31 A woman whose husband is unfaithful.

32 Dr. Crane (Howard Duff) diagnoses the matron in this way: "You are a borderline psychopath, Warden. And you are very close to the border." Ida Lupino will resuscitate this character as Claire Tyson in the made-for-television exploitation women-in-prison (WIP) movie *Women in Chains* (1972). Tyson quits a better-paying administrative position to stay on the block so she can torment the prisoners. Similarly, in *So Young, So Bad* (1950), Matron Beuhler (Grace Coppin) uses a fire hose to punish the girls.

33 Mrs. Stoner (Virginia Brissac) imparts similar wisdom to her charges in *Lady Gangster* (1942): "The quicker you realize that this is neither a country club nor a concentration camp, the better. It's up to the women themselves how they're treated. If you behave yourself, we'll meet you more than halfway, but if you want to be tough, we can be tough with you."

34 Compare with the film *Paid* (1930), which features Joan Crawford as Mary Turner, a naive shopkeeper wrongfully convicted of stealing from her employer. While incarcerated, she studies law and hatches a plan to use the system to enact revenge.

35 "Original Theatrical Release for *Ladies They Talk About*" (video), *YouTube*, posted by Warner Archive on July 11, 2012, https://www.youtube.com/watch?v=4tW4c6H6j1A.

36 Anita Loos's screenplays in *Hold Your Man* (1933), *The Women* (1939), and *Gentlemen Prefer Blondes* (1953) depict multidimensional women navigating multiple normative commitments. In *Hold Your Man*, one of Ruby's cellmates is a socialist organizer who calls out the race, class, and gender biases embedded in the criminal justice system. Similarly, while Sidney Sutherland wrote the screenplay for *Ladies They Talk About* (1933), it is actually an adaption of Dorothy Mackaye's play, *Women in Prison* (Los Angeles, 1932). Mackaye's work is a personal account inspired by the twenty-five months she spent in San Quentin for her part in the death of her husband. The film deploys euphemisms to get around the Production Code's obscenity provisions. For instance, Aunt Maggie (Maude Ebern) is incarcerated for running a brothel; she claims she was entrapped by a sergeant who came into her "beauty parlour" "to get a manicure." *Ladies They Talk About* also introduces some of the WIP genre's recurring themes, such as sexual deviance, institutional racism, and abject femininity. Nan is warned when she enters prison to be wary of Linda (Lillian Roth), a cigar-smoking butch who "likes to wrestle." Another noteworthy feature is the presence of several African American performers, though none were integral to the plot and only one has a small speaking part: Mustard (Madame Sul-Te-Wan), whose character is unfortunately locked into the antebellum caricatures of Black women.

37 Lewis, *Ann Vickers*, 85, 86, 140, 146, 151–52.

38 See, for instance, Mick Lasalle, *Complicated Women: Sex and Power in Pre-Code Hollywood* (New York: Thomas Dunne Books/St. Martin's Press, 2000); Stephen Murray, "Prison Reform and Unwed Professional Woman in a Rushed and Toned-Down Sinclair Lewis Adaptation," *Toxic Universe*, toxicuniverse.com (no longer active); Gehring, *Irene Dunne*, 51.

39 The practice was fairly common among more affluent American women when Cuba and the United States signed a treaty to add abortion to the list of crimes for which extradition could be granted. In 1938, however, Cuba's Social Defense Code would eventually strictly regulate abortion, limiting access to cases where the woman's

health was at risk or for eugenic motivations when the foetus showed signs of severe physical malformation. To terminate a pregnancy, a woman required the approbation of two doctors. Havana-based physicians generally charged a fee for such a medical opinion. Sergio Diaz-Briquets, Kenneth H. Hill, and Paula E. Hollerbach, "Fertility Determinants in Cuba," *International Family Planning Perspectives* 10 (1984): 12–20. Consequently, working-class Cuban women were often denied access to safe and medically supervised abortions.

40 Sources estimate between eight hundred thousand and three million abortions were being done annually in the United States in the early 1930s. Abraham Jacob Rongy, *Abortion: Legal or Illegal* (New York: Vanguard Press, 1933), 89, 102. Research conducted between 1931 and 1933 with 1,328 New York women found that 30 percent of the "pregnancy wastage" was attributable to illegal abortions, which were either self-induced or through an abortion provider. Science News, "Abortions Common among Women Using Birth Control," *The Science Newsletter* 31, no. 842 (1937): 349.

41 New York Penal Law § 80 (1909). In 1970, New York State passed legislation to decriminalize abortion, with some restrictions. There remain two offences targeting providers (New York Penal Law § 125.40 [1965]): abortion in the second degree when the procedure is performed for a reason other than to preserve the pregnant woman's life and abortion when the woman is over twenty-four-weeks pregnant.

42 Abortion came under attack in political, religious, and legal discourses that linked women's reproductive bodies – white women's, in particular – to nation building after the Civil War. In 1821, Connecticut became the first state to ban the use of poison to induce miscarriage, and other states followed. The national campaign to ban abortions led by the American Medical Association, with the support of Christian organizations, culminated with the Suppression of Trade in, and Circulation of, Obscene Literature and Articles of Immoral Use Act, 1873, 17 Stat. 599, being passed by the US Congress in 1873. It criminalized the possession, publication, and distribution of obscene materials, which included information on abortifacient medications or devices, on pain of a prison sentence of five years or a two thousand dollar fine.

43 *Hunter v Wheate,* 289 F 604 (Ct App DC 1923); *Nash v Meyer,* 31 P (2d) 273 (Sup Ct Idaho 1934); *Bowlan v Lunsford,* 54 P (2d) 666 (Sup Ct Okla 1936).

44 *State v Carey,* 76 Conn 342, 352 (Sup Ct Err Conn 1904).

45 This exception was also recognized in common law. The necessity of the procedure to save the pregnant woman's life was a requirement, and a good faith presumption was insufficient to shield an abortion provider from criminal liability. *State v Rudman,* 136 A 817 (Sup Jud Ct Me 1927). Colorado, the District of Columbia, Mississippi, and New Mexico had broader exceptions that ranged from the prevention of "serious and permanent bodily injury" to the pregnant woman to any abortion performed on the advice of a physician. Thomas E. Harris, "A Functional Study of Existing Abortion Laws," *Columbia Law Review* 35, no. 1 (1935): 90, n. 11.

46 Four other states did not include a medical necessity exception (California, Connecticut, Indiana, and Minnesota), and about one-third of states also criminalized women who self-induced abortions. Early decisions reveal courts inviting their legislators to criminalize women in this way because "if the good of society requires that the evil should be suppressed by penal infliction, it is far better that it should be done

by legislative enactment than [by] the courts." *State v Cooper,* 22 NJL 52 (Sup Ct NJ 1849).

47 New York Penal Law § 295 (1884): "A pregnant woman, who takes any medicine, drug, or substance, or uses or submits to the use of any instrument or other means, with intent thereby to produce her own miscarriage, unless the same is necessary to preserve her life, or that of the child whereof she is pregnant, is punishable by imprisonment for not less than one year, nor more than four years."

48 *Commonwealth v Weible,* 45 Pa Sup Ct 207 (1910). The indictment was overturned on appeal because statutory and common law provided that a woman could not be convicted of "committing an abortion upon herself." One judge dissented and would have upheld the conviction. See also *Crissman v State,* 245 SW 438 (Ct Crim App Tex 1922). Similarly, in *Trent v State,* 73 So 834 (Ct App Ala 1916), the Alabama District Court wrote that, under that state's amended statute, a woman who knowingly consents to an abortion ought to "be guilty of aiding or abetting, and indictable as a principal."

49 Harris, "Functional Study," 91. The criminalization of abortion endured for decades in New York. In *People v Blank,* 29 NE (2d) 73 (Ct App NY 1940) and *People v Candib,* 129 NYS (2d) 176 (Co Ct NY 1954), women were charged with the "killing of a child in attempt of miscarriage." As recently as 2011, women in New York State were being charged with "attempting to abort" a foetus when the abortion was unsuccessful. Kim Carollo, "Woman Charged with Self-Abortion after Fetus Found in Trash," *ABC News,* December 2, 2011, http://abcnews.go.com/blogs/health/2011/12/02/woman-charged-with-self-abortion-after-fetus-found-in-trash.

50 *State v Carey,* 351. Similarly, in *Moore v State,* 40 SW 287 (Ct Crim App Tex 1897), the court found that "our law does not hold the woman, whether she consents or not, a principle" and that she is consequently "guilty of no crime known to the law." See also *Dunn v People,* 29 NY 523 (Ct App NY 1864); *State v Cragun,* 38 P (2d) 1071 (Sup Ct Utah 1934); *Martin v Morris,* 42 SW (2d) 207 (Sup Ct Tenn 1931).

51 *State v Carey,* 351. It is estimated that in the early 1930s midwives performed approximately 20 percent of illegal abortions and that women self-induced in approximately 5 percent of cases. Regine K. Stix, "A Study of Pregnancy Waste," *Milbank Memorial Fund Quarterly* 13, no. 4 (1935): 360. According to Leslie Reagan, between 1890 and 1930, there was organized repression (by the primarily male obstetrics specialists) against the (primarily female) practitioners and midwives who had until the 1850s offered the procedure legally in the pre-quickening phase. Leslie Reagan, *When Abortion Was a Crime: Women, Medicine, and Law in the United States, 1867–1973* (Berkeley: University of California Press, 1997).

52 Thompson's Shannon's Code of Tennessee, § 6464 (1918), provided for imprisonment in the penitentiary "not less than one nor more than three years," whereas New York's act provides for manslaughter in the case of a completed abortion (New York Penal Law § 80 1909), and Kentucky's penalties range from two to twenty years (Kentucky Statutes § 1219(a)(2) [Carroll, 1930]). See, for instance, *Smartt et al. v State,* 80 SW 586 (Sup Ct Tenn 1904) (where the abortion provider was sentenced to eleven months in jail). Statutory ranges varied from state to state. The anti-abortion statutes in the District of Columbia, Kansas, Kentucky, and Massachusetts explicitly bar women from being accomplices. In most states, a woman's consent was not a defence. *State v Carey.*

53 *Commonwealth v Bricker,* 74 Pa Super 234 (1920).

54 *State v Shaft,* 81 SE 932 (Sup Ct NC 1914).

55 Stix, "Study of Pregnancy Waste"; Dorothy G. Wiehl, "A Summary of Data on Reported Incidence of Abortion," *Milbank Memorial Fund Quarterly* 16, no. 1 (1938): 80–88.

56 Irvine Loudon, "Abortion," in *Death in Childbirth: An International Study of Maternal Care and Maternal Mortality 1800–1950* (Oxford: Oxford Scholarship Online, 2011), 26.

57 Loudon, "Abortion," 26. B.B. Tolnai, "The Abortion Racket," *Forum and Century* 94, no. 3 (1935): 176–81. Indeed, between 1925 and 1934, the United States had one of the highest maternal mortality rates in the world in large part because of the criminalization of abortion. Loudon, "Abortion," 26.

58 Reagan, *When Abortion Was a Crime,* 76, 113, 126.

59 Between 1892 and 1932, there were forty indictments in Alabama but only five convictions; Minnesota saw one hundred prosecutions between 1911 and 1930 with thirty-one convictions. Harris, "Functional Study," 88. See, for instance, *People v Rongetti,* 163 NE 373 (Sup Ct Ill 1928) (where a physician's guilty verdict was overturned).

60 New York's Board of Medical Examiners reviewed forty-one cases of criminal abortion between 1928 and 1934. Of these, thirty-six were dismissed, four physicians had their licences revoked, and one had their licence suspended. Harris, "Functional Study," 90, n18.

61 In Ohio, for instance, women who launched civil litigation for malpractice could be threatened to be added as a "party to the crime." *Glovka v Fortun,* 163 NE 309 (8th Dist Ct App Ohio 1928).

62 *Hunter v Wheate,* 289 F 604 (Ct App DC 1923); *Nash v Meyer,* 31 P (2d) 273 (Sup Ct Idaho 1934); *Goldnamer v O'Brien,* 33 SW 831 (Ct App Ky 1896); *Szadiwicz v Cantor,* 154 NE 251 (Sup Jud Ct Mass 1926); *Larocque v Conheim,* 87 NYS 625 (Sup Ct NY 1904); *Androws v Coulter,* 1 P (2d) 320 (Sup Ct Wash 1931). A few exceptions can be found. In one case – *Martin v Morris* – an abortion provider who used unsterilized instruments was held liable for damages. In another – *Androws v Coulter* – a doctor abandoned his patient after the procedure and was found to have no right to do so, regardless of whether the procedure was illegal. In another case, the "seducer" of a seventeen-year-old girl was found guilty of fraud and deceit for convincing a minor to have an abortion; he had persuaded her that she would die if she brought her pregnancy to term. *Gunder v Tibbits,* 55 NE 762 (Sup Ct Ind 1899). The abortion provider in that same case was found to have done so to help the "seducer" rather than to save the young woman's life; consequently, he was also liable for damages. See also *Milliken v Heddesheimer,* 144 NE (2d) 264 (Sup Ct Ohio 1924). Finally, in cases where consent was obtained fraudulently, most notably when the victim was a minor, there could be recovery in damages. *Hancock v Hullett,* 82 So 522 (Sup Ct Ala 1919).

63 In *Bowlan v Lunsford,* para. 4, a woman was found to be *in pari delicto* (in equal fault) with her sexual partner and was stopped from recovering damages from him for injuries sustained as a result of a botched abortion. See also *Androws v Coulter.* See Gail Hollister's thought-provoking work on judicial bias in claims by women

who sustained injuries during abortions. Gail Hollister, "Tort Suits for Injuries Sustained during Illegal Abortions: The Effects of Judicial Bias," *Villanova Law Review* 45, no. 387 (2000): 387–462.

64 *Goldnamer v O'Brien.*

65 *Bowlan v Lunsford,* para. 2.

66 *Androws v Coulter.*

67 *Larocque v Conheim* (where there was no remedy for wrongful death because the woman consented to the procedure).

68 *McCreighton v American Catholic Union,* 71 Pa Super 332 (1919); *Wells v New England Mutual Life Ins. Co.,* 43 A 126 (Sup Ct Pa 1899).

69 Diana Fuss, *Identification Papers: Readings on Psychoanalysis, Sexuality, and Culture* (New York: Routledge, 1995), 25.

70 Motion Picture Production Code, Part III(4) "Sex" (as amended in December 1956).

71 *Men in White* (1934), based on Sidney Kingsley's play of the same name, which sought to highlight the dangers inherent in the criminalization of abortion, was significantly toned down and included no reference to Barbara's decision to illegally terminate her pregnancy. Sidney Kingsley and Waldemar Young, *Men in White* (New York: Twentieth Century Drama, 1934). Alfred Hitchcock in his film *Rebecca* (1940) also cut the abortion scene from his pictorial translation of Daphne Du Maurier's novel of the same name without protest. Daphne Du Maurier, *Rebecca* (London: Victor Gollancz, 1938). Geoffrey M. Shurlock, who was then director of the Production Code Administration, was unequivocal that the "[Production] Code forbids the use of the word abortion." In a letter to Producer Frank McCarthy regarding *Peyton Place* (1957), he insisted that the script include the word "miscarriage, so that there will be no mistake about what the Doctor is doing." Letter from Geoffrey M. Shurlock to Frank McCarthy, January 28, 1957, *Peyton Place,* Production Code Administration Archives, Academy of Motion Pictures Arts and Sciences Library, Los Angeles, California.

72 For an example of the former, see *Detective Story* (1951); of the latter, see *Blue Denim* (1959). This latter film differs from the original play, written by James Leo Herlihy and William Noble, in which the same character has an abortion and goes on to lead a fulfilling life. James Leo Herlihy and William Noble, *Blue Denim* (New York: Random House, 1958).

73 Letter from James Wingate to Merian Cooper, May 27, 1933, *Ann Vickers,* Production Code Administration Archives, Academy of Motion Pictures Arts and Sciences Library, Los Angeles, California.

74 Letter from Merian Cooper to James Wingate, May 11, 1933, *Ann Vickers,* Production Code Administration Archives, Academy of Motion Pictures Arts and Sciences Library, Los Angeles, California.

75 Letter from James Wingate to Merian Cooper, June 3, 1933, *Ann Vickers,* Production Code Administration Archives, Academy of Motion Pictures Arts and Sciences Library, Los Angeles, California.

76 Letter from James Wingate to Merian Cooper, June 22, 1933, *Ann Vickers,* Production Code Administration Archives, Academy of Motion Pictures Arts and Sciences Library, Los Angeles, California.

77 Letter from Benjamin Kahane to William Hays, June 10, 1933, *Ann Vickers,* Production Code Administration Archives, Academy of Motion Pictures Arts and Sciences

Library, Los Angeles, California. An earlier scene that would have had Lafe and Ann in bed together was also removed from the script. In addition to the changes made regarding Ann's romantic unions, RKO was asked to remove several "excessively brutal" scenes from the prison sequences, which they did. They also eliminated all of the subtle lesbian cues from the prison scenes. Breen to Wingate, May 5, 1933.

78 Letter from Benjamin Kahane to William Hays, June 10, 1933.

79 Letter from Benjamin Kahane to William Hays, June 27, 1933, *Ann Vickers,* Production Code Administration Archives, Academy of Motion Pictures Arts and Sciences Library, Los Angeles, California.

80 Letter from William Hays to Benjamin Kahane, July 5, 1933, *Ann Vickers,* Production Code Administration Archives, Academy of Motion Pictures Arts and Sciences Library, Los Angeles, California.

81 Ann and Barney, until then, will presumably present themselves as husband and wife. In actuality, under New York law, their union would be void until Barney's previous marriage was annulled or dissolved, which seems unlikely given that adultery was not an acceptable cause for annulment or dissolution. New York Dom. Rel. Law § 6, art. 2 (2017). If they went through with a marriage, they could be vulnerable under laws against bigamy or polygamy; the "custom or practice, as in a group, of having a plurality of wives or husbands at the same time" had been a crime in New York since 1881 and remains a Class E felony (non-violent) today. New York Penal Law § 255.15 (2008).

82 "Review of Ann Vickers," *Variety,* October 1933, http://archive.org/details/variety112-1933-10.

83 David Nusair, "Three Dramas with Irene Dunne," *Reel Film Reviews,* January 1, 2007, http://www.reelfilm.com/.

84 Levine, "The Folklore of Industrial Society," 1391.

85 Hascal R. Brill, "§ 1056: Living or Cohabiting in Adultery or Fornication," in *Cyclopedia of Criminal Law,* vol. 2 (Chicago: Callaghan and Company, 1922–23), 1644–67.

86 Cahill's Consolidated Laws of New York, being the consolidated laws of 1909, as amended to July 1, 1930, ch. 41, art. 8, para. 100 (1930). Adultery remains a Class B misdemeanour in New York State today under paragraph 255.17, punishable by ninety days in jail and/or a five hundred dollar fine. New York Penal Law § 255.17 (2017). Adultery remained grounds for divorce until 2010, when the state adopted a "no fault" regime. See generally Deborah Rhode, "Adultery: An Agenda for Legal Reform," *Stanford Journal of Civil Rights and Civil Liberties* 179 (2015): 179–206.

87 Specifically, the regulation of adultery sought to shield married men from having to provide for another man's child. It was defined as sexual intercourse between a married man and a married woman. Sex between a married man and a single woman was fornication rather than adultery. Fornication was only illegal in common law when it amounted to nuisance (an outward and publicly known act of indecency). Winfield B. Ohlson, "Adultery: A Review," *Boston University Law Review* 17, no. 2 (1937): 328–68. The tort of "criminal conversation" within a martial relationship, which protected married men's property rights in their spouses and their services, has been abolished in most states. Stuart M. Speiser, Charles F. Krause, and Alfred W. Gans, *American Law of Torts,* vol. 7 (Rochester, NY: Lawyers Co-Operative Publishing, 2017), para. 22:7

88 Ohlson, "Adultery," 328.
89 Ohlson, "Adultery," 241.
90 In Maryland, adultery is currently subject to a ten dollar fine. Maryland Code Ann., Criminal Law § 10-501 (2017). See also Alabama, Delaware, Missouri, Texas, and Vermont. See generally Brill, "§ 1056."
91 *State v Avery,* 7 Conn 266 (Sup Ct Err Conn 1828) (referring to Connecticut's laws). Brill, "§ 1056."

Chapter 3: The Unattainability of Reform

1 *Caged!* (1950). Dir. John Cromwell; Screenplay: Virginia Kellogg and Bernard C. Schoenfeld. Warner Bros. (NR). This chapter relies heavily on an earlier version of this article. Suzanne Bouclin, "Women in Prison Movies as Feminist Jurisprudence," *Canadian Journal of Women and the Law* 21, no. 1 (2009): 19–34.
2 Intersectionality is often deployed in feminist research and activism to better understand how our multiple subject positions shift according to social, cultural, juridical, political, and aesthetic contexts and are thus embedded in intersecting systems of power and domination. In law, the intersectional method has been attributed to Kimberlé Williams Crenshaw, "Mapping the Margins: Intersectionality, Identity Politics, and Violence against Women of Colour," *Stanford Law Review* 43, no. 6 (1991): 1241–99; see also Mari Matsuda, "When the First Quail Calls: Multiple Consciousness as Jurisprudential Method," *Women's Rights Law Reporter* 11, no. 7 (1989): 7–10; Patricia Hill-Collins, "Piecing Together a Genealogical Puzzle: Intersectionality and American Pragmatism," *European Journal of Pragmatism and American Philosophy* 3, no. 2 (2011): 88–112. On how the myth of female sisterhood masks and perpetuates racism, see Angela Y. Davis, *Women, Culture, and Politics* (New York : Vintage Books, 1990); heterosexism, see Adrienne Rich, *Compulsory Heterosexuality and the Lesbian Existence* (London: Only Women Press, 1981); ableism, see Nasa Begum, "Disabled Women and the Feminist Agenda," *Feminist Review* 40 (1992): 70–84. On how it exhibits condescension to women in the global South, see Chandra Talpade Mohanty, "Under Western Eyes: Feminist Scholarship and Colonial Discourses," in *Dangerous Liaisons: Gender, Nation, and Postcolonial Perspectives,* ed. Ann McClintock et al., 255–77 (Minneapolis: University of Minnesota Press, 1997); on how it has been complicit with colonial and imperial oppression, see Patricia Monture, *Thunder in My Soul: A Mohawk Woman Speaks* (Toronto: Fernwood Books, 2003). For an attempt to apply the intersectional legal method to a close reading of a film, see Suzanne Bouclin, "Women's Suffrage: A Cinematic Study," *Revue LISA/LISA e-journal* 12, no. 7 (2014): 39, https://lisa.revues.org/6918.
3 Film scholar Andre Bazin reviewed *Caged!* shortly after its release. Andre Bazin, "Notes sur d'autres films: Femmes en cages," *Cahiers de Cinema* (July 1953), reprinted and translated in Andre Bazin, *Bazin on Global Cinema,* trans. and ed. Bert Cardullo (Austin: University of Texas Press, 2014). Compare "Bleak Picture of Women's Prison," *New York Times,* May 20, 1950. Eleanor Parker, Hope Emerson, and Virginia Kellogg received Academy Award nominations in 1950 for best actress, supporting actress, and screenplay, respectively.
4 Kellogg's methodology was dangerous and illegal, as she points out: "I had no more than the governor's permission to visit the prison as an observer; it was illegal for

anyone to be committed without due process of law; but this honest and courageous official wanted me to see the corruption and brutality at firsthand. Next day I was smuggled inside the walls of the state pen." Virginia Kellogg, "Inside Women's Prison," *Collier's Weekly,* June 3, 1950, 14–16. In collaboration with Bernard Schoenfeld, she transformed this story into the screenplay produced by Warner Brothers. *Caged! Shooting Script* (Los Angeles: Alexander Street Press, 1990), https://search.alexanderstreet.com/view/work/bibliographic_entity%7Cbibliographic_details%7C3049861.

5 For quantitative data on the sentences handed down to women housed in Framingham, see Mary Jean Bowman, "Causes of Arrest of Women Committed to the Massachusetts State Reformatory," *Journal of Criminal Law and Criminology 30* (May 1939): 77. The public hearings against Dr. Miriam Van Waters were initiated in the late 1940s by Commissioner Robert McDowell and Deputy Commissioner Frank Dwyer. "Report of the Special Commission Established to Make an Investigation of the Conduct of the Reformatory for Women at Framingham" (Senate Bill 0521, 1949). DSpace, State Library of Massachusetts, https://archives.lib.state.ma.us/handle/2452/237857.

6 Estelle Freedman's biography on Van Waters includes a discussion of the hearings and correspondence between her subject and Warner Brothers concerning the *Caged!* screenplay. Estelle Freedman, *Maternal Justice: Miriam Van Waters and the Female Reform Tradition* (Chicago: University of Chicago Press, 1996), 316, 329, 332. For a thoughtful account of Van Waters's radical penology, see Joan Sakalas, *Toward Fellow Sinners: An Ethical and Historical Exploration of the Penology of Miriam Van Waters* (Master's thesis, Episcopal Divinity School, 1993).

7 "Innocents thrown in with female bully-boys!!!!" Tagline from *House of Women* (1962), an inferior reboot of *Caged!* (1950).

8 On the historical regulation of lesbianism in prison and especially how women racialized as Black were more closely scrutinized and coded as natural and menacing "butches" because of racist assumptions about Black women's sexuality, see Estelle Freedman, "The Prison Lesbian: Race, Class and the Free Construction of the Aggressive Female Homosexual 1915–1965," *Feminist Studies* 22 (1996): 397–423; see also Teresa Severance, "The Prison Lesbian Revisited," *Journal of Gay and Lesbian Social Sciences* 17, no. 3 (2004): 39–57; Shoshana Pollack, "Lesbian Relationships," in *Encyclopedia of Prisons and Correctional Facilities,* ed. Mary Bosworth (London: Sage Publications, 2005). For a legal interpretation, see Ruthann Robson, *Lesbian (Out)law: Survival under the Rule of Law* (Ithaca, NY: Firebrand Books, 1992). The groundbreaking queer study of Hollywood narrative also mentions the film *The Celluloid Closet* (1995); see also Eve Kosofsky Sedgwick, *Epistemologies of the Closet* (Berkeley: University of California Press, 1990); Suzanna Danuta Walters, *All the Rage: The Story of Gay Visibility in America* (Chicago: University of Chicago Press, 2003).

9 There are a few excellent discussions of the queer elements of *Caged!:* Judith Mayne, "Caged and Framed: The Women-in-Prison Film," in *Framed: Lesbians, Feminists, and Media Culture* (Minneapolis: University of Minnesota Press, 2000), 115–48; Patricia White, "Supporting Character: The Queen Career of Agnes Moorehead," in *Out in Culture: Gay, Lesbian, and Queer Essays on Popular Culture,* ed. C. Creekmur and A. Doty (Durham, NC: Duke University Press, 1995), 91–111; Richard Barrios,

Screened Out: Playing Gay in Hollywood from Edison to Stonewall (New York: Routledge, 2003).

10 Vito Russo, *The Celluloid Closet: Homosexuality in the Movies* (New York: Harper and Row, 1981).

11 The brutal lesbian matron became iconic with the character of Alabama (Pam Grier) in *Women in Cages* (1971) and then later in a new configuration with the Ilsa series: *Ilsa: She Wolf of the SS* (1975); *Harem Keeper of the Oil Sheiks* (1976); *Wanda, the Wicked Warden* (1977).

12 White, "Supporting Character."

13 Letter from Joseph Breen to Jack Leonard Warner, June 10, 1949, *Caged!*, Production Code Administration Archives, Academy of Motion Pictures Arts and Sciences Library, Los Angeles, California.

14 "Girls in Prison," *Monthly Film Bulletin* no. 23(264) (January 1, 1956): 116.

15 Occasionally, however, the romantic union will be between staff members. *So Young, So Bad* (1950), for instance, centres on the budding romance between a female social worker and a male warden. The more recent dramatic film *Within These Walls* (2001) explores the non-romantic relationship between two women, Joan Thomas (Ellen Burstyn) and Sister Pauline (Laura Dern). Similarly, *Four Minutes* (2006) is actually about the relationship between Jenny (Hannah Herzprung) and Traude (Monica Bleibtreu), who bond through a love of music.

16 In 1830, New York established the first women's ward in a male prison. In 1874, Indiana was the first state to create a separate women's reformatory, run by and for women. Feminist reformers of the mid-1800s tended to be married, white, devout, have children, and were often volunteers. Their focus was on protecting women's virtues and, correspondingly, Victorian standards of moral refinement, propriety, and chastity. The next wave of reformers (in 1900–30) included educated women who participated in the movement in their capacity as wardens, social workers, psychiatrists, and educators. However, as Estelle Freedman has explained, it is reductive to construct two separate and homogenous waves of reformers when women actually "entered prison reform during different decades, during different times in their life cycles, and at different stages of the movement." Estelle Freedman, *Their Sisters' Keepers: Women's Prison Reform in America, 1830–1930* (Ann Arbor: University of Michigan Press, 1981), 15–17. The following discussion borrows from Freedman's research, which remains the most thorough and historically grounded examination of early feminist prison reform.

17 Freedman, *Their Sisters' Keepers.*

18 Paradoxically, *Caged!* was released in 1950 at the height of the backlash against women who had entered into the workforce and the concerted drive to return them to the home.

19 A passing reference from one of the inmates ("who is this Pearl Harbor anyway? Is she an inmate here?") indicates that Marie entered prison in 1941; she will be released a year later.

20 While Nevada only criminalized exploitation, Wyoming regulated most aspects of commercialized sex. See Walter C. Reckless, "The Impact of War on Crime, Delinquency, and Prostitution," *American Journal of Sociology* 48, no. 3 (1942): 378 (on increased rates of prostitution near military and naval bases); Eleanor Shenehon,

"The Prevention and Repression of Prostitution in North America," *International Review of Criminal Policy* 15 (1958): 15–27 (on the regulatory role of vice squads); Gladys Bowman, *Social Factors Related to the Violation of the May Act as Revealed in the Selected Case Records of Women Committed to a Federal Reformatory* (Master's thesis, University of Southern California, June 1947) (for statistics on the number of women arrested under the May Act and state regulations).

21 Lois McNay, *Gender and Agency: Reconfiguring the Subject in Feminist and Social Theory* (Cambridge: Polity Press, 2000), 16.

22 I borrow the following taxonomy of themes and characters in films about prostitution from Russell Campbell, *Marked Women: Prostitutes and Prostitution in the Cinema* (Madison: University of Wisconsin Press, 2006). According to Campbell, the following films circulate the street angel archetype: *Street Angel* (1937), *Dédée d'Anvers* (1948), *Women without Hope* (1954), *Tainted Flowers* (1958); the gold digger archetype: *Fifty Fathoms Deep* (1931), *Woman without a Soul* (1945), *Song on a Rainy Night* (1950); the gigolette archetype: *Macadam/Back Streets of Paris* (1946), *Casque d'Or* (1952); the femme fatale archetype: *Pandora's Box* (1929), *Eva/Eve* (1962); the avenger archetype: *Wages of Sin* (1914), *Women of the Night* (1948), *Jeanne Dielman, 23 Quai du Commerce, 1080 Bruxelles* (1976). However, some feminist filmmakers have endeavoured to produce more complex depictions of women who engage in transactional sex. See *Streetwalkin'* (1985); *Working Girls* (1987); *Purge* (1994). For a rare and layered depiction of women as sex consumers, see *Miss Sloane* (2016); for a thoughtful depiction of transgender women's experiences as sellers, see *Tangerine* (2015).

23 Sex workers are stock characters in the women-in-prison (WIP) genre, and from Jeta "Smoochie" Kovsky (Jan Sterling) in *Caged!* to Lee Daniels (Pam Grier) in *Black Mama White Mama* (1973), they are most often depicted as witty and streetwise. This is the case for Maude Eburne's role as Aunt Maggie, a well-liked madam in *Ladies They Talk About* (1933), who is in for running what she calls "a beauty parlor" that was pretty successful until "a detective sergeant came to [her] place to get a manicure from one of [her] girls." Occasionally, audiences are offered a small window into how girls and women enter the transactional sex trade. In *Born Innocent* (1974), Josie (Tina Andrews), a young Black woman, was sold into a prostitution ring by her mother. Similarly, seventeen-year-old Amanda Sue Bradley (Juliette Lewis) in *Too Young to Die?* (1990) was forced to engage in sex work to escape her violent stepfather. In *Orange Is the New Black* (2013–19), Tricia Miller (Madeline Brewer), who is street involved because she left an incestuous house as a teenager and is consequently dealing with addiction, adds multiple layers of complexity to the typical figure of the "common prostitute" found throughout the WIP genre.

24 I explore both "sides" of the feminist conversation and conclude that, regardless of ideological viewpoint, decision-making around the regulation of commercialized sex is largely done without the input of those most affected by the criminal law: sex workers. Moreover, I find that racialized sex workers experience violence more frequently than do their white counterparts, especially if they are street entrenched. Suzanne Bouclin, "Regulating Sex Work in Canada," *Public Law* 3 (July 2012): 387–95. For a strong articulation of the sex worker rights' perspective, see Chris Bruckert et al., *Sex Work: Rethinking the Job, Respecting the Workers* (Vancouver: UBC Press, 2013).

25 Rebecca Johnson deconstructs and problematizes how choice discourse is deployed in similar ways in the context of motherhood in *Taxing Choices: The Intersection of Class, Gender, Parenthood, and the Law* (Vancouver: UBC Press, 2002), 124.

26 Orit Kamir, *Framed: Women in Law and Film* (Durham, NC: Duke University Press, 2006), 33.

27 The mainstream restorative justice initiatives that are most often adopted in the criminal justice system "regularly acknowledge the influence that Aboriginal concepts of justice have had on their development." Jonathan Rudin, "Aboriginal Justice and Restorative Justice," in *New Directions in Restorative Justice: Issues, Practice, Evaluation,* ed. Elizabeth Elliott and Robert M. Gordon (Cullompton, UK: Willan Publishing, 2005), 89–114; see also Josephine Savarese, "Gladue Was a Woman: The Importance of Gender in Restorative-Based Sentencing," in Elliott and Gordon, *New Directions in Restorative Justice,* 134–50; Jeffery G. Hewitt, "Indigenous Restorative Justice: Approaches, Meaning and Possibility," *University of New Brunswick Law Journal* 67 (2016): 313–35; Gerry Johnstone, *Restorative Justice: Ideas, Values, Debates,* 2nd ed. (London: Routledge, 2011); Kathleen Daly and Julie Stubbs, "Feminist Engagement with Restorative Justice," *Theoretical Criminology* 10, no. 1 (2006): 9–28.

28 Karlene Faith, "Transformative Justice versus Re-entrenched Correctionalism: The Canadian Experience," in *Harsh Punishment: International Experiences of Women's Imprisonment,* ed. Sandy Cook and Susanne Davies (Boston: Northeastern University Press, 1999), 99.

29 Sigmund Freud, *The Interpretation of Dreams* (London: Allen and Unwin, 1913), 202, cited in Diana Fuss, *Identification Papers: Readings on Psychoanalysis, Sexuality, and Culture* (New York: Routledge, 1995).

Chapter 4: Recuperating Exploitation

1 This rating system remains in place today; however, "X"-rated films have been re-categorized as "NC-17" (not suitable for audiences under the age of seventeen).

2 While the exploitation genre has always aligned itself with independent cinema, film scholar Annette Insdorf disagrees, arguing that independent features are by their nature non-commercial. Annette Insdorf, "Ordinary People, European-Style: Or How to Spot an Independent Feature," in *Contemporary American Independent Film: From the Margins to the Mainstream,* ed. Christine Holmlund and Justin Wyatt (London: Routledge, 2004), 27–33; see also Chris Holmlund, "Introduction to 'Critical Formulations,'" in Holmlund and Wyatt, *Contemporary American Independent Film,* 23–26.

3 The term "Blaxploitation" was coined by Junius Griffen, president of the National Association for the Advancement of Colored People (Beverly Hills chapter), as a derogatory term because he believed these films circulated damaging stereotypes about Black people. It has been reappropriated by film scholars. For a theoretical discussion of exploitation films, see generally Pam Cook, "Film Culture: 'Exploitation' Films and Feminism," *Screen* 17, no. 2 (July 1976): 122–27; Yvonne Tasker, *Spectacular Bodies: Gender, Genre, and the Action Cinema* (London: Routledge, 1993);

Annette Kuhn and Guy Westwell, *A Dictionary of Film Studies* (Oxford: Oxford University Press, 2012) (who provide a definition of "exploitation film"); Eric Schaefer, *"Bold! Daring! Shocking! True!": A History of Exploitation Films, 1919–1959* (Durham, NC: Duke University Press, 1999); see also Gerald Martinez, Diana Martinez, and Andres Chavez, *What It Is ... What It Was! The Black Exploitation of the 70s in Words and Pictures* (New York: Hyperion Miramaz Books, 1998).

4 Jonathan Kaplan paraphrasing Roger Corman and cited in Jim Hillier and Aaron Lipstadt, *Roger Corman's New World* (London: British Film Institute, 1981). Stephanie Rothman described her experience working with Corman as follows: "I stopped working for Roger Corman because he did not pay me a living wage. In his opinion ... he was giving [directors] the chance to have their work seen widely, which might lead to more and better paid work, maybe even with a major studio. And for a very few, it did. For most, it did not." Stephanie Rothman, interview by Henry Jenkins, *Confessions of an Aca-Fan,* October 16, 2007, http://henryjenkins.org/blog/2007/10/exploiting_feminism_an_intervi.html.

5 Mary Murphy, "Pam's Stranglehold on Violent Roles," *Los Angeles Times,* January 4, 1976.

6 *Caged Heat* (1974). Dir. and Screenplay: Jonathan Demme. New World Pictures (R).

7 My decision to include *Terminal Island* as a women-in-prison (WIP) movie is because it is set in what remains a correctional institution for men and the female protagonists are introduced through their mug shots and a brief description of their crime. Stephanie Rothman's first film, *The Student Nurses* (1970), advocated for access to free and safe abortions and explored racial tensions and privilege. While not tackling women in prison, a remarkable number of women directed exploitation flicks and explored feminist themes through their films at the peak of the genre's popularity. See, for instance, *Bad Girls Go to Hell* (1965); *Gator Bait* (1973); *Bury Me an Angel* (1972).

8 Stephanie Rothman, "The Cult of Stephanie Rothman," interview by Colleen Kelsey, *Interview Magazine,* March 7, 2016, https://www.interviewmagazine.com/film/stephanie-rothman# [emphasis mine].

9 Danny Peary, *Cult Midnight Movies: Discover the 37 Best Weird, Sleazy, Sexy and Crazy Good Cinema Classics* (New York: Workman Publishing, 2014). For a recent iteration of the classic exploitation WIP movie without the campiness, see *Jailbait* (2014).

10 Walter O'Hara, "The Changing Face of the WIP Film," *Videooze,* Winter 1991, 20.

11 The Australian television program *Prisoner* (1979–86), which was called *Prisoner: Cell Block H* in the United States and *Caged Women* in Canada, as well as its reboot *Wentworth* (2013–present), is a counter-weight to this assessment. Similarly, while *Women in Chains* (1972) drew on several of the exploitation cycle's traditions, minus the graphic violence and nudity, it was made for television and told from the perspective of an undercover parole officer, and it feels more like a kitschy endeavour than a serious exposé of prison conditions.

12 O'Hara, "Changing Face," 20.

13 A plain language search in April 2019 on the *Million Short* search engine (https://millionshort.com/) without any limitations showed there are currently 14,400 websites devoted to "women in prison films," 17,000 results for "women in prison movies," and 729,010 for "*Orange Is the New Black*." I conducted a similar search at the

beginning of this project, doing a plain language search on Google© in 2007. That search retrieved 9,500 hits for "women in prison films" and 11,400 for "women in prison movies." A number of these websites are no longer available, but their content remains on file with the author. See "Bad Cinema Diary: Women in Prison," http://www.cathuria.com/bcd/bcWIP.htm; "Women in Prison," http://www.prisonflicks.com (site discontinued), quoted in Suzanne Bouclin, "Caging Women: Punishment, Judgment, Reform, and Resistance in Women in Prison Films" (Master's thesis, University of Manitoba, 2007), 62. Some commercial vendors such as Amazon© and more obscure websites such as Sinister Cinema© sell VHS, DVD, and Blu-ray media under the heading "Women-in-prison movies."

14 James Robert Parish, *Prison Pictures from Hollywood: Plots, Critiques, Casts, and Credits for 293 Theatrical and Made-for-Television Releases* (Jefferson, NC: McFarland and Company, 1991), 26.

15 Cited in Rikke Schubart, *Super Bitches and Action Babes: The Female Hero in Popular Cinema, 1970–2006* (Jefferson, NC: McFarland and Company, 2007), 76.

16 Jim Morton, "Women in Prison Films," in *Incredibly Strange Films*, ed. V. Vale, Andrea Juno, and Jim Morton (San Francisco: Re/Search Publications, 1986), 151.

17 Morton, "Women in Prison Films," 151.

18 Gary Morris, "Roger Corman's New World Pictures: Notes toward a Lexicon," *Bright Lights Film Journal* 27 (January 2000). https://brightlightsfilm.com/roger-cormans-new-world-pictures-notes-toward-lexicon/#.X20YYsJKiM9.

19 O'Hara, "Changing Face," 22.

20 Morris, "Roger Corman's New World Pictures."

21 Their work is inspired by Molly Haskell's *From Reverence to Rape* (which demonstrates how mainstream Hollywood films offer a limited range of roles for women, usually conventional or caricatured) and Laura Mulvey's "Visual Pleasure and Narrative Cinema" (which argues that films are intentionally constructed to generate and endorse a "masculine" gaze). Molly Haskell, *From Reverence to Rape: The Treatment of Women in the Movies*, 3rd ed. (Chicago: University of Chicago Press, 2016); Laura Mulvey, "Visual Pleasure and Narrative Cinema," *Screen* 16, no. 3 (1975): 6–18.

22 Cook, "Film Culture," 122–27; Carol J. Clover, *Men, Women, and Chain Saws: Gender in the Modern Horror Film* (Princeton, NJ: Princeton University Press, 1992).

23 Mulvey, "Visual Pleasure," 6.

24 Mulvey reworked her initial formulation to account for women's ways of knowing and experiencing pleasure through their viewing experience. Laura Mulvey, "Afterthoughts on 'Visual Pleasure and Narrative Cinema' Inspired by King Vidor's Duel in the Sun," in *Visual and Other Pleasures*, 2nd ed. (London: Macmillan, 1989). In other fields, feminists have challenged the gendered lens through which scholarship is developed and constituted, and they have offered an alternative epistemology to so-called "objective," "rational," and "universal" methods and methodologies. See especially Sandra G. Harding, *Whose Science, Whose Knowledge? Thinking from Women's Lives* (Ithaca, NY: Cornell University Press, 1991); see also Maggie Humm, *Feminism and Film* (Edinburgh: Edinburgh University Press, 1997).

25 Nicole Rafter, *Shots in the Mirror: Crime Films and Society* (New York: Oxford University Press, 2006), 172. This perspective is shared by Karlene Faith and Bruce Crowther. Karlene Faith, *Unruly Women: The Politics of Confinement and Resistance,*

rev. ed. (New York: Seven Stories Press, 2011). Crowther argues that it cannot be doubted that exploitation cycles "harm ... the image of women," whether or not they are "being made tongue-in-cheek." Bruce Crowther, *Captured on Film: The Prison Movie* (London: BT Batsford, 1989), 65.

26 Boris Lugosi, "Women in Cages (1971)," July 2, 2007, http://www.girlsgunsandghouls.com/womenincages.html.

27 Faith, *Unruly Women,* 258.

28 Cook, "Film Culture," 123.

29 Cook, "Film Culture," 124.

30 Cook, "Film Culture," 124–25.

31 See Judith Mayne, "Caged and Framed: The Women-in-Prison Film," in *Framed: Lesbians, Feminists, and Media Culture* (Minneapolis: University of Minnesota Press, 2000), 115–45 (race and sexual orientation are mutually constituted and mutually constitute the narrative elements of WIP movies). For instance, Vestron Video released *Chained Heat* (1983) and *Vendetta* (1986) on VHS in 1984 and 1986, respectively, and *Red Heat* (1985) in direct-to-video format in 1985. *Naked Cage* (1986) was a direct-to-video production by the Cannon Group, and *Stranger Inside* (2001) premiered on cable and was distributed through Home Box Office.

32 A number of WIP exploitation films can be accessed through various streaming technologies, and, of course, *OITNB* is an original Netflix series.

33 In the former, a woman has herself arrested intentionally so that she can be reunited with her partner who is serving a long sentence in a women's reformatory; the latter follows a similar storyline insofar as a young lesbian is intentionally locked up because she wants to find her mother, who is also a lesbian. Both films feature a number of normalized lesbian relationships.

34 Clover, *Men, Women, and Chain Saws.*

35 Mayne, "Caged and Framed," 117.

36 Mayne, "Caged and Framed," 115.

37 Clover, *Men, Women, and Chain Saws,* 64.

38 *The Concrete Jungle* (1982); *Chained Heat; Purgatory* (1988).

39 Regarding the feminist potential of the exploitation WIP cycle, see Beverley Zalcock and Jocelyn Robinson, "Inside Cell Block H: Hard Steel and Soft Soap," *Continuum* 9, no. 1 (1996): 95–96; Mayne, "Caged and Framed"; Didi Herman, "'Bad Girls Changed My Life': Homonormativity in a Women's Prison Drama," *Critical Studies in Media Communication* 20, no. 2 (2003): 141–59; Jenni Millibank, "It's about *This:* Lesbians, Prison, Desire," in *Law and Popular Culture,* vol. 7, ed. Michael D. Freeman (Oxford: Oxford University Press, 2005), 449–69; Henry Jenkins, "Exploiting Feminism in Stephanie Rothman's *Terminal Island,*" in *The Wow Climax: Tracing the Emotional Impact of Popular Culture* (New York: New York University Press, 2007), 102–24; Suzanna Danuta Walters, "Caged Heat: The (R)evolution of Women-in-Prison Films," in *Real Knockouts: Violent Women in the Movies,* ed. Martha McCaughey and Neal King (Austin: University of Texas Press, 2001), 106–23.

40 Compare *Ladies They Talk About* (1933) and *Condemned Women* (1938) with *Caged Heat* and *Vendetta* (1986).

41 This assessment may require some nuance. While, in *Caged Heat,* there are no long-standing rivalries or so-called tribal wars between the women, other films do

feature women having to first "transcend" race and class lines before advancing a unified resistance to oppression. Compare *Chained Heat* and, more recently, *OITNB*, which contain explicit race-based clans.

42 Matt Mulcahey, "Caged Heat," *EFilmCritic.com*, accessed August 12, 2020, http://efilmcritic.com/review.php?movie=7200&reviewer=255.

43 Gerald Peary, "Caged Heat," *Boston Phoenix*, December 7, 1999, accessed August 12, 2020, http://www.filmvault.com/filmvault/boston/c/cagedheat1.html.

44 Roger Corman has claimed that "the producer is more important than the director." He argues that, unlike in Europe where the director is seen as the film's auteur and the person who "comes up with the subject matter, works on the screenplay and supervises the cutting and casting as well as the directing ... most American pictures are not conceived by the director." In fact "the producer works with the writer, casts the film, and supervises the editing. The director comes in simply to direct."

45 Compare other films that feature a brutalizing lesbian guard (*Women in Cages* [1971]; *Caged Fury* [1990]) or a predatory lesbian cellmate (*The Big Doll House* [1971]). In other features, the genre has afforded lesbian characters more range and certainly some of its most campy dialogue. In *False Arrest* (1991), a "new fish" is told by the "queen bee," "I'm gonna treat you so good, I'm gonna wish I was you," and, in *Reform School Girls* (1986), Charlie (Wendy O. Williams) tells the protagonist: "I'm all the stud that you need."

46 Strictly speaking, melodrama is thought to be inimical to realism. However, as I argue throughout this book, one of the features that makes the social problem/melodrama cycle of WIP films so compelling is that the stories are often grounded in real facts and are shot on location in actual prisons. For instance, *The Story of Molly X* (1949) was shot at Tehachapi Institution for Women, and Dr. Norman Fenton, then assistant director of the State Department of Corrections, served as a technical adviser. *Caged Heat* was shot at Lincoln Heights Jail.

47 Quoted in Morris, "Roger Corman's New World Pictures."

48 The constitutional validity of racial segregation in male prison "reception centres" was upheld as recently as 2005 in California. *Johnson v California*, 543 US 499 (2005).

49 See Ruthann Robson, *Lesbian (Out)law: Survival under the Rule of Law* (Ithaca, NY: Firebrand Books, 1992).

50 *People v Lovercamp*, 118 Cal. Rptr 110 (1974). Two incarcerated women who had been given the alternative to "fuck or fight" had been provided no recourse to the administrative complaints procedure and, given that they committed no acts of violence during their attempted escape, were found to have behaved out of necessity. Later WIP films will capitalize on such discourse. In *Vendetta*, for instance, the innocent protagonist will be murdered by a lesbian for refusing her advances.

51 Orit Kamir, *Framed: Women in Law and Film* (Durham, NC: Duke University Press, 2006), 27.

52 Regarding the regulation of lesbians during the progressive prison reform movements, see Margaret Otis, "A Perversion Not Commonly Noted," *Journal of Abnormal Psychology* 8, no. 2 (1913): 113; Estelle Freedman, "The Prison Lesbian: Race, Class, and the Construction of the Aggressive Female Homosexual, 1915–1965," *Feminist Studies* 22, no. 2 (1996): 397; Sarah Potter, "'Undesirable Relations': Same-Sex Relationships and the Meaning of Sexual Desire at a Women's Reformatory during the

Progressive Era," *Feminist Studies* 30, no. 2 (2004): 394–415. Authors who have explored the use of close friendships between Black and white women as a signifier of lesbianism include Linda Nochlin, *The Politics of Vision: Essays on Nineteenth-Century Art and Society* (New York: Harper & Row, 1989); B. Ruby Rich, *New Queen Cinema: The Director's Cut* (Durham, NC: Duke University Press, 2013), especially chapter 6, "True Stories of Forbidden Love"; Mayne, "Caged and Framed," 115–45.

53 bell hooks, *Reel to Real: Race, Sex and Class at the Movies* (New York: Routledge, 1996), 299.

54 Michel Foucault, *The History of Sexuality* (New York: Pantheon Books, 1978); Michel Foucault, *Discipline and Punish: The Birth of the Prison* (New York: Vintage Books, 1995); Carol Smart, "Women, Crime and Mental Illness," in *Women, Crime and Criminology: A Feminist Critique* (London: Routledge, 1977), 146–75.

55 Electroconvulsive treatment (ECT) induces a convulsive seizure; it was developed to treat depression. Alan N. Polasky, "Regulation of Electroconvulsive Therapy," *Michigan Law Review* 75, no. 2 (1976): 364.

56 James McConnell, "Criminals Can Be Brainwashed – Now," *Psychology Today* (April 1970), cited in Jessica Mitford, *Kind and Usual Punishment: The Prison Business* (New York: Alfred A. Knopf, 1974), 125.

57 *Aden v Younger,* 57 Cal App 3d 622 (1976); *Kaimowitz v Department of Mental Health for the State of Michigan,* 42 USLW 2063 (1976) (persons in custody have the right to refuse psychosurgery, and circumstances in which involuntarily detained persons cannot be deemed to give informed consent to treatment); *Sanchez v Ciccone,* No 20182-4, 3061-4 (WD Mo 1973) (the Federal Bureau of Prisons announces the termination of the behaviour modification program); *Washington v Harper,* 759 P (2d) 358 (1988), 494 US 210, 236 (1996) (the state's security interests relating to administering treatment may outweigh a prisoner's liberty interest/right to refuse). See generally Edward M. Opton, "Psychiatric Violence against Prisoners: When Therapy Is Punishment," *Mississippi Law Journal* 45, no. 3 (1974): 605–44 (the distinction between punishment and treatment in prison is "spurious"). In the late 1940s, Canadian penitentiaries began the use of ECT; the practice has also been challenged in that jurisdiction. *Proctor v Canada,* [2000] OJ No 658, 95 ACWS (3d) 37 (Sup Ct); *Proctor v Canada (Attorney General),* [2002] OJ No 350, 111 ACWS (3d) 713 (Sup Ct).

58 Maggy Lee, "Over-prescription of Drugs," in *Encyclopedia of Prisons and Corrections,* ed. Mary Bosworth (London: Sage Publications, 2005), 659.

59 See *Liles v Ward,* 424 F. Supp. 675 (NY Dist. Ct. 1976) (women who had been deemed "disciplinary problems" and who had had a series of violent altercations with guards attempted to escape; they were transferred from the Bedford [New York] State Prison for women to a mental hospital, where some underwent forced treatment).

60 See generally Smart, "Women, Crime and Mental Illness," 146–75; Dorothy E. Chunn and Robert Menzies, "Out of Mind, Out of Law: The Regulation of 'Criminally Insane' Women inside British Columbia's Public Mental Hospitals, 1888–1973," *Canadian Journal of Women and the Law* 10, no. 2 (1998): 306–37; Kathleen Auerhahn and Elizabeth Dermody Leonard, "Docile Bodies? Chemical Restraints and the Female Inmate," *Journal of Criminal Law and Criminology* 90, no. 2 (2000): 599–634.

61 One study has found that over 80 percent of incarcerated women who pleaded guilty to the offence for which they were serving time "illustrate a series of life course characteristics which makes them much more susceptible to poor health – including unmet medical needs, drug/alcohol use, and mental health issues – that have the potential to be treated, or exacerbated, by incarceration." Noelle E. Fearn and Kelly Parker, "Health Care for Women Inmates: Issues, Perceptions and Policy Considerations," *Californian Journal of Health Promotion* 3, no. 2 (2005): 6.

62 Compare *Big Bird Cage* (1972); *The Big Doll House; Women in Cages;* and the entire *Isla* franchise beginning with *Ilsa: She Wolf of the SS* (1975).

63 Elizabeth Comack, "Part I: Women, Criminology and Feminism," in *Criminalizing Women: Gender and (In)justice in Neo-Liberal Times,* ed. Gillian Balfour and Elizabeth Comack, 2nd ed. (Halifax: Fernwood Publishing, 2014), 11–46; Elizabeth M. Schneider, "Feminism and the False Dichotomy of Victimization and Agency," *New York Law School Law Review* 38 (1993): 387–99.

64 But see Annalise Acorn, "Reclaiming a Restorative Understanding of the Victim-Offender Dichotomy," *Restorative Justice: An International Journal* 5, no. 2 (2017): 468–80 (reclaims the victim/offender dichotomy to pressure governments to protect the procedural rights of people who have been victimized by structural inequality, poverty, and marginalization).

65 Ivory (Louise Beavers) in *Ladies of the Big House* (1931) is serving a one-hundred-year sentence; Emma (Ellen Corby) in *Caged!* (1950) fought back a number of times but eventually killed her abusive husband; Bonnie (Michelle Newkirk) in *Vendetta,* Maria (Maria Rangel) in *Dangerous Women* (1991), and Frances (LisaRaye McCoy) in *Civil Brand* (2002) are all serving sentences for killing abusive husbands; Lil' Mama (Lark Voorhies) in *Civil Brand* killed her sexually abusive stepfather; Bea (Danielle Cormack) in *Wentworth* was sent to prison for attempting to kill her abusive husband. Compare *Against Their Will: Women in Prison* (1994), in which a woman who kills her abusive husband is bullied by the other prisoners because of her crime.

66 Ray Kuszelewski and Dianne Martin document cases of women being given cheques that bounce or getting "stiffed" by clients in other ways and attempting to sue. Such lawsuits are framed as "immoral contracts." Ray Kuszelewski and Dianne L. Martin, "The Perils of Poverty: Prostitutes' Rights, Police Misconduct, and Poverty Law," *Osgoode Hall Law Journal* 35, no. 3–4 (1997): 835–63; Anna-Louise Crago, *Arrest the Violence: Human Rights Abuses against Sex Workers in Central and Eastern Europe and Central Asia* (Budapest: Sex Workers' Rights Advocacy Network, 2009), http://www.opensocietyfoundations.org/sites/default/files/arrest-violence-20091217.pdf.

67 New York Civil Liberties Union, "Legislative Memo: An Act to Amend the Criminal Procedure Law, in Relation to Admissibility of a Complainant's Sexual Conduct," May 18, 2010, https://www.nyclu.org/en/node/1523/print; see also Bennett Capers, "Rape, Truth and Hearsay," *Harvard Journal of Law and Gender* 40, no. 1 (2017): 183–228.

68 Compare *Betrayed Women* (1955), *Violent Women* (1960), and *Big Bird Cage.*

69 Crowther, *Captured on Film,* 67, 65.

70 While no doubt performative, she is in fact in costume to help her friend Suzanne Warren, who suffers from mental illness and is increasingly vulnerable after the loss

of a mother figure (Season 2) and friend (Season 4). Cindy and Alison Abdullah (Amanda Stephen) create an imaginary prison they call Bitchfield to provide a sense of normalcy for Suzanne during the riot.

71 She also played Carol in *Chained Heat* (for which she was awarded the Golden Raspberry for Worst Actress) and Christine in *Red Heat.*

72 In *Niemi v National Broadcasting Corporation,* 458 US 1108 (1982), a nine-year-old girl had been attacked and raped with a beer bottle by three girls and a boy – ages ten, twelve, thirteen, and fifteen, respectively. The child's mother filed suit for $11 million, charging that the National Broadcasting Company (NBC) was negligent for broadcasting *Born Innocent* (1974) during family hours. The Superior Court ruled in favour of NBC, not calling for a jury, but the California Court of Appeals overturned that decision. According to Elana Levine, "this case and the incendiary rhetoric surrounding it helped cement the film's reputation as the embodiment of the threats to America's youth from television and the new sexual culture." Elana Levine, *Wallowing in Sex: The New Sexual Culture of 1970s American Television* (Durham, NC: Duke University Press, 2007), 89.

73 Levine, *Wallowing in Sex,* especially chapter 3 ("The Sex Threat: Regulating and Representing Sexually Endangered Youth").

Chapter 5: Representing Incarcerated Black Women

1 Women have written women-in-prison (WIP) screenplays throughout the genre's existence, with the exception perhaps of the exploitation cycle. For instance, in the melodramatic cycle, see *Chicago* (1927) and its adaptation *Roxie Hart* (1942), both based on Maurine Dallas Watkins's 1926 play. Jeanie MacPherson wrote the screenplay for Cecil B. DeMille's *The Godless Girl* (1929), Anita Loos wrote *Hold Your Man* (1933), and Dorothy Mackaye wrote *Ladies They Talk About* (1933). More recently, the National Broadcasting Corporation's movie *Girl Called Hatter Fox* (1977) is an adaptation of the novel by Marilyn Harris; Shelagh Delaney wrote the screenplay for *Dance with a Stranger* (1985), and Elizabeth Gill wrote the television movie *Convicted: A Mother's Story* (1987).

2 Stephanie Rothman, interview by Henry Jenkins, *Confessions of an Aca-Fan,* October 16, 2007, accessed August 27, 2020, http://henryjenkins.org/blog/2007/10/exploiting_feminism_an_intervi.html; see also Henry Jenkins, "Exploiting Feminism in Stephanie Rothman's *Terminal Island,*" in *The Wow Climax: Tracing the Emotional Impact of Popular Culture* (New York: New York University Press, 2007), 102–24.

3 Katja von Garnier directed the Home Box Office's (HBO) film *Iron Jawed Angels* (2004), which chronicles the work and activism of American suffragists Alice Paul (Hilary Swank) and Lucy Burns (Frances O'Connor). Its title refers to these political prisoners, who, after a hunger strike for better living conditions in the prison, were force fed and placed in solitary confinement. However, it does not feature enough scenes in prison for it to be considered within the WIP genre.

4 While difficult to find, a few episodes are available on streaming sites such as Youtube©: https://www.youtube.com/watch?v=iIqNMWxjhg0.

5 Linda K. Fuller, "Louise Beavers," in *Harlem Renaissance Lives from the African American National Biography,* ed. Henry Louis Gates and Evelyn Brooks Higginbotham (Oxford: Oxford University Press, 2009), 42–43.

6 K. Sue Jewell, *From Mammy to Miss America and Beyond: Cultural Images and the Shaping of US Social Policy* (New York: Routledge, 1993), 38, cited in Melissa V. Harris-Perry, *Sister Citizen: Shame, Stereotypes, and Black Women in America,* Kindle Edition (New Haven, CT: Yale University Press, 2011), 1063. See also Jeanine Weekes Schroer, "The Terrifying Tale of the Philosophical Mammy," *The Black Scholar* 43, no. 4 (2013): 101–7; and Douglas Flamming, *Bound for Freedom: Black Los Angeles in Jim Crow America* (Berkeley: University of California Press, 2005).

7 Gallery of Great Black Kentuckians, "Nellie Conley," *Kentucky Commission on Human Rights,* https://kchr.ky.gov/ggbk/Documents/GBK43.pdf. A similar quote has also been attributed to Hattie McDaniel, the first African American actor to receive an Academy Award: "Why should I complain about making $700 a week playing a maid? If I didn't, I'd be making $7 a week being one." Ronald Bergan, "Juanita Moore Obituary," *The Guardian,* January 2, 2014, https://www.theguardian.com/film/2014/jan/02/juanita-moore.

8 These films and the actors featured in them have generally been ignored by mainstream film historians. See Henry T. Sampson, *Blacks in Black and White: A Source Book on Black Films,* 2nd ed. (Lanham, MD: Scarecrow Press, 1995); Charlene B. Regester, *African American Actresses: The Struggle for Visibility, 1900–1960* (Bloomington: Indiana University Press, 2010).

9 *Reform School* (1939) was rereleased as *Prison Bait* (1944).

10 Promotional poster for *Reform School,* http://www.imdb.com/title/tt0031843/mediaviewer/rm1086852608.

11 Regester, *African American Actresses,* 34.

12 Chris Holmlund, "Wham! Bam! Pam! Pam Grier as Hot Action Babe and Cool Action Mama," *Quarterly Review of Film and Video* 22, no. 2 (2005): 97–112.

13 In *Women in Cages* (1971), however, she incarnates Alabama, a sadistic, sex-crazed warden. She also played opposite Margaret Markov in *Black Mama White Mama* (1973) and has a small part in the made-for-television movie *A Mother's Right: The Elizabeth Morgan Story* (1992).

14 Regarding Pam Grier's construction as a feminist icon, see Cedric J. Robinson, "Blaxploitation and the Misrepresentation of Liberation," *Race and Class* 40, no. 1 (1998): 1–12; Yvonne D. Sims, *Women of Blaxploitation: How the Black Action Film Heroine Changed American Popular Culture* (Jefferson, NC: McFarland and Company, 2006). Chris Holmlund writes that stars like Grier "cannot easily be hailed as simply 'pro-feminist' or purely 'pro-black,'" but they do nevertheless "disrupt conventions common to exploitation action films, whether directed by whites or blacks." Holmlund, "Wham! Bam! Pam!" 102.

15 Pam Grier, with Andrea Cagan, *Foxy: My Life in Three Acts* (New York: Grand Central Publishing, 2010).

16 Sims, *Women of Blaxploitation,* 45.

17 Yvonne Sims relies on bell hooks's theory of the oppositional gaze. Namely, Black spectators not only may mine films for small subversive moments and contradictions in the cinematic texts but also respond to the "conventional representations of [B]lack women" by blocking those images out, "looking the other way," and "accord[ing] cinema no importance in their lives." Others still look at films with an "oppositional gaze" that positions them to "assess the cinema's construction of white womanhood as the

object of phallocentric gaze and choose not to identify with either the victim or the perpetrator" and "looked from a location that disrupted." bell hooks, "The Oppositional Gaze: Black Female Spectators," in *Reel to Real: Race, Sex and Class at the Movies* (New York: Routledge, 1996) 202, 205; Sims, *Women of Blaxploitation,* 29.

18 Sims, *Women of Blaxploitation,* 29, 30, 47.

19 However, some films reinforced negative stereotypes about Black women. In *Born Innocent* (1974), Josie (Tina Andrews) is a Black girl who has been sold into a prostitution ring by her drug-addicted mother. Moreover, Jesse Algeron Rhines's political economy of American popular culture found that acting roles for Black actors decreased significantly in the 1980s. Jesse Algeron Rhines, *Black Film White Money* (New Brunswick, NJ: Rutgers University Press, 1996).

20 hooks, "Oppositional Gaze," 201.

21 Shonda Rhimes is perhaps the best-known African American woman screenwriter, having created and executive produced the American Broadcasting Corporation's award-winning *Grey's Anatomy* (2006–present). Rhimes has since created and produced the political thriller *Scandal* (2012–present) and the legal drama *How to Get Away with Murder* (2014–present). Before Rhimes's ascension, the 1990s saw Julie Dash who, with *Daughters of the Dust* (1991), became the first Black woman director to have a full-length feature with a general theatrical release. More recently, Ava DuVernay was the first Black woman to be nominated for best director at the Golden Globes, for *Selma* (2015), which was in the Best Picture category at the Academy Awards. Neema Barnette was also the first African American woman to direct a situational comedy for Season 2, episode 7 ("Shirley's Little Sister") of *What's Happening Now!* (1986).

22 *Stranger Inside* (2001). Dir. Cheryl Dunye; Screenplay: Cheryl Dunye and Catherine Crouch. HBO Films (NR); and *Civil Brand* (2002). Dir. Neema Barnette; Screenplay: Preston Whitmore and Joyce Renee Lewis. Lions Gate Films (R).

23 Season 4 of *Orange Is the New Black* (2013–19) grappled with race when one of the most beloved Black characters, Poussey, was suffocated, albeit accidentally, by a white guard; the season went on to explore privilege, power, and the #BlackLivesMatter Movement. However, the series came under fire when it was revealed that its writing staff are almost entirely white. Ellen McGirt, "An Uproar over 'Orange Is the New Black' Shows the Problem with Diversity," *Fortune,* June 22, 2016.

24 Dunye identifies as a Liberian-born, Black lesbian American. Equality Forum, "Meet LGBT History Month Icon Cheryl Dunye," October 14, 2019, access August 26, 2020, https://sdlgbtn.com/causes/2019/10/14/meet-lgbt-history-month-icon-cheryl-dunye.

25 Maria St. John, "Making Home/Making 'Stranger': An Interview with Cheryl Dunye," *Feminist Studies* 30, no. 2 (2004): 332.

26 *The Watermelon Woman* (1997) won Best Feature Film at the Berlin International Film Festival in 1996 and Outstanding Narrative Feature at the Los Angeles Outfest in 1996.

27 Allison Perlman, "*Deadwood,* Generic Transformation and Televisual History," in *Westerns: The Essential Journal of Popular Film and Television Collection,* ed. Gary R. Edgerton and Michael T. Marsden (London: Routledge, 2012), 251.

28 St. John, "Making Home/Making 'Stranger,'" 329.

29 St. John, "Making Home/Making 'Stranger,'" 325.
30 *Cage without a Key* (1975) features a similar prison family, where a Black woman is the head. Tommy (Jonelle Allen) self-identifies as "Papa." Although Tommy is a cool head and generally non-violent, when the queen bee attacks one of her "little sisters," she gives up a well-crafted escape plan and comes to her defence. Tommy is stabbed to death as a result.
31 It is nine times more common for a Black child to have an incarcerated parent than it is for a white child. Lauren E. Glaze and Laura M. Maruschak, "Parents in Prison and Their Minor Children," Bureau of Justice Statistics, Office of Justice Programs, US Department of Justice, 5, last updated March 30, 2010, accessed August 26, 2020, https://www.bjs.gov/content/pub/pdf/pptmc.pdf.
32 See generally Megan L. Comfort, "In the Tube at San Quentin: The 'Secondary Prisonization' of Women Visiting Inmates," *Journal of Contemporary Ethnography* 32, no. 1 (2002): 77–107; Donald Braman, *Doing Time on the Outside: Incarceration and Family Life in Urban America* (Ann Arbor: University of Michigan Press, 2004). On the effects of high imprisonment rates on communities, see Joseph Murray and David P. Farrington, "The Effects of Parental Imprisonment on Children," *Crime and Justice* 37, no. 1 (2008): 133–206; Dorothy Smith Ruiz and Albert Kopak, "The Consequences of Parental Incarceration for African American Mothers, Children, and Grandparent Caregivers," *Journal of Pan African Studies* 7, no. 6 (November 2014): 9–24; John Hagan and Holly Foster, "Children of the American Prison Generation: Student and School Spillover Effects of Incarcerating Mothers," *Law and Society Review* 46, no. 1 (2012): 37–69.
33 Gail T. Smith, "The Adoption and Safe Families Act of 1997: Its Impact on Prisoner Mothers and Their Children," in *Women and Girls in the Criminal Justice System*, ed. Russ Immarigeon (Kingston, NJ: Civic Research Institute, 2006), 15.
34 Patricia Hill Collins, "The Meaning of Motherhood in Black Culture and Black Mother-Daughter Relationships," in *Double Stitch: Black Women Write about Mothers and Daughters*, ed. Patricia Bell-Scott et al. (New York: Harper Perennial, 1993), 42–60.
35 The term "Latinas" includes, among others, women of Mexican, Puerto Rican, Cuban, and Dominican descent as well as women from across Latin America (South and Central).
36 Joanne Minaker and Bryan Hogeveeen, "From Criminalizing Mothering to Criminalized Mothers: An Introduction," in *Criminalized Mothers, Criminalizing Mothering*, ed. Joanne Minaker and Bryan Hogeveeen (Bradford, ON: Demeter Press, 2015), 2.
37 A similar trend is seen for Latinas. See Linda C. Fentiman, "Pursuing the Perfect Mother: Why America's Criminalization of Maternal Substance Abuse Is Not the Answer – A Comparative Legal Analysis," *Michigan Journal of Gender and Law* 15, no. 1 (January 2009): 389–469; Erika Derkas, "'Don't Let Your Pregnancy Get in the Way of Your Drug Addiction': CRACK and the Ideological Construction of Addicted Women," *Social Justice* 38, no. 3 (2012): 125–44. Regarding sanctions for substance use during pregnancy, see Katrina Hui, Cara Angelotta, and Carl E. Fisher, "Criminalizing Substance Use in Pregnancy: Misplaced Priorities," *Addiction* 112, no. 7 (2017): 1123–25.
38 See generally Evelyn Nakano Glenn, "Social Constructions of Mothering: A Thematic Overview," in *Mothering: Ideology, Experience, and Agency*, ed. Evelyn Nakano

Glenn and Grace Chang (New York: Routledge, 1994), 1–29. There is an equally troubling level of intervention into Indigenous mothers' lives, most notably through the Eurocentric interpretation of the "best interests of the child" principle. Regarding how the existence of the Indian Child Welfare Act, 1978, 92 Stat. 3069, which begins from the premise of Indigenous nations' sovereignty, challenges "dominant conceptions of kinship grounded in Euro American ideologies of possessive individualism and the nuclear family," see Pauline Turner Strong, *American Indians and the American Imaginary: Cultural Representation across the Centuries* (Boulder, CO: Paradigm Publishers, 2012), especially 102–17.

39 See generally Dorothy E. Roberts, "Prison, Foster Care, and the Systemic Punishment of Black Mothers," *University of California, Los Angles Law Review* 59, no. 1 (August 2012): 1474–1500; Eliza Duggan, "A Velvet Hammer: The Criminalization of Motherhood and the New Maternalism," *California Law Review* 104, no. 1 (2016): 1299–1332; Suzanne Allen, Chris Flaherty, and Gretchen Ely, "Throwaway Moms: Maternal Incarceration and the Criminalization of Female Poverty," *Affilia: Journal of Women and Social Work* 25, no. 2 (2010): 160–72. But see Ebonie Cunningham Stringer, who investigates the intersections of race, gender, religion, spirituality, and mothering to argue that African American mothers use their faith to cope with the damage that incarceration may have on their relationships with their children. Ebonie Cunningham Stringer, "'Keeping the Faith': How Incarcerated African American Mothers Use Religion and Spirituality to Cope with Imprisonment," *Journal of African American Studies* 13, no. 3 (September 2009): 325–47.

40 The trauma of losing a child is a recurring theme in later films. In *House of Women* (1962) and *Wentworth* (2013–present), the protagonists suffer a mental break when their children die on the outside. In HBO's *Prison Stories: Women on the Inside* (1991), a pregnant prisoner (Rae Dawn Chong) is forced to join a gang to ensure her child will be adopted into a safe home.

41 A number of excellent documentaries are also devoted to the subject. See, for instance, *Voices from Inside: Women Prisoners and the Children Speak Out: Prison Lullabies* (2005).

42 In the British film *Weak and the Wicked* (1954), the protagonist witnesses the trauma inflicted on young women who are forced to give birth in prison and then put their children up for adoption. In the Argentinian film *Leonera* (2008) and the Belgian film *Ombline* (2012), each protagonist is redeemed by the death of her child while behind bars.

43 The fresco appears to be one of the many "Madonna and Child" paintings of the Italian Baroque period from the sixteenth century.

44 In the made-for-television movie *Cage without a Key* (1975), one of the prisoners has a bisexual mother, who, troublingly, is characterized as a drug addict and an incestuous sexual predator.

45 St. John, "Making Home/Making 'Stranger,'" 332.

46 Andrew Billingsley, *Climbing Jacob's Ladder: The Enduring Legacy of African-American Families* (New York: Simon & Schuster, 1994); Patricia Hill Collins, "Black Women and Motherhood," in *Black Feminist Thought: Knowledge, Consciousness, and the Politics of Empowerment*, 2nd ed. (New York: Routledge, 2000), 173–200.

47 Michelle Alexander, *The New Jim Crow: Mass Incarceration in the Age of Colorblindness* (New York: New Press, 2012).
48 St. John, "Making Home/Making 'Stranger,'" 332.
49 See generally Lawrence O. Gostin, Cori Vanchieri, and Andrew Pope, eds., *Ethical Considerations for Research Involving Prisoners* (Washington, DC: National Academic Press, 2007). Neema Barnette was already familiar with some of the genre's conventions. She had, for instance, directed *Better Off Dead* (1993), in which Kit (Mare Winningham) is redeemed in prison and waits for her execution. While not technically a WIP film, it is certainly part of the "death row" genre. Notably, this film was produced by feminist icon Gloria Steinem.
50 This trope goes back to Hope Emerson, who personified brutality in her portrayal of Matron Evelyn Harper in *Caged!* (1950). It is later seen in Ida Lupino's chilling depiction of Superintendent Amilia Van Zant in *Women's Prison* (1955); Lupino brought back this character in the form of Claire Tyson in *Women in Chains* (1972).
51 Jacqueline Bobo, "*Civil Brand* (2002) and the Prison Industrial Complex," *Communication, Culture and Critique* 1, no. 1 (2008): 63. The film won the Blockbuster Audience Award at the Black American Film Festival in Miami in 2002.
52 Neema Barnette, interview, *The Auburn Avenue* no. 2 (Spring/Summer 2017), https://www.theauburnavenue.com/issue-ii.
53 Afiya X, "Black Women Directors: Neema Barnette," *Grandmother: The Definitive Record of Africa,* July 27, 2011, http://grandmotherafrica.com/black-women-directors-neema-barnette/. Following the "three strikes" law implemented in 1994 in California, any woman found guilty of two or more serious felonies could receive an indeterminate sentence, usually between twenty-five years and a life sentence. The three strikes policy remained intact and forcefully implemented until 2012 when it was modified to apply only to serious and violent felonies.
54 Ruth Gilmore, *Golden Gulag: Prison, Surplus, Crisis and Opposition in Globalizing California* (Berkeley: University of California Press, 2007). The concept was first introduced by Mike Davis, "Hell Factories in the Field: A Prison-Industrial Complex," *The Nation* 260, no. 7 (February 1995): 229; see also Angela Davis, *The Prison Industrial Complex* (Chico, CA: AK Press, 1999); Genevieve LeBaron, "Rethinking Prison Labor: Social Discipline and the State in Historical Perspective," *Journal of Labor and Society* 15, no. 3 (2012): 327–51.
55 Justice System Improvement Act, 1979, Pub. L. 96-157. The prison industrial complex is derived from the term "military industrial complex." Dwight Eisenhower introduced the term to refer to the co-existence of a government-endorsed military and a privatized arms industry. Dwight D. Eisenhower, "Military Industrial Complex Speech," *Public Papers of Presidents,* 1035–40, http://avalon.law.yale.edu/20th_century/eisenhower001.asp. Julia Sudbury sees links between the military and the prison industrial complex in the use of prison as a sentencing tool for political speech, which "undermine[s] peace activism [against] the deployment of technology and weaponry developed by the arms industry," as well as in the industry's reliance on inexpensive weapons production through prisoner labour. Julia Sudbury, "A World without Prisons: Resisting Militarism, Globalized Punishment, and Empire," *Social Justice* 31, nos. 1–2 (2004): 17.

56 Beth E. Richie, *Arrested Justice: Black Women, Violence, and America's Prison Nation* (New York: New York University Press, 2012).

57 Black slaves were subject to the arbitrary rules of plantation owners, charged with crimes that only attached to people living in slavery (running away, harbouring runaways, disobeying orders) and tried in "Negro Courts." With the emergence of prisons for women in the mid-1800s, Black women would be sent to workhouses/penitentiaries, whereas white women who also committed non-violent offences would find themselves in reformatories, where they could follow vocational training in the hope of reintegration. After the Civil War, criminalized Black women could be leased out to private employers where they would serve out their term. See generally Anne M. Butler, "Still in Chains: Black Women in Western Prisons, 1865–1910," *Western Historical Quarterly* 20, no. 1 (1989): 19–35; Catherine F. Collins, *The Imprisonment of African American Women: Causes, Experiences, and Effects* (Jefferson, NC: MacFarland and Company, 2010). Today, the prison has been characterized by Black activists and scholars as the natural extension of the plantation/slavery system. Ava Duvernay's documentary *13th* (2016), for instance, makes reference to the constitutional amendment that abolished slavery in all cases except for punishment for crime.

58 As Lisa Marie Cacho has argued, these practices, such as California's Proposition 21 (which added penalties to gang-related crimes), "attached to statuses that invoke race (gang member), ethnicity ("illegal alien"), and/or national origin (suspected terrorist)." Lisa Marie Cacho, *Social Death: Racialized Rightlessness and the Criminalization of the Unprotected* (New York: New York University Press, 2012), 43.

59 Calvin John Smiley and David Fakunle, "From 'Brute' to 'Thug': The Demonization and Criminalization of Unarmed Black Male Victims in America," *Journal of Human Behavior in the Social Environment* 26, nos. 3–4 (May 2016): 350–66.

60 See generally Khalil Gibran Muhammad, *The Condemnation of Blackness: Race, Crime, and the Making of Modern Urban America* (Cambridge, MA: Harvard University Press, 2010); Naomi Murakawa, *The First Civil Right: How Liberals Built Prison America* (Oxford: Oxford University Press, 2014).

61 Angela Y. Davis, "Masked Racism: Reflections on the Prison Industrial Complex," *Color Lines*, September 10, 1998, https://www.colorlines.com/articles/masked-racism-reflections-prison-industrial-complex; Angela Y. Davis and Cassandra Shaylor, "Race, Gender, and the Prison Industrial Complex: California and Beyond," *Meridians: Feminism, Race, Transnationalism* 2, no. 1 (2001): 1–25; Sudbury, "World without Prisons"; Paula Johnson, *Inner Lives: Voices of African American Women in Prison* (New York: New York University Press, 2003).

62 Lauren E. Glaze and Laura M. Maruschak, *Parents in Prison and Their Minor Children* (Washington, DC: Bureau of Justice Statistics, Office of Justice Programs, US Department of Justice), last updated March 30, 2010, https://www.bjs.gov/content/pub/pdf/pptmc.pdf.

63 On the intersection of the foster and prison systems and the impact on Black American women especially, see Roberts, "Prison, Foster Care." Adoption and Safe Families Act, 1997, Pub. L. 105–89.

64 Shimica Gaskins, "'Women of Circumstance': The Effects of Mandatory Minimum Sentences on Women Minimally Involved in Drugs Crimes," *American Criminal Law Review* 41, no. 4 (2004): 1533–53.

65 Alexander, *New Jim Crow;* Kali Nicole Gross, "African American Women, Mass Incarceration, and the Politics of Protection," *Journal of American History* 102, no. 1 (2015): 25–33.

66 Richie, *Arrested Justice,* 23–63; see also Shatema Threadcraft and Lisa L. Miller, "Black Women, Victimization, and the Limitations of the Liberal State," *Theoretical Criminology* 21, no. 4 (2017): 480.

67 Beth Richie explains the concept that she developed in 1985 as "(1) the obligation that Black women feel to buffer their families from the impact of racism in the public sphere; (2) the pressure to live up to the expectation that they, as Black women, will be able to withstand abuse and mistreatment more than other members of their households; and (3) an acceptance of the community rhetoric that argues that Black women are in a more privileged position than are Black men (including those who abuse them)." Richie, *Arrested Justice,* 36, referring to Beth Richie, "Battered Black Women: A Challenge for the Black Community," *Black Scholar* 16, no. 2 (1985): 40–44.

68 Angela Y. Davis, *Are Prisons Obsolete?* (New York: Seven Stories Press, 2003), 84 (emphasis added).

69 Erica Jones (Constance Shulman) offers yoga and meditation classes.

70 The labour is organized by race, ethnicity, and class and shifts with each clan's power status. When Galina "Red" Reznikov (Kate Mulgrew), matriarch of the white faction, loses her influence with the prison administration, Gloria Mendoza (Selenis Leyva) takes over as head chef/queen bee and the "Spanish Harlem" takes charge of kitchen duties. At the same time, Yvonne "Vee" Parker (Lorraine Toussaint) strategically takes over custodial duties from Gloria's girls. The electrical maintenance crew is racially diverse and requires a certain level of education. It consists of Janae Watson (Vicky Jeudy), a young Black high-school track star who, in one moment of youthful rebellion, lost her college scholarship and saw her chance for a better life ripped away; Nicky, a white, upper-middle-class recovering drug addict; and, of course, entitled protagonist Piper Chapman (Taylor Schilling). The laundry is, for the time being at least, run by Tiffany "Pennsatucky" Doggett (Taryn Manning), a poor white evangelical Christian, and her disciples, Loretta Fisher (Christina Huie), Angie Rice (Julie Lake), and Leanne Taylor (Emma Myles).

71 In Season 3, the Management and Corrections Corporation assumes control of the prison and makes significant staff changes in an effort to cut costs. Correctional officers are required to apply for their previously held positions, thus losing seniority and their union. Existing staff have their hours cut, and the new guards are not adequately trained. The season ends with a mass exodus of competent guards, including rule-bound Wade Donaldson (Brendan Burke). Wanda Bell (Catherine Curtin), one of the few skilled and sensible correctional officers who stayed on during the transition, also walks out in Season 4 after working conditions deteriorate even further.

72 Black girls also face more severe charges despite any evidence that they engage in more serious crimes; they have more difficult hurdles to jump through when trying to get bail and are unlikely to be diverted to a restorative justice initiative. Richie, "Queering Antiprison Work," 73–85.

73 The GEO Group, a private company offering mental and other health treatments in correctional and detention facilities, settled with the family of a woman who took her

life after being raped by a male prisoner who was housed in the same cellblock as her in a facility it was managing. *Tapia v Dugger,* 2006 US Dist. LEXIS 69356 (WD Tex., September 7, 2006). In 2015, the Corrections Corporation of America (CCA), the largest privatized prison company in the United States, faced over four million dollars in liabilities related to such lawsuits. Gary Hunter, "Guards Rape of Prisoners Rampant, No Solution in Sight," *Prison Legal News,* August 15, 2006, https://www.prisonlegalnews.org/news/2006/aug/15/guards-rape-of-prisoners-rampant-no-solution-in-sight/; *Escalante v CCA,* USDC, DCA Case no. 05-CV-0022WQH; Lonnie Burton, "Female Prisoner Raped by Florida Sheriff's Deputy Settles Lawsuit for $91,666," *Prison Legal News,* August 24, 2017, https://www.prisonlegalnews.org/news/2017/aug/24/female-prisoner-raped-florida-sheriffs-deputy-settles-lawsuit-91666/. There are similar cases involving male and juvenile institutions. In May 2013, a class action was filed on behalf of more than 1,100 prisoners of the East Mississippi Correctional Facility (EMCF). *Dockery v Epps,* 2014 US Dist. LEXIS 190937 (SD Miss., November 4, 2014). The prisoners alleged that the EMCF deliberately or tacitly failed to address life-threatening conditions – malnourishment, overcrowding, infestations, and a lack of infrastructure (including running water and electricity) to provide basic health care – in a prison operated by the Management and Training Corporation. In another case in 2012, GEO was sued for malpractice in a juvenile prison, where young people were "kicked and punched while handcuffed, and others have been stripped naked and placed in solitary confinement for weeks." Brendan Fischer, "Violence, Abuse, and Death at For-Profit Prisons: A GEO Group Rap Sheet," *Centre for Media and Democracy's PR Watch,* September 26, 2013, https://www.prwatch.org/news/2013/09/12255/violence-abuse-and-death-profit-prisons-geo-group-rap-sheet. There is a class action involving male prisoners. In *Gonzalez v CoreCivic Inc.,* 2018 US Dist. LEXIS 36753 (SD Cal., March 6, 2018), two male prisoners sued CoreCivic, arguing that using prisoners to clean and maintain the institution (clean the jail, prepare and serve meals, run the law library, do laundry, and cut hair at the maximum rate of one dollar per day with threats of punishment for failure to work) amounted to forced labour, rights-infringements under the Trafficking Victims Protection Act, violations of the Labor Code, negligence, unjust enrichment, and unfair competition. The decision has not yet been rendered. "Owino et al v. CoreCivic, Inc.," *Pacer Monitor,* March 23, 2017, https://www.pacermonitor.com/public/case/21591650/Owino_et_al_v_CoreCivic,_Inc. Women's labour rights in the context of privatized prisons, however, remain precarious.

74 Bobo, *"Civil Brand,"* 65 (the American Black Film Festival in Miami, the Urbanworld Film Festival in New York, and the Pan African Film Festival in Los Angeles to name a few).

75 In 2000, on the fourteenth day of a shoot scheduled for twenty-five days, Trimark merged with Lions Gate Entertainment (Lionsgate), and the production company informed Barnette that she had one day to get the film in the can.

76 See generally Neema Barnette, "Director's Commentary," *Civil Brand* (2002), DVD; David Geffner, "Indies Lock-Up: Re-Creating Indie Life on an Indie Film Budget," *Directors Guild of America Magazine,* retrieved February 15, 2011; and Andre Chautard, "A Story That Couldn't Stay Locked Up," *Los Angeles Times,* August 23, 2003, http://articles.latimes.com/2003/aug/25/entertainment/et-chautard25.

77 A.O. Scott, "Film Review: Tough Women in the Pen Decide to Get Tougher," review of *Civil Brand*, directed by Neema Barnette, *The New York Times*, October 10, 2003, http://www.nytimes.com/movie/review?res=9C05E6DC173FF933A25753C1A9659C8B63.

78 The film won the Audience Awards at the Philadelphia Festival of World Cinema (2002) and the San Francisco International Film Festival (2002). Lisa Crooms and Judith Kegan Gardiner, "Preface," *Feminist Studies, The Prison Issue* 30, no. 2 (Summer 2004): 267.

79 Lydia Marcus, "Cheryl Dunye's Lesbian Prison Drama, *Stranger Inside*, Suffers by Comparison with Other Jail Tales," *The Advocate* 841 (July 2001): 54.

80 St. John, "Making Home/Making 'Stranger,'" 336.

81 Bobo, "*Civil Brand*," 67, citing E. Iverem, "Q &A: Director Neema Barnette. The Odyssey of *Civil Brand*, A New Film with Mos Def, Da Brat, LisaRaye About the 'Prison Industrial Complex,'" *Seeing Black* (2003), http://www.seeingblack.com/2003/x91203/neema_barnette.shtml (website discontinued).

82 Frann Michel makes this observation. Frann Michel, "Eating the (M)Other: Cheryl Dunye's Feature Films and Black Matrilineage," *Rhizomes* 14 (Summer 2007), http://www.rhizomes.net/issue14/michel/michel.html.

Chapter 6: Representation and Recalibrating the WIP Genre

1 *Orange Is the New Black* (2013–19). Creator and original screenplay: Jenji Kohan. Netflix (TV-MA).

2 It was the first series to win Emmy Awards in both the comedy and drama categories. In its first year, *Orange Is the New Black* (*OITNB*) (2013–19) received three Emmy Awards (out of twelve nominations). In its second, Uzo Aduba won the award for Outstanding Supporting Actress in a Drama Series (2013); she then took home the same award for a comedy series the following year (2014). *OITNB* has been nominated by the Golden Globes, the Writers Guild of America, and the British Academy of Television and has won, among others, the Screen Actors Guild's Award for Outstanding Performance by an Ensemble in a Comedy Series (2015, 2016, 2017) and the Producers Guild of America Award for Best Episodic Comedy (2015).

3 To Suzanne Ennk and Megan Morrissey, the show "enables [a] poignant but limited critique" of prison. Suzanne Ennk and Megan Morrissey, "If *Orange Is the New Black*, I Must Be Color Blind: Comic Framings of Post-Racism in the Prison-Industrial Complex," *Critical Studies in Media Communication* 32, no. 5 (2015): 303–17. Michelle Kelsey Kearl "celebrate[s] and criticize[s]" its depiction of intersecting power structures. Michelle Kelsey Kearl, "Prison Is Bullshit: An Intersectional Analysis of Popular Culture Representations of the Prison Industrial Complex in *Orange Is the New Black*," in *Communication Perspectives on Popular Culture*, ed. Andrew F. Herrmann and Art Herbig (Lanham, MD: Lexington Books, 2016), 66–70. Throughout its tenure, Netflix has engaged in some troubling practices such as promotional campaigns (including the "Crazy Pyes" food truck, with servers dressed in orange prison jumpers) that commodify fictional and actual incarcerated women. Lauren DeCarvalho and Nicole Cox make a strong argument that despite *OITNB*'s "potential to mobilize social awareness and activist sensibilities amongst its target audience," such unfortunate advertising strategies "emphasize stereotypes that the

program itself problematizes." Lauren J. DeCarvalho and Nicole B. Cox, "Extended 'Visiting Hours': Deconstructing Identity in Netflix's Promotional Campaigns for *Orange Is the New Black,*" *Television and New Media* 17, no. 6 (2016): 504–19; see also Anna Smith, "*Orange* is the Same White: Book Review of *Orange Is the New Black: My Year in a Woman's Prison* by Piper Kerman," *New Political Science* 37, no. 2 (2015): 276; Christina Belcher, "There Is No Such Thing as a Post-racial Prison: Neoliberal Multiculturalism and the White Savior Complex on *Orange Is the New Black,*" *Television and New Media* 17, no. 6 (2016): 491–503; Katerina Symes, "*Orange Is the New Black:* The Popularization of Lesbian Sexuality and Heterosexual Modes of Viewing," *Feminist Media Studies* 17, no. 1 (2017): 29–41; Shirley Jackson and Laurie Gordy, eds., *Caged Women: Incarceration, Representation and Media* (Boca Raton, FL: Routledge, 2018).

4 Thankfully, Suzanne's character is depicted with more nuance and care in later seasons. She resists the label "crazy," even when used affectionately, and introduces herself by her given name. She also develops into a self-aware, intelligent, creative, compassionate, and loyal truth teller. Uzo Aduba has won several awards for her compelling and layered portrayal of Suzanne. Moreover, Lorraine Toussaint defends the role of Vee for its complex exploration of psychopathy. Quoted in Kevin Fallon, "OITNB's New Villain Vee, Played by Lorraine Toussaint Speaks for the First Time," *The Daily Beast,* July 12, 2017.

5 As I complete this book, there are seven full seasons of *OITNB;* Seasons 6 and 7 had not yet been released when I completed this chapter.

6 Interview with Jenji Kohan on National Public Radio's *Fresh Air:* "You're not going to go into a network and sell a show on really fascinating tales of black women, and Latina women, and old women ... instead [you] sell them on the 'girl next door, the cool blonde.'" Cited in T.F. Charlton, "'Orange Is the New Black,' and How We Talk about Race and Identity," *Rewire.News,* September 3, 2013, https://rewire.news/article/2013/09/03/orange-is-the-new-black-and-how-we-talk-about-race-and-identity/.

7 Danielle Turchiano, "From 'Girls' to 'GLOW': Casting Director Jennifer Euston on the Importance of 'Authenticity,'" *Variety,* August 3, 2017, http://variety.com/2017/tv/news/jennifer-euston-girls-glow-orange-is-the-new-black-casting-interview-1202488659/.

8 I maintain this assertion despite the understandable controversy around the homogeneity of the writer's room. Shamira Ibrahim, "Yeah, I'm Finished with the Black Suffering Trauma Porn of *Orange Is the New Black,*" *The Root: Black News, Opinions, Politics, and Culture,* June 23, 2016, https://verysmartbrothas.theroot.com/yeah-im-finished-with-the-black-suffering-trauma-porn-1822523097.

9 *OITNB,* Season 1, episode 3 ("Lesbian Request Denied"); episode 5 ("The Chickening"); episode 7 ("Blood Donut"); episode 8 ("Moscow Mule"); episode 11 ("Tall Men with Feelings"); Season 2, episode 2 ("Looks Blue, Tastes Red"); episode 6 ("You Also Have a Pizza"); Season 3, episode 5 ("Fake It Till You Fake It Some More"); Season 4, episode 3 ("(Don't) Say Anything").

10 *OITNB,* Season 1, episode 6 ("WAC Pack") (in reference to Kathryn Stockett's novel *The Help* [New York: Penguin Books, 2009] and its film adaptation).

11 Throughout the series, Janae expresses righteous indignation about gender inequality, the systematic erasure of Black women's contribution to American society, and racism within the criminal justice system. After being invited to attend a private high school on a field trip, she is left numb by the discrepancies in resources and infrastructure between her public (mostly Black) school and the (mostly white) prep school. Thereafter, her grades start to slip, and her interest shifts away from scholarly pursuits (*OITNB,* Season 5, episode 5 ["Sing it, White Effie"]). In high school, Janae is a track star, but her father, to protect her modesty, forbids her from running (Season 3, episode 13 ["Trust no Bitch"]). In prison, she is falsely accused of stealing a screwdriver that was actually taken by a white woman. For that offence and for speaking up against being discriminated against (for example, a white guard refers to her as "one of those" and a "monkey in a cage"), she is systematically thrown in solitary confinement (Season 1, episode 4 ["Imaginary Enemies"]; episode 7 ["Blood Donut"]).

12 *OITNB,* Season 2, episode 11 ("Take a Break from Your Values").

13 None of the women of "Spanish Harlem" is racialized as Black.

14 Charles Ramirez Berg provided an early taxonomy of these stereotypes including Clown/Spitfire, Half breed Harlot, and Dark Lady. Charles Ramirez Berg, "Stereotyping in Films in General and of the Hispanic in Particular," *Howard Journal of Communications* 2, no. 3 (1990): 286–300. They were made more complex by Angharad N. Valdivia, *A Latina in the Land of Hollywood and Other Essays on Media Culture* (Tucson: University of Arizona Press, 2000). Such stereotypes can be located within what Frances Aparicio and Susana Chavez-Silverman call "tropicalism" or "the system of ideological fictions," through which Anglo-European representations "trope Latin American and U.S Latino/a identities and cultures." Frances Aparicio and Susana Chavez-Silverman, *Tropicalizations: Transcultural Representation of Latinidad* (Hanover, NH: University Press of New England, 1997), 1; see also Debra Merksin, *Media, Minorities, and Meaning: A Critical Introduction* (New York: Peter Lang, 2011).

15 She adds, however, that these roles have afforded her the opportunity to reflect and resist the social construction of Latinas: "But, you know what? These are all opportunities for us to show that we have the skill set even though maybe they [the roles] seem stereotypical. If we play those stereotypical characters in a non-stereotypical way [then] slowly but surely maybe things will begin to change." Vanessa Erazo, "This Actress from 'Orange Is the New Black' Moonlights as a Singer in a Death Metal Band," *Remezcla,* October 30, 2014.

16 Incidentally, this made-for-television movie is the only mainstream American feature I found that had an Asian queen bee, Suzy Kurosawa (Susie Elene).

17 Hispanic women and Latinas in the United States are over-policed and under-protected by law enforcement, subjected to sexism and gender-based violence within their communities, and racialized as non-status migrant workers. Latina/Hispanic women in America face discrimination beyond their interaction with law enforcement. They remain segregated in lower-paying occupations and industries and face disparate access to higher education and training; moreover, those Latinas with post-secondary education face pay inequalities compared to their white

counterparts. Marie T. Mora and Alberto Dávila, "The Hispanic-White Wage Gap Has Remained Wide and Relatively Steady," *Economic Policy Institute,* July 2, 2018.

18 *OITNB,* Season 4, episode 4 ("Doctor Psycho").

19 While in American Indigenous activism and scholarship, the nomenclature Native Indian, Native American, and American Indian are used, I use the term Indigenous, which, in Native Studies, has "become interchangeable with the word indigeneity" and "fosters an understanding of how power shapes specific identities through various discourses." Unlike "native," the term "Indigenous/Indigeneity," scholars suggest, is more fluid, "always changing [and] signifies a process of constant transformation." Maile Arvin, "Analytics of Indigeneity," in *Native Studies Keywords,* ed. Stephanie Nohelani Teves, Andrea Smith, and Michelle Raheja (Tucson: University of Arizona Press, 2015), 114. There are currently approximately 560 recognized Indigenous nations in the United States, including American Indian communities (for example, Algonquin, Choctaw, Haudenosaunee, Lakota, and Navaho), Arctic peoples (for example, Inuit, Inupiat, Yupik, Aleut, Eyak, Tlingit, Haid, and Tsmishian), and Native Hawaiians. I note, however, Kimberly TallBear's caution, when racializing Indigenous peoples into one category, "not to violate [the] political and cultural integrity ... distinct beliefs, histories, and cultural practices" of particular communities. Kimberly TallBear, "Racialising Tribal Identity and the Implications for Political and Cultural Development" (Paper presented at the Indigenous Peoples and Racism Conference, Sydney, Australia, February 2001). On Indigeneity as an analytic, rather than an identity, marker, see Arvin, "Analytics of Indigeneity."

20 In a recent interview, Joanelle Romero discusses her lasting legacy as an activist, community organizer, and artist that started with her role in *Girl Called Hatter Fox* (1977). Joanelle Romero, "A Girl Called Hatter Fox," *Bedrosian Center* (May 10, 2018), accessed August 27, 2020, https://bedrosian.usc.edu/tag/a-girl-called-hatter-fox/.

21 Maureen Trudelle Schwarz, *Fighting Colonialism with Hegemonic Culture: Native American Appropriation of Indian Stereotypes* (Albany, NY: State University of New York Press, 2013), 1.

22 Sandra Ego was born and raised in New Mexico and played minor roles like "Indian Maiden" in *The Trial of Billy Jack* and Joanie Little Bird in the police drama *Cade's County.* She began her career playing a Navajo teenager in *Born Innocent* (1974) three years before the release of *Girl Called Hatter Fox.*

23 *City of Dreams* (2005).

24 Malika Saada Saar, Rebecca Epstein, Lindsay Rosenthal, and Yasmin Vafa, *The Sexual Abuse to Prison Pipeline: The Girls' Story* (Washington, DC: Center for Poverty and Inequality: Georgetown University Law Center), accessed August 27, 2020, http://rights4girls.org/wp-content/uploads/r4g/2015/02/2015_COP_sexual-abuse_layout_web-1.pdf.

25 Julie C. Abril, "Native American Indian Women: Implications for Prison Research," *Southwest Journal of Criminal Justice* 4, no. 2 (2007): 133–44. Native Americans make up approximately 1.6 percent of the American population. US Census Bureau, *2010 Census Redistricting Data (Public Law 94-171) Summary File: 2010 Census of Population and Housing* (Washington, DC: US Department of Commerce, 2011).

26 David W. Adams, *Education for Extinction: American Indians and the Boarding School Experience* (Lawrence: University Press of Kansas, 1995).

27 "Standing Rock Legal Defense," *Lakota People's Law Project,* September 27, 2018, accessed August 27, 2020, https://www.lakotalaw.org/our-campaigns/justice-and-sovereignty. But see *Dollar General Corp v Mississippi Band of Choctaw Indians,* 136 S Ct 2159 (2016) (the tribal court has jurisdiction to adjudicate civil tort claims brought by tribal members against a non-member); see also Sarah Deer, "'Criminal Justice in Indian Country,' in 'Heeding Frickey's Call: Doing Justice in Indian Country' (Conference transcript, Berkeley, CA, September 27–28, 2012)," *American Indian Law Review* 37, no. 2 (2012): 374–84.

28 There are approximately 560 recognized Indigenous nations in the United States. In New York, these include the Cayuga, Oneida, Onondaga, Seneca, Shinnecock, St. Regis Mohawk, Tonawanda, Tuscarora, and Unkechaug (Poospatuck) nations. It is estimated that Native Americans make up 2.3 percent of the prison population in the United States and 2.6 percent of people under the jurisdiction of state correctional authorities. See generally "Inmate Race," *Federal Bureau of Prisons,* last updated June 22, 2019, https://www.bop.gov/about/statistics/statistics_inmate_race.jsp; E. Ann Carson, "Prisoners in 2016," *Bureau of Justice Statistics, Office of Justice Programs, US Department of Justice,* last updated August 7, 2018, accessed August 27, 2020, https://www.bjs.gov/content/pub/pdf/p16.pdf. Moreover, between 2000 and 2016, women's incarceration in American Indian country jails increased by 20 percent. Todd D. Minton and Mary Cowhig, "Jails in Indian Country, 2016," Bureau of Justice Statistics, Office of Justice Programs, US Department of Justice, last updated December 2017, accessed August 27, 2020, https://www.bjs.gov/content/pub/pdf/jic16.pdf.

29 Jodi Byrd has found that some Hawaiian sovereignty activists refuse to self-identify as Indigenous because they associate the concept with American domination. Jodi A. Byrd, *The Transit of Empire: Indigenous Critiques of Colonialism* (Minneapolis: University of Minnesota Press, 2011).

30 Staff discuss how they will "tame" Sarah, and the other prisoners fear she will use ancient magic on them (*Prisoner* [1979–86], episode 659). Sarah is violently attacked and covered in white paint by two white women (episode 660). Pamela's authority is frequently undermined, and she is called a "coconut" (episode 666). Sarah's backstory includes that her Maori mother is dead, her white alcoholic father abandoned her, and she was raised in foster care by a white family. Little to nothing is known about Pamela's life.

31 Letter from Joseph Breen to James Wingate, May 5, 1933, *Ann Vickers,* Production Code Administration Archives, Academy of Motion Pictures Arts and Sciences Library, Los Angeles, California.

32 Joyce Lukezic and Ted Schwarz, *False Arrest: True Story of Kidnapping, Contract Murder, Police Corruption and Innocence* (Far Hills, NJ: New Horizon Press, 1990).

33 The depth of his homophobia is shown when, after discovering that Piper Chapman (Taylor Schilling) is bisexual, he orchestrates an attack on her life by Tiffany. *OITNB,* Season 1, episode 1 ("I Wasn't Ready"); episode 13 ("Can't Fix Crazy").

34 *OITNB,* Season 4, episode 3 ("(Don't) Say Anything"). Moreover, Asia Kate Dillon, who plays Brandy Epps, identifies as gender non-binary in real life.

35 Joel Luschek (Matt Peters), while occasionally likeable, is shown to be a scheming opportunist and an alcoholic who carries racist animus. George "Pornstache" Mendez (Pablo Schreiber) incites a drug addict to take her own life and is never brought to justice for that abusive exercise of power (although he will eventually get his own). And Desi Piscatella (Brad William Henke) and Thomas Humphreys (Michael Torpey) regularly display sociopathic tendencies.

36 Counsellor Berdie Rogers (Marsha Stephanie Blake) is fired after Sam Healey (Michael Harney) finds out that Suzanne's "Time Hump Chronicles" has become extremely popular among the other prisoners. *OITNB*, Season 3, episode 7 ("Tongue Tied").

37 Guard Susan Fisher (Lauren Lapkus) confesses to Piper that "the only difference between us is when I made bad decisions in life, I didn't get caught." She is sexually harassed by Warden Caputo and attacked by Miss Claudette Pelage (Michelle Hurst) after her request for early release is denied. *OITNB*, Season 1, episode 11 ("Blood Donut"); episode 12 ("Fool Me Once").

38 Alex Vause (Laura Prepon) and Piper rekindle their relationship in Season 1; Nicole "Nicky" Nichols (Natasha Lyonne) and Big Boo have a "sex off" trying to bag as many orgasms as possible in Season 2, episode 4 ("A Whole Other Hole"), episode 5 ("Low Self Esteem City"), and episode 6 ("You Also Have a Pizza"); Soso and Poussey come out as a couple in Season 4, episode 3 ("(Don't) Say Anything").

39 Tiffany is an evangelical Christian who comes to believe that she has the power to heal. Cindy Hayes asserts her rights under the Religious Land Use and Institutionalized Persons Act, 2000, 114 Stat. 803, first as an effort to gain access to kosher meals but ultimately when she converts in earnest to Judaism. Yoga Jones is a practising Buddhist. Sister Jane Ingall (Beth Fowler) is a fallen nun and practices pragmatic Catholicism anchored in social justice advocacy. Alison Abdullah (Amanda Stephen), the show's only Muslim character who dons a headscarf, engages in daily prayer. While Janae Watson was raised in a conservative Muslim home, she finds God not through prayer but by running.

40 Creativity comes out through the Christmas play (Season 1, episode 13 ["Can't Fix Crazy"]), theatre class, Suzanne's sci-fi porn (and the universal enjoyment of it), and a talent show in Season 4 (albeit with correction officer hostages). In Season 3, episode 6 (Ching Chon Chang), Mei Chang (Lori Tan Chinn) makes a herb garden and converts everyday commissary items into gourmet meals.

41 In Season 1, Janae (the young Black star athlete) and Yoga Jones (the white middle-class hippy) become close after each exposes the other's vulnerabilities: the former will be eaten alive if she gives in to her righteous anger, and the latter's air of Buddhist superiority masks a deep shame for having murdered a child. In that same season, women of all the factions engage in a ritualistic gift giving to Red's girls after Tricia Miller's (Madeline Brewer) death. In Season 2, Red and Gloria become allies and strategize how to rid themselves of their common enemy, Correctional Officer Pornstache. In Season 3, Big Boo and Tiffany become loyal friends in large part because of their ostracism: Boo for having double-crossed Red and Tiffany for having found God. These friendship/loyalty lines even cross the lines of guards and prisoners. In Season 4, after Sister Jane is unsuccessful in getting a photo of Sophia in solitary to prove she is being

subjected to inhumane treatment, Warden Caputo surreptitiously takes the photo and leaks it to the media.

42 Sister Jane is serving a sentence for having protested against the nuclear war and the School of the Americas. In Season 4, episode 12 ("The Animals"), Soso tries to organize a peaceful protest in response to discrimination and guard brutality. Season 5 unfolds over a three-day riot that stems from this failed protest and the accidental suffocating of Poussey by a white guard.

43 Some commentators have argued that the relationship between Daya and Corrections Officer John Bennett (Matt McGorry) is also rape because there can never be consent in conditions of confinement. I am of the opinion that their relationship reveals the power dynamics between prisoners and guards, no matter how endearing or well meaning the guard may be. In most of their interactions, however, she wields more authority, controls the pace of their romance, and explicitly calls him out for not being attentive to his own privilege. These interactions indicate the possibility of a measure of consent on her behalf. However, Daya ends up a single mother and is forced to hand her child over to another woman when John abandons her and all responsibility for their child; this fact is far more powerful in conveying how infinitesimal these moments of exercised power can be for women whose bodies are controlled and disciplined through prison regimes. Compare, however, Correctional Officer Pornstache, who extorts oral sex from Leanne Taylor (Emma Myles) in exchange for drugs.

44 *OITNB*, Season 1, episode 10 ("Bora Bora Bora").

45 *OITNB*, Season 2, episode 9 ("40 Oz. of Furlough") and episode 12 ("It Was the Change").

46 *OITNB*, Season 3, episode 10 ("A Tittin' and a Hairn").

47 *OITNB*, Season 5 culminates with Tiffany, having escaped during the riot, finding her way to Charlie's house. Unphased, he wraps his arms around her, and they watch television in silence.

48 Linda Ferguson (Beth Dover), the ruthless and self-serving director of the Management and Corrections Corporation (MCC) that privatized the prison, may also have committed involuntary manslaughter or at least criminal negligence in her twenties when she let one of her drunken sorority sisters freeze to death.

49 The members of the "White Power Group" introduced in Season 4 include Jennifer Digori (Olivia Luccardi), who is illiterate; Kasey Sankey (Kelly Karbocz), who insists that she is a white nationalist unlike others who are unabashedly neo-Nazi white supremacists (such as Brandy and "Skinhead Helen" [Francesca Curran]); and two tagalong/meth addicts: Leanne, who was homeschooled in her Amish community, and Angie, who paradoxically has had at least one Black boyfriend. Piper is the group's "accidental" founder. Leanne and Angie function as the Statler and Waldorf of show. For instance, in response to the influx of incarcerated women, they offer up this insight into the variances within Latina communities:

> LEANNE: There's so many Mexicans now. It's like a Home Depot parkin' lot in here.
>
> ANGIE: Dominicans. If you're gonna be racist, you gotta be accurate, or you just look dumb.

LEANNE: Is Dominicans the ones that wear gold chains and smoke cigars – and swim to Florida?
ANGIE: No.
LEANNE: Is it the coffee and the coke and the "Hips Don't Lie"?
ANGIE: No, they talk a lot and play baseball, and they're always like, "I'm super not black," even though Haiti is the exact same island.
LEANNE: That's right. Yeah, I hate them.

50 First, Judith "Judy" King (Blair Brown) is white and famous though she does not appear to come from wealth or education; she has committed tax evasion. Second, Big Boo is white but gender non-confirming; she is firmly middle class but has presumably committed extortion. Third, Soso is mixed ancestry Scottish and Japanese; she is middle class and educated. Finally, Sister Jane is a white nun who has presumably taken a vow of poverty. They are respectively incarcerated for tax evasion, extortion, environmentalist and anarchist activism, and social-justice advocacy.
51 *OITNB,* Season 3, episode 5 ("Fake It Till You Make Some More").
52 Soso assumes that she is the abandoned daughter of a crack addict, and Judy does not question this characterization despite all evidence to the contrary.
53 *OITNB,* Season 4, episode 12 ("The Animals").
54 This refers to Eric Garner's death from a police chokehold. The creator's choice to use a sympathetic white character as the agent of Poussey's death has been criticized by some critical race commentators. For instance, Shamira Ibrahim writes that the scene positions viewers "to relive a facsimile of tragic real-life events" – the killing of innocent Black people at the hands of police – "under the most infantilizing and insulting context possible." Shamira Ibrahim, "Yeah, I'm Finished with the Black Suffering Trauma Porn of *Orange Is the New Black,*" *The Root: Black News, Opinions, Politics, and Culture,* June 23, 2016. Others, such as Soraya Nadia McDonald, consider the entire season to be "the strongest yet" because it "reflects and explores the subjugation of black Americans, past and present." Soraya Nadia McDonald, "In Its Strongest Season So Far, 'Orange Is the New Black' Yells 'Say Her Name!,'" *The Undefeated,* June 20, 2016.
55 Andrea J. Ritchie et al., "Say Her Name: Resisting Police Brutality against Black Women," *African American Policy Forum* (2015); Michelle S. Jacobs, "The Violent State: Black Women's Invisible Struggle against Police Violence," *William and Mary Journal of Women and the Law* 24, no. 1 (2017): 39–100.
56 It is watched on a video-streaming platform by MCC staff members and again by Desmond Piscatella (Brad William Henke) on his mobile phone (*OITNB,* Season 5, episode 1 ["Riot FOMO"]).
57 Victoria Law, "Dilemma Faced in 'Orange Is the New Black' All Too Real for Mothers behind Bars," *Rewire.News,* June 12, 2015; Victoria Law, "Can 'Orange Is The New Black' Change the Way Congress Thinks about Prisons?" *Bitch Media,* June 5, 2014.
58 *OITNB,* Season 1, episode 8 ("Moscow Mule"); episode 12 ("Fool Me Once)". In Season 5, Aleida Diaz (Elizabeth Rodriguez) is also released on parole and is optimistic about a new career as a nail artist. She is unable to find work other than an unpaid apprenticeship in a salon.

Conclusion

1 Christine Gledhill, "Genre and Gender: The Case of Soap Opera," in *Representation: Cultural Representations and Signifying Practices,* ed. Stuart Hall (London: Sage Publications, 1997), 355.

2 Jessica Silbey, "Patterns of Courtroom Justice," *Journal of Law and Society* 28, no. 1 (2001): 98.

3 Alexandra Juhasz, "Victim Stories: Documenting Pain, Punishment, Prison and Power," *Studies in Law, Politics, and Society* 30 (2004): 247.

4 Angela Y. Davis, *Are Prisons Obsolete?* (New York: Seven Stories Press, 2003), 17.

Selected Filmography

Acquitted. Directed by Frank R. Strayer. Columbia Pictures, 1929. Marion (Margaret Livingston) is wrongfully convicted and sentenced to a mixed prison. She falls in love with Bradford (Lloyd Hughes), the prison physician who has also been framed. Upon her dispense, Marion discovers that both crimes were committed by Egan (Sam Hardy), her ex-boyfriend/notorious crime boss. Egan arranges to have Bradford released in exchange for Marion spending the night with him. She refuses Egan's advances and, in a struggle, shoots him. True to his Hippocratic oath, Bradford saves Egan's life. A changed man, Egan turns himself in.

Against Their Will: Women in Prison. Directed by Karen Arthur, 1994. In a maximum-security prison for women, guards regularly extort sexual favours from their charges, until one prisoner, Alice Needham (Judith Light) decides to fight back. With the help of a lawyer (Stacy Keach), Alice becomes a prisoners' rights activist, leads a class action against the institution, and exposes the violence and corruption.

Bad Girls Dormitory. Directed by Tim Kincaid. Entertainment Concepts, 1986. Three girls in a juvenile reformatory – run by a corrupt warden (Teresa Farley) and her violent staff – decide to escape (after taking several showers and attending a dance party).

Betrayed Women. Directed by Edward Cahn. Allied Artists Pictures, 1955. The Bayou Reformatory for Women is run by an incompetent head matron

Mrs. Ballard (Esther Dale); the women warehoused there are brutalized by a sadistic guard (Sara Haden). Jeff (Tom Drake), the district attorney charged with an investigation into events at the reformatory, recognizes one of the prisoners: Nora (Peggy Knudsen), his former fiancée, serving a sentence for a petty crime. Fed up with the violence, Kate (Beverly Michaels) and Honey (Carole Mathews), two opposing queen bees, join forces, take Jeff, Nora, and Mrs. Ballard as hostages, and escape. In a police chase, Kate will be killed, but Honey, upon Jeff's assurances that the prison will be reformed, turns herself in. Nora and Jeff rekindle their relationship.

Big Bird Cage. Directed by Jack Hill. New World Pictures, 1972. A group of activists, most of whom are women, including Blossom (Pam Grier), heist a bar to fund their revolution. Some of the women are captured and taken to a jungle work camp run by Zappa (Andres Centenera), a particularly brutal warden. Other prisoners include Terry Rich (Anitra Ford), a white occasional escort, Mickie (Carol Speed), a Black woman who has committed crimes against the state, and Karen (Karen McKevic), a lesbian so violent she must be chained to her bed. Blossom and her boyfriend attempt to rescue their imprisoned comrades but fail horribly. The film closes with only two surviving women prisoners and Blossom's whereabouts unknown.

The Big Doll House. Directed by Jack Hill. New World Pictures, 1971. Collier (Judith Brown) has killed her abusive husband. She is sentenced to a women's work camp in the Philippines. There, she meets Grear (Pam Grier), incarcerated because she had sensitive information on government officials, her girlfriend Harrad (Brooke Mills), a heroine addict navigating mental illness, who may have committed infanticide, and Bodine (Pat Woodell), a political prisoner. The women are routinely tortured and sexually assaulted by guards. Grear will be killed by Harrad, who has hallucinated that Grear is abandoning her. A group of prisoners manages to escape, but the prison doctor inadvertently informs the warden. All of the fugitives will be murdered, except Collier, who is returned to the prison.

Black Mama White Mama. Directed by Eddie Romero. American International Pictures, 1973. Two prisoners – Lee (Pam Grier), a Black sex worker and Karen (Margaret Markov), a white activist – are serving time in a work camp. They escape while being transferred to another institution. While they loathe each other, they are handcuffed together and must collaborate to evade authorities and a vicious crime boss. Unlike the conventional racial coding in which the Black protagonist will be sacrificed for her white buddy, Karen is killed in the final scene, and Lee will find freedom.

Blonde Bait. Directed by Elmo Williams. Howco Exchange, 1956. Angela (Beverly Michaels) is engaged to Randall (Jim Davis), who is, unbeknownst to her, a murderer and a Nazi collaborator. She is sent to prison for assault, having rebuked a man's sexual advances by slapping him in the face. A detective who has been trying to pin Randall for years, sets a plan in motion to have Angela escape, so that she can lead him to Randall.

Blonde Sinner. Directed by J. Lee Thompson. Allied Artists Pictures, 1956. Mary Hilton (Diana Dors) has had a string of abusive relationships. When she finally believes to have found love, she discovers he has been unfaithful and plans to leave her. Mary murders her boyfriend's mistress and is sentenced to hang. While waiting her execution, she reflects upon her difficult life circumstances.

The Bridge of Sighs. Directed by Phil Rosen. Chesterfield Motion Pictures Corporation, 1936. Marion Courtney (Dorothy Tree) arranges to have herself arrested and sent to a woman's prison to collect evidence establishing that her brother has been framed.

Cage without a Key. Directed by Buzz Kulik. Columbia Broadcasting System, 1975. In this telemovie, with a notably diverse cast, Susan Dey (of the *Partridge Family*) plays Valerie, a high school student who is framed for armed robbery and murder. At the reformatory, she meets girls from unfortunate circumstances as well as more hardened criminals. Valerie is terrorized and victimized throughout and will ultimately become jaded and succumb to a life of crime.

Chained Heat. Directed by Paul Nicholas. Jensen Farley Pictures, 1983. Carol Henderson (Linda Blair) is sent to an overcrowded women's prison and finds herself in the middle of a racially divided gang war motivated by a warden who forces his charges into prostitution.

Chicago. Directed by Frank Urson. DeMille Pictures Corporation, 1927. Roxie Hart (Phillis Haver) shoots her lover when he ends their affair. Despite all evidence pointing to her, the police arrest her husband Amos (Victor Varconi) who has confessed to the crime. An investigator tricks Roxie into incriminating herself. Her trial is widely covered by the media, who are drawn to Roxie's glamour. She uses her feminine wiles to convince the all-male jury of her innocence. Roxie is acquitted, but Amos leaves her for another woman.

Chicago. Directed by Rob Marshall. Miramax, 2002. When Roxie Hart's (Renée Zellwegger) lover breaks it off unceremoniously, she protests. He gets violent. She shoots him. When her husband Amos (John C. Reilley) gets home, she convinces him that she has shot a burglar in self-defence. Amos is about to confess but puts two and two together and hands Roxie over to the police instead. While her case attracts a media frenzy, she is found guilty and sentenced to be hanged on "murderesses' row." She meets the glamorous Velma (Katherine Zeta Jones) who has killed her husband and her sister who were having an affair. Initially, Velma hates Roxie because she has stolen the media's attention from her case; she even testifies against her at the appeal hearing. However, Roxie's lawyer and her charms lead the jury to acquit her. Velma will also be found innocent. The two rivals join forces and become a Chicago headliner.

The Concrete Jungle. Directed by Tom DeSimone. Motion Picture Marketing, 1982. Elizabeth (Tracy Bregman) is framed by her boyfriend for cocaine trafficking. She is sent to a hellish women's prison where Warden Fletcher (Jill St. John) and her favourite charge Cat (Barbara Luna) use the other prisoners to supply a prostitution ring. Shelly Meyers (Nita Talbot) will infiltrate the prison and rescue Elizabeth. Together, they gather evidence to have Fletcher fired.

Condemned. Directed by Oren Shai. Rocking Oren, 2010. Prisoner 1031 (Margaret Anne Florence) has accidentally snitched on a fellow inmate and consequently sits in a cell alone expecting retaliation. She is convinced that her beautiful new cellmate is in fact her "executioner."

Condemned Women. Directed by Lew Landers. RKO Pictures, 1938. Linda (Sally Eilers) is an unemployed nurse who, out of desperation, steals some food. Sentenced to three years in prison and embittered by life, she attempts suicide. Dr. Phillip Duncan (Louis Hayward) saves her life; together, they stave off a typhoid outbreak in the prison and eventually fall in love. The head matron tells Linda she will ruin Phillip. Out of despair, she agrees to help the queen bee escape. The plan fails, a riot ensues, and many are killed. Linda survives, but her sentence has been extended. Phillip promises to wait for her.

Convicted. Directed by Bille August. DEJ Productions, 2004. Charlotte (Connie Nielsen) awaits execution for having kidnapped and murdered a child. Her attorney Susan (Kelly Preston) works with Frank (Aidan Quinn), a disbarred lawyer, to prove her innocence and save her before time runs out. Charlotte and Frank fall in love in the process.

Convicted: A Mother's Story. Directed by Richard Heffron. National Broadcasting Company, 1987. Billie (Ann Jillian) is a single mother who is tricked by her boyfriend into stealing money from her boss. While trying to cope with prison life, she is forced to face the queen bee, Angie (Jenny Gago). Billie's problems continue after release: the custody of her children is put into question, and her boyfriend re-emerges, wanting to start over.

Convicted Woman. Directed by Nick Grinde. Columbia Pictures, 1940. Betty (Rochelle Hudson) is sent to the Curtiss House of Correction for a theft she did not commit. She discovers corruption in the prison and her lawyer Mary (Freida Inescort) and a reporter Jim (Glenn Ford) bring it to light. Mary will be named the new matron and will bring about sweeping reforms. However, the prisoners who lost the privileges they once had under the old regime retaliate and take it out on Betty. Jim will uncover information establishing her innocence. The film closes with Jim and Betty beginning a romance.

Conviction: The Kitty Dodds Story. Directed by Michael Tuchner. Columbia Broadcasting System, 1993. Based on the true story of Katherine Dodds (Veronica Hamel), who was sent to prison for life for killing her abusive husband (a police officer). She escapes prison but is discovered when she saves a man's life. While her death sentence is vacated and her sentence is reduced to thirty years, she navigates taken-for-granted assumptions about women's victimization when she finally applies for parole.

Dance with a Stranger. Directed by Mike Newell. Samuel Goldwyn Company, 1985. Ruth Ellis (Miranda Richardson) is the last woman hanged in Britain. The film is a remake of *Blonde Sinner* (1956) based on Joan Henry's novel *Yield to the Night* (1954). It provides nuance to Ruth's crime.

False Arrest. Directed by Bill L. Norton. American Broadcasting Company, 1991. Joyce Lukezic (Donna Mills) is found guilty of a gruesome double murder. While awaiting execution and trying to clear her name, she witnesses and experiences sexual and physical violence. Based on the memoir of the same name.

Forgotten Girls. Directed by Phil Rosen. Republic Pictures, 1940. Judy (Louise Platt) is sentenced to prison for a murder that her stepmother committed. A reporter (Donald Woods) covers the story, believes Judy to be innocent, and sets out to clear her name.

Four Minutes (Vier Minuten). Directed by Chris Kraus. Autobahn (Germany), 2006. Jenny (Hannah Herzprung), a twenty-something musical prodigy, is incarcerated for murder. Traude (Monica Bleibtreu), an octogenarian with a mysterious past works as a piano instructor in prison. Despite adversity, Jenny and Traude strive to find redemption through music.

Gallant Lady. Directed by William Beaudine. Producers Releasing Corporation, 1942. Dr. Rosemary Walsh (Rose Hobart) is incarcerated for having assisted a patient's suicide. She gets caught up in a prison break during which she gives a stranger medical attention. She is, as a result, discovered by Steve (Sidney Blackmer), a local doctor who offers to hide her. They fall in love, and, on the day of their wedding, she is recognized, and they are arrested. However, during Steve's trial, a catastrophic event occurs at the courthouse and the two doctors save several lives. The governor pardons Rosemary, and Steve is found not guilty.

Girls in Chains. Directed by Edgar G. Ulmer. Producers Releasing Corporation, 1943. Helen (Arline Judge) loses her job as a teacher because her brother-in-law is the notorious racketeer Johnny (Allan Byron). Frank (Roger Clark) is a detective eager to see Johnny behind bars. He helps Helen secure a teaching gig at a girl's reformatory. There, she discovers that the superintendent Marcus (Clancy Cooper) is embezzling funds and that Johnny is involved. With Frank's help, Helen will bring the men to justice; she will be appointed head of the reformatory.

Girls in Prison. Directed by Edward L. Cahn. American International Pictures, 1956. Anne (Joan Taylor) unintentionally becomes an accessory to robbery. At the women's prison, her chaplain (Richard Denning) and the kindly matron (Jane Darwell) suspect Anne is innocent because the loot was never found. Ann gets swept into a prison break by women who believe she will lead them to the money. The plan goes south; Anne turns herself in with the chaplain's help.

Girls in Prison. Directed by John McNaughton. Showtime Networks, 1994. Aggie (Missy Crider), a young musician, is framed for killing her manager; she is sentenced to life in prison at the California State Penitentiary for Women.

Jennnifer (Anne Heche), the person who actually committed the murder, infiltrates the prison to tie up loose ends and kill Aggie. The prisoners unite to protect Aggie, and her name is cleared.

Girls of the Big House. Directed by George Archainbaud. Republic Pictures, 1945. Jeanne (Lynne Roberts) is framed for larceny. Even thought her boyfriend Barton (Tom Keene) is a lawyer, she self-represents, using a pseudonym to keep her father's name out of the papers. In the women's reformatory, she gets caught up in a territorial battle between Bernice (Virginia Christine) and Alma Vlasek (Tala Birell). Jeanne escapes to attend a ceremony honouring her father but is discovered and severely punished. When news hits that she is incarcerated, Barton sets a plan in motion to prove her innocence.

The Godless Girl. Directed by Cecil B. DeMille. Pathé Exchange, 1929. Judith (Lina Basquette) runs an atheist youth organization; Bob (Tom Keene) heads a rival Christian organization. When a fight ensues between the two groups, a young woman is killed. Judith and Bob are labelled the instigators and sent to a mixed reform school. When a fire breaks out, Judith and Bob save a guard's life. The state pardons them; they fall in love, and Judith converts to Christianity.

Good-Time Girl. Directed by David MacDonald. General Film Distributors, 1948. This is a cautionary tale about Gwen (Jean Kent), a rebellious, but harmless teenager, who is sent to a Borstal detention centre. Rather than being reformed by the well-meaning matron (Nora Swinburn), Gwen learns all about criminality. She and some other girls escape and go on a crime spree that culminates in manslaughter. Gwen will be arrested and sentenced to fifteen years in prison.

The Green-Eyed Blonde. Directed by Bernard Girard. Warner Brothers, 1957. Betsy (Linda Plowman), a teenager and mother to two-month-old Buddy is labelled sullen by the Head Matron of a girl's reformatory, when in fact she is carrying a terrible secret: her pregnancy resulted from a rape by her stepfather. When Betsy's mother threatens to put Buddy up for adoption, one of the other inmates secretly kidnaps him and hides him at the reformatory. The girls work together to provide Buddy with love and stability, but when the administration discovers him, a riot erupts.

Guilt by Association. Directed by Graeme Campbell. Court Television, 2002. Based on actual events, Susan (Mercedes Ruehl) is found guilty of serious drug offences committed by her boyfriend. At the women's prison, she navigates violence and sexual advances while trying to establish her innocence.

Hold Your Man. Directed by Sam Wood. Metro-Goldwyn-Mayer, 1933. Ruby (Jean Harlow) and Eddie (Clark Gable) are in love. Eddie's got a checkered past but wants to go clean. He decides to do one last heist. The plan goes awry, and the pair gets caught up in an accidental homicide. Ruby is sent to a state institution where she pines over Eddie, who goes on the lam. Ruby begins to attend church regularly and has a near mystical experience that transforms her into a law-abiding citizen. When Eddie discovers Ruby is pregnant, he sneaks into her prison to marry her. Ruby finishes out her sentence and leaves prison determined to be a good person.

I Want to Live! Directed by Robert Wise. United Artists, 1958. Barbara Graham was executed in 1955 for having killed an elderly woman. She maintained her innocence until her death. This film, which is based on actual events, recounts the moments leading up to her execution and the circumstances of her life. Barbara (Susan Hayward) made some bad choices, lived in extreme poverty, and experienced intimate partner violence.

I Want to Live! Directed by David Lowell Rich. American Broadcasting Company, 1983. In this made-for-television adaptation of the 1953 film by the same name, Barbara Graham (Lindsay Wagner) is a young woman with no family, who grew up in a girls' reformatory. After a lifetime of unwanted attention from men, she becomes a single mother. The depiction of Barbara's death in the gas chamber is a direct indictment of capital punishment.

Jackson County Jail. Directed by Michael Miller. New World Pictures, 1976. Dinah (Yvette Mimieux) picks up two hitchhikers who attack her, steal her wallet, and take off in her car. She finds her way to the police station only to be thrown in a holding cell. While being raped by the deputy, she manages to escape with the help of the only other detainee, Coley (Tommy Lee Jones). The deputy is killed in the struggle, and Dinah and Coley flee. He is killed in a police shoot-out; she survives but will likely spend the rest of her life behind bars.

Jailbait. Directed by Jared Cohn. The Asylum, 2014. Anna (Sara Malakul Lane) is a teenager who has killed her sexually abusive stepfather. In an adult women's prison, she is quickly initiated into the world of illicit drugs, sapphic desire, and sadism.

Johnny Greyeyes. Directed by Jorge Manzano. Wolfe Video, 2000. Johnny (Gail Maurice) is a two-spirited Cree woman. Recently released from prison, she contemplates the life circumstances – intergenerational trauma, poverty, and the vestiges of colonialism – that lead to her criminalization. She also revisits the connections she made, and the love she found, while in prison.

Ladies of the Big House. Directed by Marion Gering. Paramount Pictures, 1931. On the day that Kathleen (Sylvia Sidney) and Standish (Gene Raymond) are to be married, they instead get framed for murder by Kid (Earle Foxe), a violent gangster who fancies Kathleen. Standish is sentenced to death, while Kathleen, found to be an accessory to murder, receives a life sentence. Unable to adapt to prison life and devastated by Standish's imminent death, Kathleen escapes, with the help of the other women. She successfully brings new facts to light, and she and Standish are cleared of all wrongdoing.

Ladies They Talk About. Directed by Howard Bretherton and William Keighley. Warner Brothers, 1933. Nan (Barbara Stanwyck) is charged for her connection to a bank robbery. Her childhood friend David Slade (Preston Foster), a respected preacher, believes she is innocent and convinces the prosecutor to release her into his custody. Moved by Slade's kindness, Nan confesses that she did the crime. Honour bound, he rescinds his support, and Nan is forced to serve her sentence in prison. In the women's ward at San Quentin, Nan seems to oscillate between wanting to "go straight" and enacting her revenge on Slade. When two of the other members of her gang are arrested and thrown into the men's quarters, she orchestrates a prison break. The plan is thwarted, and Nan is convinced that it is Slade's doing. Upon dispense, she finds Slade and is determined to kill him. The ambivalent ending indicates that she may instead give marriage a chance.

Lady Gangster. Directed by Robert Florey. Warner Brothers, 1942. Dot (Faye Emerson) gets embroiled with some unsavoury types and finds herself an accessory to a bank robbery. Rather than cut a deal with the district attorney, she pleads her innocence. She is found guilty but manages to hide the money before being incarcerated; her intent is to give it all back. To extort the money from her, the mob puts a hit on her new boyfriend, but she stages an escape and helps return the money. Granted early parole as a result, she can finally marry her boyfriend.

Love, Mary. Directed by Robert Day. Columbia Broadcasting System, 1985. Mary (Kristy McNichol) is housed at a reformatory for having committed a string of misdemeanours. Rachel (Rachel Ticotin), the school's social worker, discovers that Mary actually has a learning disability. With Rachel's help, Mary develops a new approach to learning, and her grades and interest in school increase dramatically. The film, which is based on the life of Dr. Mary Groda-Lewis, ends with Mary having enrolled in university.

The Lullaby. Directed by Chester Bennett. Film Booking Offices of America, 1924. Felipa (Jane Novak), who is pregnant, receives a twenty-year sentence for manslaughter. She gives birth to Antoinette (Dorothy Brock), who, at the age of three, is taken out of the prison and placed in an orphanage. Antoinette will be adopted by the judge who sentenced Felipa to life. Once her full sentence expires, Felipa attempts to relocate her now-grown daughter. Reunited at last, Felipa becomes part of Antoinette's new family.

Manslaughter. Directed by Cecil B. DeMille. Paramount Pictures, 1922. Lydia (Leatrice Joy) refuses to give Evans (Lois Wilson), her domestic worker, money to pay some medical bills. Evans steals Lydia's jewellery and is charged with larceny. Daniel (Thomas Meighan), the district attorney on the file, and Lydia's love interest, asks her to appear in court to ask for clemency for Evans. However, Lydia forgets to attend. Evans is sentenced to Auburn Prison. Lydia's reckless ways land her in a police chase, in which an officer dies. At her trial, Daniel asks the court for Lydia to serve the maximum sentence for manslaughter. Enraged, Lydia vows to enact revenge, but incarceration will change her. After her release, she and Evans open a shelter for homeless people, and she reunites with Daniel.

Manslaughter. Directed by George Abbott. Paramount Pictures, 1930. Dan (Fredric March), a lawyer driven by the rule of law, prosecutes his love interest Lydia (Claudette Colbert) for her part in a vehicular death. In prison, Lydia learns compassion, forgiveness, and self-discipline. Once released, rather than enact revenge on Dan as she had planned, she falls in love with him, and they begin a romance. A remake of Cecil DeMille's film of the same name.

The Midnight Flower. Directed by Leslie T. Peacocke. Aywon Film, 1923. In a heist gone wrong, Myra (Vola Vale) is left holding the bag. While serving her sentence in a women's prison, she meets an evangelist minister (Gaston Glass) who helps her go straight. Upon release, Myra is rewarded when she discovers that she is the long-lost daughter of the city's wealthiest family.

A Mother's Right: The Elizabeth Morgan Story. Directed by Linda Otto. American Broadcasting Company, 1992. Dr. Elizabeth Morgan (Bonnie Bedelia) is sent to prison after refusing to reveal the whereabouts of her daughter, maintaining that she was protecting her from her abusive ex-husband. A fictionalized account of the actual events, which resulted in the passing of the Elizabeth Morgan Act.

The Naked Cage. Directed by Paul Nicholas. Cannon Film Distributors, 1986. Michelle (Shari Shattuck) is wrongfully convicted of armed robbery. In prison, she realizes that the warden (Angel Tompkins) is a racist sexual predator. She and her guards, with the help of the queen bee, are running a drug ring. The one decent guard, Rhonda (Lucinda Crosby), turns out to be an undercover cop. Michelle will help Rhonda bring the corruption to light and, in turn, will have her sentence overturned.

Paid. Directed by Sam Wood. Metro-Goldwyn-Mayer, 1930. Mary (Joan Crawford) is wrongfully convicted of theft and sent to jail for three years. While incarcerated, she studies law. Upon dispense, Mary runs an extortion racket against the rich men who have harmed her and negotiates legal settlements on their behalf.

Prison-A-Go-Go! Directed by Barak Epstein. Independent Cinema, 2003. Janie (Laurie Walton) has herself arrested to rescue her little sister who is confined in a women's prison. The film is intended as a comedic iteration of the exploitation genre.

Prison without Bars. Directed by Brian Desmond Hurst. United Artists Corporation, 1938. Yvonne (Edna Best) is a compassionate reform-minded warden. Her long-time fiancé George (Barry Barnes), who happens to be the prison doctor, falls for Suzanne (Corrinne Luchaire), one of their charges. George resigns and asks Suzanne to meet him overseas upon her release. Yvonne will eventually support their union and help Suzanne receive a pardon and return to a lonely personal life but a fulfilling career.

Purgatory. Directed by Ami Artzi. New Star Entertainment, 1988. Two Peace Corps workers, Carly (Tanya Roberts) and Melanie (Julie Pop), are wrongfully convicted of drug smuggling. In prison, they are victimized by the sadist warden, Commandant Bledsoe (Hal Orlandini). Melanie takes her own life, but Carly recruits other women to riot and escape.

Red Heat. Directed by Robert Collector and Ernst Ritter von Theumer. International Screen, 1985. In a case of mistaken identity, Christine (Linda Blair), who is visiting Germany, is picked up by the East German police. They torture her into a false confession. She is sent to a notorious women's prison, which is run by a sadistic warden (Elisabeth Volkmann) and is full of sexual predators. Luckily, her fiancé will stage a rescue.

Red Hot Tires. Directed by Erle C. Kenton. Warner Brothers, 1925. Elizabeth's (Patsy Ruth Miller) father is the chief of police. He sends her to jail to teach her a lesson for speeding and for injuring Al (Monte Blue). Al has a crush on Elizabeth and gets himself arrested too so he can be in the cell next to hers. Although he is released, Elizabeth is kept under lock and key because she refuses to repent. Al convinces a gang to break her out, but they end up taking her hostage. Al is able to save her, but, fearing her father's wrath, they elope.

Reform School Girl. Directed by Edward Bernds. American International Pictures, 1957. Donna (Gloria Castillo) is framed for manslaughter and sentenced to a girls' reformatory. Josie (Luana Anders), a gun moll, has herself arrested so that she can keep tabs on her. Josie recruits the other girls to make Donna's life unbearable. In a struggle, Donna will stab Josie in self-defence and be transferred to a state prison. The prison teacher, convinced of her innocence, sets a plan in motion to have her name cleared.

Reform School Girls. Directed by Tom DeSimone. New World Pictures, 1986. Jenny (Linda Carol) finds herself wrapped up in a robbery staged by her boyfriend. She is sentenced to Pridemore Reform School for Girls, where she suffers inhumanities from a leather-clad warden (Sybil Danning) and a brutal head matron as well as unwanted sexual advances by the other inmates. Dr. Norton (Charlotte McGinnis) is a prison psychiatrist who, out of concern for the girls' treatment, writes a report to the commissioner. During the ensuing investigation, prisoners take a guard hostage, and several girls will be killed in a shootout. However, Jenny's name will be cleared, and Dr. Norton will take on the role of warden.

Roxie Hart. Directed by William A. Wellman. Twentieth Century-Fox Film, 1942. A man is found dead in Roxie's (Ginger Rogers) apartment. Her husband Amos (George Chandler) is initially the prime suspect. However, when Homer (George Montgomery), a crime reporter, discovers that Roxie and the dead guy had a relationship, he convinces her to confess. Even though Amos has in fact killed the man, Roxie turns herself in, believing that the press could bolster her career. After spending months in prison, she is eventually acquitted. Amos will flee. Roxie and Homer will begin a romance.

Slammer Girls. Directed by Chuck Vincent. Lightning Pictures, 1987. Melody (Devon Jenkin) shoots Governor Caldwell (Ron Sullivan) during a public event. She is sentenced to twenty years at a particularly brutal women's institution. Harry (Jeffrey Hurst) is a reporter who discovers that Caldwell owns a company that supplies the prison with electric chairs. He dons women's clothing and infiltrates the prison to collect evidence and to find out Melody's motives. It turns out that she is the out-of-wedlock child of the governor's. In a twist, rather than denying his paternity, the governor embraces Melody and even stands as best man in her wedding to Harry.

So Young, So Bad. Directed by Bernard Vorhaus and Edgar G. Ulmer. United Artists, 1950. Dr. Jason (Paul Henreid), a prison psychiatrist, vows to help reform a school for wayward girls. He learns that many of the charges are being housed for minor offences (running away, vagrancy) and, while there, are being forced to work long hours and are punished with solitary confinement. Another staff member, Ruth (Catherine McLeod), believes in his approach but has compromised her values in order to survive in the institution. Eventually, they join forces, expose the corruption within the prison, and make plans to marry.

The Story of Molly X. Directed by Crane Wilbur. Universal Pictures, 1949. Molly's (June Havoc) gangster husband is murdered; she in turn shoots the man who has confessed to the crime. Because of insufficient evidence, she will be found guilty of a lesser crime. In prison, Molly is a model prisoner, but the police are unmoved. A moll is sent in to trick her to confess, without effect. Molly is released but when she discovers another person will face a life sentence for the murder she committed, she turns herself in. It is revealed that her shot was not fatal; she is set free and begins a new life.

Sweet Sugar. Directed by Michael Levesque. Dimension Pictures, 1972. Sugar (Phyllis Davis) is a sex worker who is set up by a corrupt politician. Convinced that she will not get a fair hearing, she volunteers for a diversion program run by Dr. John (Angus Duncan). The doctor uses the work camp to recruit subjects for his torturous medical experiments. Sugar rallies the other women and manages to escape.

Terminal Island. Directed by Stephanie Rothman. Dimension Pictures, 1973. In a near future, violent criminals are relocated to a remote island without any law enforcement. A group of prisoners form a community, lead by Bobby (Sean Kenney), a murderer who rules with an iron fist. When Carmen (Ena Hartman), an independent thinker, is sent to the island to serve her sentence, Bobby's reign comes to an action-filled end. Carmen and the other women will overthrow Bobby and build a more egalitarian society.

Vendetta. Directed by Bruce Logan. Concorde Pictures, 1986. Bonnie (Michelle Newkirk) kills a rapist and is sentenced to the Duran Correctional Institute. There, guards rape prisoners with impunity, prisoners beat other prisoners, and drugs are everywhere. Kay (Sandy Martin), the queen bee, makes advances towards Bonnie who does not reciprocate. Kay and her gang drug, beat, and kill Bonnie. The prison calls it an overdose suicide. Bonnie's sister Laurie (Karen Chase) intentionally has herself arrested and sent to the prison. She gains the trust of the other prisoners, and, one by one, she enacts revenge on each of the women responsible for her sister's death.

Violent Women. Directed by Barry Mahon. Joseph Brenner Associates, 1960. Five violent offenders plan an escape from prison through a drainpipe into the streets of New York. Whether through double-crossings, a freak death, or a shoot-out with the police, all five women will die.

Within the Law. Directed by Frances Marion. Associated First National Pictures, 1923. Mary (Norma Talmage) is wrongfully convicted of stealing. In prison, she learns the law and plots her revenge. When she is dispensed, she and her friend Aggie (Eileen Percy) seduce wealthy men and then collect money from them for having breached a contract (a promise to marry). Even though she falls for Dick, one of her victims, her time in jail has hardened her, and she sticks with the plan. However, when he finds himself embroiled in some legal issues, Mary confesses that she loves him and helps clear his name.

Within the Law. Directed by Gustav Machatý. Metro-Goldwyn-Mayer, 1939. Mary (Ruth Hussey) is framed for stealing from her boss. In prison, she studies criminal law and, when released, she becomes a legal consultant to a gang boss, teaching him about loopholes and possible defences. She eventually puts into motion a revenge plot against her former boss – namely, she seduces his son Richard and marries him. However, Richard only sees the good in her, and they live happily ever after.

Within These Walls. Directed by Mike Robe. Lifetime Television, 2001. Joan Thomas (Ellen Burstyn) is sent to prison on drug charges. There she meets Sister Pauline (Laura Dern), who helps her find redemption through a pet rehabilitation program. Based on a true story.

Woman against the World. Directed by David Selman. Columbia Pictures Corporation, 1937. Anna (Alice Moore) accidentally kills her aunt. Larry (Ralph Forbes), a young lawyer, assists her in regaining custody of her daughter Betty (Sylvia Welsh) upon release. She finds herself engaging in sex work to pay the bills. By the time she discovers her daughter's whereabouts, she is arrested again. When she is paroled, Anna kidnaps her daughter but, wracked with guilt, brings Betty back and turns herself in. At trial, Larry argues that she cannot be convicted of kidnapping her own child, and she is released on probation. Learning that the adoption was done illegally, the judge also grants Anna custody; however, Betty wants to stay with her adoptive family. Heartbroken, Anna relinquishes custody, and Larry comforts her.

The Woman Condemned. Directed by Dorothy Davenport. Willis Kent Productions, 1934. Barbara (Claudia Dell) takes the rap for a murder. Jerry (Richard Hemmingway) is a journalist who does not believe she is the real perpetrator of the crime. They fall in love, and Jerry goes on a mission to prove Barbara's innocence while she waits in prison. It turns out, however, that Barbara is an undercover detective, working the same case as Jerry, only from within the walls of the prison.

Women in Cages. Directed by Gerardo De Leon Gerardo. New World Pictures, 1971. Carol (Jennifer Gan) is framed by her boyfriend and sent to a women's prison. Alabama (Pam Grier) is a vicious warden who subjects her charges to psychological and physical abuse. Carol and her cellmates set in motion an escape plan, using Alabama as a hostage. But when they finally get out, they discover their escape vessel is actually a floating brothel run by the mob.

Women in Chains. Directed by Bernard L. Kowalski. American Broadcasting Company, 1972. Claire (Ida Lupido) is a psychopathic matron who torments her charges. After a prisoner dies under suspicious circumstances, Sandra (Lois Nettleton), a parole officer, goes undercover to find evidence of foul play. The only person on the outside who knows about Sandra's work is killed. Trapped on the inside, she must use all of her wits to uncover the truth and survive.

Women in Prison. Directed by Lambert Hillyer. Columbia Pictures Corporation, 1938. Daisy (Mayo Methot) is a gun moll who intentionally gets arrested in an effort to get away from the mob from whom she has stolen. When Barney (Arthur Loft), the mob boss, offers the superintendent (Sarah Padden) money if she will give Daisy early parole, she refuses. Barney frames Martha's daughter Anne (Wyn Cahoon) for manslaughter, and she is locked in the same cell as Daisy. The two become close, and they successfully plan an escape. However, Barney intercepts them and kills Daisy. Anne agrees to tell him where the money is if he confesses to having her framed. When the police catch up to them, Barney is shot, but, in his final breath, he clears Anne of wrongdoing.

Women without Names. Directed by Robert Florey. Paramount Pictures, 1940. Joyce (Ellen Drew) and her husband Fred (Robert Paige) find themselves embroiled in a murder committed by Joyce's ex-husband Walter (John McGuire), a con-artist, and his new moll Peggy (Judith Barrett). They are found guilty: he is sentenced to be hanged, and she is sent to the women's prison. Coincidentally, Peggy is charged with forging cheques and is sent to the same prison. She initiates a quarrel with Joyce but convinces the guards that it was the other way around. Joyce is sent to solitary confinement, but the other prisoners intimidate Peggy until she confesses. The two women eventually become allies. Peggy tricks Walter into admitting the truth in front of witnesses. Joyce and Fred are released and are free to live happily ever after.

Women's Prison. Directed by Lewis Seller. Columbia Pictures, 1955. Helen (Phyllis Thaxter) is a first offender who is traumatized by her crime (the accidental killing of a child). She is sent to a maximum-security prison that houses men and women in separate facilities. The women's superintendent, Amelia van Zandt (Ida Lupino), is particularly brutal. Despite the prison doctor's (Howard Duff) warning about Helen's fragile mental state, Amelia has her sedated and put into isolation. When she discovers that one of her charges has been sneaking to the men's prison to see her husband and is pregnant as a result, Amelia cancels all programs, denies the women basic privileges, and eventually beats the pregnant inmate to death. A hunger strike turns into a riot. The prison doctor intervenes and files an official complaint against the superintendent. Helen will be paroled and reunited with her family.

Index